Antitrust
Health Care Handbook

Third Edition

 Section of Antitrust Law

**Defending Liberty
Pursuing Justice**

This volume should be officially cited as:
ABA SECTION OF ANTITRUST LAW,
Antitrust Health Care Handbook, 3d Edition (2004)

Cover design by ABA Publishing

Printed in the United States of America.

08 07 06 05 04 5 4 3 2

Library of Congress Control Number: 2004101704

ISBN 1-59031-371-2

Discounts are available for books ordered in bulk. Special consideration is given to state bars, CLE programs, and other bar-related organizations. Inquire at Book Publishing, ABA Publishing, American Bar Association, 750 North Lake Shore Drive, Chicago, Illinois 60611.

www.ababooks.org

CONTENTS

FOREWORD

The Section of Antitrust Law is pleased to publish the *Antitrust Health Care Handbook III*. The *Handbook* is primarily intended for use by health-care professionals and administrators, as well as their counsel, as an introduction and general guide to the application of federal antitrust law to issues that arise in health care. Obviously, the *Handbook III* is not a substitute for competent legal advice, but we hope those in the health-care industry will find it to be a useful overview of how federal antitrust laws apply to the health-care industry.

This represents the third edition of the *Handbook*. I was pleased to chair the Health Care Committee the last time the *Handbook* was updated in 1993, and I know how much hard work and effort go into a publication like this. I commend Doug Ross, current Chair of the Committee, as well as all the others who have worked so hard to bring this publication to you. I particularly want to express the Section's thanks to Greg Wrobel, who began the revisions to the earlier edition, and Jeff Miles, who completed the project in a masterful fashion.

If the last year or two are any indication of the type of antitrust activity in the health-care industry we can expect in the future, I have no doubt that the Section will be considering an *Antitrust Health Care Handbook IV* in the not-too-distant future. If we do, I know we will once again draw on the talent and dedication of the members of the Section's Health Care Committee, which has consistently been one of the Section's leading committees in publishing top-quality publications and newsletters. If you are not already a member, I urge you to consider joining and participating in the wide range of activities supported by this Committee.

Kevin E. Grady
Chair, Section of Antitrust Law
American Bar Association 2003-2004

PREFACE

The *Antitrust Health Care Handbook III* was prepared by the Health Care Committee of the ABA Section of Antitrust Law for use by health-care lawyers and health-care professionals alike. This *Handbook*, like the two earlier editions, is aimed primarily at those who do not specialize in antitrust law, yet who confront antitrust issues in health care on a frequent basis, either as lawyers who counsel their clients or as health-care professionals in their business activities.

The Original *Handbook* was prepared in 1988, and a second edition was released in 1993. Ten years have passed since the second edition, however. In that time, the federal antitrust enforcement agencies have issued statements of their enforcement policy in health care, the most recent of which were issued in 1996, and continue to be very influential. The agencies also have published myriad business review and staff advisory opinion letters, and have filed numerous civil actions in the health-care field. Private litigation in health care continues to account for a substantial amount of all antitrust litigation. Over the last decade the courts, including the Supreme Court, have issued important decisions that have substantially reshaped large areas of health-care antitrust law.

Because of the substantial passage of time since the last *Handbook*, the Health Care Committee realized that a new edition would have to be written that could not simply represent an update of the last edition. The Committee wishes to acknowledge the important contributions of Howard M. Ullman, D. Matthew Allen, Michael Farber, Jennifer Gladieux, and Greg Wrobel, who began the process of revising the prior *Handbook*, and of Neil Imus, Jonathan Jacobson, and Dara Diomande, who provided valuable editorial assistance. Jeff Miles is deserving of the Committee's special thanks, as he took on this project when a great deal of work remained to be done and devoted a tremendous amount of time and energy to its completion. Without Jeff's efforts, the *Antitrust Health Care Handbook III* would not have become a reality.

The Appendix lists Web sites with current information on court decisions, governmental enforcement, and legislation on the application of antitrust law to health care, many of which can be accessed through the Section of Antitrust Law's own Web site at *www.abanet.org/antitrust.*

Douglas C. Ross
Chair, Health Care Committee
Section of Antitrust Law
American Bar Association 2003-2004

INTRODUCTION

No sector of the United States economy is more important to American consumers than the health-care sector. Not only are health-care services indispensable, having no reasonable substitutes, but in 2002, the latest year for which statistics are available, expenditures for health care were $1.6 trillion, or some 14.9 percent of United States Gross Domestic Product, amounting to $5,440 per person.[1] The average consumer spent approximately 6 percent of disposable income on health care. More disturbing, after several years of relative stability in health-care expenditures, spending on health care has accelerated in recent years. For example, while expenditures on health care grew only about 5 percent per year between 1995 and 1999, they increased by some 8.5 percent in 2002 and 9.3 percent in 2002. In comparison, Gross Domestic Product grew by only 3.6 percent in 2002.[2]

Because the United States, unlike many other countries, relies primarily on market forces to allocate health-care resources, it comes as no surprise that the recent rapid increases in health-care costs have attracted the attention of state and federal antitrust enforcement agencies, whose job is to examine whether conduct adversely affecting competition is a significant cause of this phenomenon. Accordingly, the chairman of the Federal Trade Commission (FTC) has indicated that antitrust issues in the health-care sector will be a priority of the FTC,[3] and FTC actions appear to corroborate this. For example, the FTC is conducting a hospital-merger retrospective, in which it

---

1. *See* Katherine Levit et al., *Health Spending Rebound Continues in 2002,* HEALTH AFFAIRS, Jan.–Feb. 2004, at 147, 149.
2. *See generally* Sara Munoz, *U.S. Health-Care Spending Rose 9.3% in 2002,* WALL ST. J., Jan. 9, 2004, at A2; David Brown, *Health Care Spending Increases for 6th Year,* WASHINGTON POST, Jan. 9, 2004, at A3.
3. *See* William M. Sage, *Protective Competition and Consumers: A Conversation With Timothy J. Muris,* HEALTH AFFAIRS, Nov.–Dec. 2003, at 101, 102 ("When I took over as chairman [of the FTC], I wanted to emphasize health care. . . . On the antitrust side, we have close to doubled our resources on health care."); Timothy J. Muris, Chairman, Federal Trade Commission, "Opening Remarks," Prepared Remarks Before the Federal Trade Commission and U.S. Depart-

is examining consummated hospital mergers and attempting to determine their actual effect on competition.[4] Antitrust Division officials also have indicated that the Division will actively enforce the antitrust laws in the health-care sector.[5] The FTC and the Antitrust Division concluded some 30 days of joint hearings from February through October 2003 to study competition in the health-care sector and the proper role of the antitrust laws,[6] after holding two days of hearings on health-care competition and antitrust in September 2002.[7]

This *Antitrust Health Care Handbook III* outlines and discusses the basic antitrust principles applicable to providers and others in the health-care sector, many of the antitrust issues that frequently arise, and methods to minimize antitrust problems. The *Handbook* emphasizes federal antitrust

---

ment of Justice Hearings on Health Care and Competition Law and Policy (Feb. 26, 2003), *at* http://www.ftc.gov/ogc/healthcarehearings/docs/030226muris.htm; Timothy J. Muris, Chairman, Federal Trade Commission, "Everything Old Is New Again: Health Care and Competition in the 21st Century," Prepared Remarks Before the Northwestern University School of Law Annual Competition in Health Care Forum (Nov. 7, 2002), *at* http://www.ftc/gov/speeches/muris/murishealthcarespeech0211.pdf.

4. *See* FTC Press Release, "FTC Announces Formation of Merger Litigation Task Force" (Aug. 28, 2002), *at* http://www.ftc.gov/opa/2002/08/mergerlitigation/htm; *see also* Payton M. Sturgis, *FTC Staff Recommends Case Closures, Statement to Give Guidance, Attorneys Say*, Health L. Rep. (BNA), Dec. 18, 2003, at 1885.

5. *See generally* Deborah Platt Majoras, Deputy Assistant Attorney General, Antitrust Division, Prepared Remarks Before the Federal Trade Commission Health Care Competition Law and Policy Workshop (Sept. 9, 2002), *at* http://www.usdoj.gov/atr/public/speeches/200195.pdf.

6. The agenda, hearing transcripts, and related documents from the hearings are on the FTC's Web site *at* http://www.ftc.gov/ogc/healthcarehearings/index.htm. For summaries of the hearing presentations prepared by the ABA Section of Antitrust Law's Health Care Committee, *see* http://www.aba.net.org/antitrust/committees/health/hearings.html.

7. *See* Federal Trade Commission Public Workshop: Federal Trade Commission Workshop on Health Care and Competition Law and Policy, *at* http://www.ftc.gov/ogc/healthcare/index/htm.

principles; state antitrust statutes and legal principles largely parallel federal law and are not discussed separately.[8]

The application of antitrust principles to health-care markets and conduct is inherently fact-specific. Thus, the overview presented here is not a substitute for focused and detailed analysis of specific conduct by qualified antitrust counsel knowledgeable about health-care markets, regulation, and current governmental enforcement policies.

---

8. For an in-depth discussion of state antitrust laws and principles, *see* ABA SECTION OF ANTITRUST LAW, STATE ANTITRUST PRACTICE AND STATUTES (3d ed. 2004) [hereinafter *ABA State Antitrust Practice*].

CHAPTER 1

ANTITRUST OVERVIEW

A. Application of the Antitrust Laws to Health Care

The health-care sector comprises numerous industries providing a broad array of products and services, including medical care by licensed physicians and other health-care professionals, inpatient and outpatient services of hospitals and other facilities, prescription drugs, durable medical equipment, home-health services, and a variety of arrangements for delivering and paying for health-care services, ranging from traditional indemnity insurance to health maintenance organizations (HMOs). These varied products and services are delivered to consumers by health-care providers and payers through a complex web of contractual and regulatory relationships.

Until the mid-1970s, antitrust cases in the health-care sector were rare. For many years after passage of the Sherman Act, the practice of medicine was considered a "learned profession," rather than "trade or commerce," and thus it was debatable whether the antitrust laws applied to it.[1] In addition, the delivery of health care is often a local activity, and thus it was questionable whether the rendering of health-care services affected interstate commerce sufficiently for courts to have subject-matter jurisdiction over cases brought under the federal antitrust laws.

The U.S. Supreme Court issued important decisions in 1975 and 1976, however, settling these issues. In its 1975 *Goldfarb v. Virginia State Bar* decision,[2] the Court held that there is no "learned professions" exemption from antitrust coverage, although it also noted that there may be differences in antitrust treatment between the activities of professions and other occupations.[3] The next year, the Court decided *Hospital Building Co. v. Trustees of*

---

1. *See, e.g.,* FTC v. Raladam Co., 283 U.S. 643, 653 (1931) (noting that medical practitioners "follow a profession and not a trade"); *but cf.* Am. Med. Ass'n v. United States, 317 U.S. 519 (1943) (suggesting that antitrust laws apply to activities of physicians).
2. 421 U.S. 773 (1975).
3. *Id.* at 788 n.17.

Rex Hospital,[4] in which it explained that the activities of a local hospital might affect interstate commerce sufficiently to fall within the purview of federal antitrust law. In succeeding years, the Supreme Court issued other important decisions establishing the federal antitrust laws' broad application to health care.[5] Now, antitrust claims frequently are asserted against the conduct of health-care providers and payers, and it is clear that the antitrust laws apply to activities in the health-care sector just as they do to activities in other sectors of the economy.[6]

---

4. 425 U.S. 738 (1976).
5. *See* Cal. Dental Ass'n v. FTC, 526 U.S. 756 (1999) (discussing application of the "quick look" rule of reason in the context of a professional association's restraints on advertising); Summit Health Ltd. v. Pinhas, 500 U.S. 322 (1991) (discussing the interstate commerce requirement in the context of a hospital staff-privilege exclusion); Patrick v. Burget, 486 U.S. 94 (1986) (discussing the state-action exemption in the context of a hospital staff-privilege peer-review proceeding); FTC v. Ind. Fed'n of Dentists, 476 U.S. 447 (1986) (discussing application of the rule of reason in the context of a concerted provider effort to thwart cost containment by payers); Jefferson Parish Hosp. Dist. No. 2 v. Hyde, 466 U.S. 2 (1984) (discussing tying arrangements in the context of an exclusive hospital-physician contract); Arizona v. Maricopa County Med. Soc'y, 457 U.S. 332 (1982) (discussing horizontal price-fixing in the context of a physician contracting network); Am. Med. Ass'n v. FTC, 455 U.S. 676 (1982) (affirmance by equally divided court) (discussing ethical provisions affecting advertising and solicitation of patients and modes of practice by physicians); Union Labor Life Ins. Co. v. Pireno, 458 U.S. 119 (1982) (discussing the McCarran Act exemption for the business of insurance in the context of a fee peer-review program); Nat'l Gerimedical Hosp. & Gerontology Ctr. v. Blue Cross, 452 U.S. 378 (1981) (discussing the implied-repeal doctrine in the context of health planning); Group Life & Health Ins. Co. v. Royal Drug Co., 440 U.S. 205 (1979) (discussing the McCarran Act exemption for the business of insurance in the context of provider-payer agreements); St. Paul Fire & Marine Ins. Co. v. Barry, 438 U.S. 531 (1978) (discussing the McCarran Act exemption for the business of insurance in the context of malpractice insurance).
6. *E.g.,* Boulware v. Nevada, 960 F.2d 793, 796 (9th Cir. 1992) (emphasizing that "[h]ealth-care providers are exposed to the same liability and entitled to the same defenses as businesses in other industries"); *cf.* Timothy J. Muris, Chairman, Federal Trade Commission, "Opening Remarks," Prepared Remarks Before the Federal Trade Commission and U.S. Department of Justice Hearings on Health Care and Competition Law and Policy (Feb. 26, 2003)

B. Purpose of the Antitrust Laws

Antitrust law encourages and protects competition as this country's mechanism for allocating resources by prohibiting conduct that unreasonably interferes with competition among sellers and among buyers. As the Supreme Court has stated:

> The Sherman Act was designed to be a comprehensive charter of economic liberty aimed at preserving free and unfettered competition as the rule of trade. It rests on the premise that the unrestrained interaction of competitive forces will yield the best allocation of our economic resources, the lowest prices, the highest quality and the greatest material progress, while at the same time providing an environment conducive to the preservation of our democratic political and social institutions. But even were that premise open to question, the policy unequivocally laid down by the Act is competition.[7]

By protecting competition, antitrust law seeks to maximize consumer welfare by promoting the efficient use of scarce resources and thus high output, low prices, high quality, varied services, innovation, and efficiency in production and distribution.[8] Antitrust law, however, does not protect individual competitors from the consequences of normal market forces, from aggressive competition by others, from more efficient competitors,[9] or from

---

(explaining that "[c]ompetition law does not hinder the delivery of high-quality health care" and that "[a]ggressive competition promotes lower prices, higher quality, greater innovation and enhanced access. More concretely, in health care, competition results in new and improved drugs, cheaper generic drugs, treatment with less pain and fewer side effects, and treatments offered in a manner and location consumers desire"), *at* http://www.ftc.gov/ogc/ healthcarehearings/docs/030226muris.htm.

7. N. Pac. Ry. v. United States, 356 U.S. 1, 4-5 (1958).

8. *See, e.g.*, Reiter v. Sonotone Corp., 442 U.S. 330, 343 (1979) (antitrust laws are a "consumer welfare prescription"); *cf.* Stop & Shop Supermarket Co. v. Blue Cross & Blue Shield, 239 F. Supp. 2d 180, 186 (D.R.I. 2003) (the antitrust laws are "aimed at activities that interfere with competitive markets and their ability to provide adequate supplies of quality goods at reasonable prices").

9. *See* Freeman v. San Diego Ass'n of Realtors, 322 F.3d 1133, 1154 (9th Cir.) ("Inefficiency is precisely what the market aims to weed out. The Sherman

unfair or arbitrary conduct that does not harm marketwide competition and thus consumers.[10] Indeed, one of the most important of all antitrust-law principles is that "[t]he antitrust laws . . . were enacted for 'the protection of competition, not *competitors*.'"[11] Stated most succinctly, antitrust law protects consumers from the effects of market power unless that power was obtained through competition on the merits. Even where market power is achieved by competition on the merits, antitrust law prohibits maintenance or expansion of that power by conduct unreasonably excluding competitors from the market.

Most basically, antitrust law focuses on "collusion" and "exclusion." Collusion occurs when firms, usually but not necessarily competitors, reach agreements or understandings that significantly reduce competition among themselves (such as agreements about the prices they will charge) and thus adversely affect consumers by increasing prices or reducing quality, choice, or access to goods or services. Exclusion results when a single firm (or group of firms acting in concert) engages in conduct that significantly hinders or prevents competition against them from other firms already in the market or firms that would enter the market, resulting in the same types of consumer harm.

C. Competition in Health Care

In competitive markets, the optimal output, quality, prices, and other terms of purchase and sale are achieved through rivalry among suppliers seeking to

---

Act, to put it bluntly, contemplates some roadkill on the turnpike to Efficiencyville."), *cert. denied*, 124 S.Ct. 355 (2003).

10. *See, e.g.*, NYNEX Corp. v. Discon, Inc., 525 U.S. 128, 137 (1998) (explaining that other laws dealing with unfair dealing and unfair competition, business torts, and business regulation provide remedies for competitive practices that offend standards of business morality); Spectrum Sports, Inc. v. McQuillan, 506 U.S. 447, 458 (1993) (purpose of antitrust law "is not to protect businesses from the working of the market; it is to protect the public from the failure of the market"); Brooke Group Ltd. v. Brown & Williamson Tobacco Co., 509 U.S. 209, 225 (1993) (antitrust law does not create a "federal law of unfair competition"); Ehredt Underground, Inc. v. Commonwealth Edison Co., 90 F.3d 238, 240 (7th Cir. 1996) (noting that antitrust law "is designed to protect consumers from producers, not to protect producers from each other or to insure that one firm gets more of the business").

11. Brunswick Corp. v. Pueblo Bowl-O-Mat, Inc., 429 U.S. 477, 488 (1977).

satisfy consumer preferences as revealed by their dollar votes in freely negotiated transactions. Health-care markets, however, have important characteristics that influence, and arguably distort, normal market forces, sometimes preventing the market from allocating resources efficiently. Among these are:

1. "Moral hazard" resulting from the significant role of third-party payers (governmental health plans and private insurance), which makes consumers less sensitive to actual prices and costs and, as a result, likely to demand more health-care goods and services than optimal or economically efficient. This concern, coupled with the significant overall cost of health care, has made containment of cost and utilization primary goals of governmental policy and of both governmental and private payers.

2. Informational deficiencies and asymmetries, that is, a perceived lack of information necessary for consumers to make informed choices about the type, quality, quantity, and cost of the health care they need or desire. Frequently, others, particularly providers, serve as the patient's "agent," effectively making purchasing decisions on his or her behalf.

3. The highly personal nature of health care, which may make consumers reluctant to switch among rival physicians and other health-care providers based on prices, cost, or other competitive factors.

4. Ethical considerations and governmental programs mandating broad access to health care without regard to ability to pay.

5. Price controls in governmental health plans that may result in cross-subsidization through providers' higher prices to private commercial health plans.

6. Entry barriers, such as certificate-of-need, credentialing, and licensing requirements intended to limit over-investment in facilities or to maintain competence and quality, but which also may constrain entry into health-care markets and limit supply.

7. Substantial economies of scale and scope in some market settings, particularly those for hospital services, specialty care, and high-tech equipment, which may result in fewer providers serving a market or even in "natural monopolies."

8. The price inelasticity of demand for health-care services resulting from the absence of alternatives.

9. The nonprofit status of many health-care providers, particularly hospitals, which may affect their incentives to maximize profits and, because of their tax-exempt status, their costs.
10. The tax treatment of employer payments for health insurance, which may result in overinvestment in insurance.
11. Legal and practical requirements that some providers, particularly hospitals, provide certain services regardless of whether they are profitable.

These concerns or "market imperfections" notwithstanding, competition remains the primary determinant of the range, quality, quantity, and prices of health-care services offered to consumers. Moreover, antitrust analysis is sufficiently flexible to take account of these factors.

The increased prevalence of managed care has resulted in competition not only among rival providers of specific health-care goods and services, but also among rival payers offering different types of health plans with varying cost structures and choices of participating providers. Much of this competition has focused on reducing cost and utilization through price concessions, risk-sharing arrangements with providers, and medical-management programs. Providers compete, first, to participate in health plans and then for those plans' subscribers.[12]

These competitive pressures have prompted varied responses in local and regional health-care markets. Many providers have merged or entered into joint ventures to reduce operating costs and facilitate their participation in managed-care contracts with health plans. These same types of transactions, however, may also result in the providers' obtaining significant market power and thus may cause antitrust concerns.

There also has been significant consolidation among payers, prompting concerns by some that dominant sellers of health plans and dominant purchasers of health-care services will emerge.[13] Providers, particularly physi-

---

12. For a discussion, *see* Gregory Vistnes, *Hospitals, Mergers and Two-Stage Competition*, 67 ANTITRUST L. J. 671 (2000).
13. *See, e.g.*, United States v. Aetna, Inc., 1999-2 Trade Cas. (CCH) ¶ 72,730 (N.D. Tex. 1999) (consent decree and competitive impact statement) (requiring health-plan divestitures in Houston and Dallas to resolve claims that Aetna's acquisition of Prudential's health plans would create both a dominant seller of health plans and a dominant purchaser of physician services in local markets for HMO and HMO-based point-of-service health plans).

cians, have complained that they lack the bargaining power to engage in meaningful negotiations with large health plans over prices and other terms of service and that this is compromising patient care.[14] State governments, in some instances, have responded by mandating that specified services be included in health plans or by prohibiting certain practices by health plans that arguably interfere with the relationship between physicians and their patients.[15] Similar federal legislation has been considered in Congress. State and federal legislation also has been proposed to permit health-care professionals to bargain collectively in contracting with health plans, and there has been significant debate and disagreement as to whether these and other legislative proposals to alter the interplay of competitive forces in health-care markets are warranted or would benefit consumers.[16] In response, payers argue that it is the

---

14. *See, e.g.*, AMERICAN MEDICAL ASSOCIATION, COMPETITION IN HEALTH INSURANCE: A COMPREHENSIVE STUDY OF U.S. MARKETS (2d ed. 2002).

15. *See generally* 1999 STATE BY STATE GUIDE TO MANAGED CARE LAW (Stauffer & Levy eds. 1999) (in-depth summary and analysis of state managed-care laws, including laws mandating that health plans provide access to providers or specific health-care services).

16. *See* Quality Health Care Coalition Act of 2003, H.R. 1247, 108th Cong. (2003); Health Care Antitrust Improvements Act of 2002, H.R. 3897, 107th Cong. (2002). *See generally* ABA SECTION OF ANTITRUST LAW, ANTITRUST IMMUNITY LEGISLATION FOR HEALTH CARE PROVIDERS (2000); Fred J. Hellinger & Gary J. Young, *An Analysis of Physician Antitrust Exemption Legislation*, J. AM. MED. ASS'N, July. 4, 2001, at 83 (concluding that federal exemption legislation would "appreciably alter the balance of power between physicians and managed care plans").

    The FTC and Antitrust Division have consistently opposed an antitrust exemption for physician joint negotiations with payers. *See* Prepared Statement of Robert Pitofsky, Chairman, Federal Trade Commission, before the House Judiciary Committee on H.R. 1304, The Quality Health Care Coalition Act of 1999 (June 22, 1999), *at* http://www.ftc.gov/05/1999/06/healthcaretestimony.htm; Statement of Joel I. Klein, Assistant Attorney General, Antitrust Division, before the House Judiciary Committee on H.R. 1304, The Quality Health Care Coalition Act of 1999 (June 22, 1999), *at* http://www.usdoj.gov/atr/public/testimony/2502.htm. The FTC also has consistently opposed state legislation that purportedly would permit physicians to bargain collectively with payers by triggering state-action exemption protection for their activities. *See, e.g.*, FTC Staff Letter to Ohio House of Representatives (Oct. 16, 2002), *at* http://www.ftc.gov/05/2002/10/ohb325.htm; FTC Staff Letter to State of Washington House of Representa-

providers who have gained too much market power through, for example, hospital mergers and the formation of provider-controlled contracting networks.[17]

Given the importance and cost of health care, such debates will continue at many levels. At present, however, health-care providers and payers, for the most part, must conform their conduct to established antitrust principles, which are outlined in this Handbook.

D. Principal Federal Antitrust Statutes

The principal federal antitrust statutes containing substantive standards of conduct are Sections 1 and 2 of the Sherman Act[18] and Sections 2 (as amended by the Robinson-Patman Act), 3, and 7 of the Clayton Act.[19] These statutes describe prohibited conduct (rather than affirmative obligations), but do so only in general terms. Most of the antitrust principles outlined in this Handbook have been established in court decisions interpreting and applying these general provisions.

Section 1 of the Sherman Act prohibits contracts, combinations, and conspiracies that unreasonably restrain competition, and Section 2 prohibits monopolization, attempted monopolization, and conspiracies to monopolize. Section 3 of the Clayton Act prohibits exclusive dealing agreements, requirements contracts, and tying arrangements in the sale of commodities (but not services), where the effect of the arrangement may be to lessen competition substantially.[20] Section 7 of the Clayton Act prohibits mergers and acquisitions (including the formation of joint ventures) that may substantially lessen competition or tend to create a monopoly in any line of commerce in any section of the country. Section 2(a) of the Clayton Act (as amended by the

---

tives (Feb. 8, 2002), *at* http://ftc.gov/bc/v020009.pdf; FTC Staff Letter to Alaska House of Representatives (Jan. 18, 2002), *at* http://www.ftc.gov/bc/020003.pdf.

17. *See, e.g.*, Bob Cook, *Clash of the Titans*, AM. MED. NEWS, Dec. 23-30, 2002, at 19 (claiming that "hospital systems built up by consolidation are telling health plans . . . that it's payback time for years of accepting substandard reimbursement").

18. 15 U.S.C. §§ 1, 2.

19. 15 U.S.C. §§ 13, 14, 18.

20. Section 1 of the Sherman Act does apply to services and thus to tying arrangements and exclusive dealing agreements involving services.

Robinson-Patman Act) prohibits sellers from discriminating in price between different purchasers in the sale of commodities of like grade and quality, where the discrimination may lessen competition, tend to create a monopoly, or injure competition. Section 2(f) of the Robinson-Patman Act prohibits buyers from inducing such discriminatory prices.

Section 5(a) of the Federal Trade Commission Act,[21] which technically is not an "[a]ntitrust law[ ],"[22] prohibits unfair methods of competition and unfair or deceptive acts or practices. "Unfair methods of competition" include conduct prohibited by the antitrust statutes described above, as well as other anticompetitive conduct that does not, as a technical matter, violate these statutes; "unfair and deceptive acts or practices" covers a broad variety of conduct that need not violate antitrust law or amount to an unfair method of competition, but which deceives or misleads consumers.[23]

Section 7A of the Clayton Act[24] (part of the Hart-Scott-Rodino Antitrust Improvements Act of 1976) establishes notification and waiting-period requirements for certain mergers and other acquisitions that meet prescribed thresholds, requiring that the parties report them to both the Antitrust Division and FTC. The FTC's implementing regulations[25] specify information that parties must provide before such transactions may be consummated. The agencies may request additional information, and thereby extend the waiting period for specific transactions. In practice, these requirements enable the agencies to conduct substantial investigations of proposed acquisitions before they occur, and thus to challenge transactions they believe are anticompetitive or to negotiate relief (such as partial divestitures and technology licensing) as a condition to permitting them to proceed without challenge.

E. Antitrust Enforcement and Penalties

The federal antitrust laws are enforced by the Antitrust Division of the United States Department of Justice, the Federal Trade Commission, state attorneys

---

21. 15 U.S.C. § 45(a).
22. *See id.* § 12 (defining the term "[a]ntitrust laws").
23. *See generally* ABA Section of Antitrust Law, Antitrust Law Developments 616-47 (5th ed. 2002) [hereinafter *ALD V*].
24. 15 U.S.C. § 18a.
25. 16 C.F.R. §§ 801.1-803.90 & App.

general, and private plaintiffs.[26] In enforcing the Sherman Act, the Antitrust Division may bring either criminal or civil actions in federal court, seeking fines, imprisonment, and injunctive relief. The Division's antitrust investigations sometimes spawn criminal investigations for obstruction of justice, wire fraud, and mail fraud. The Division also brings civil actions challenging acquisitions under Section 7 of the Clayton Act.

The FTC is authorized to enforce the FTC Act through general rulemaking, by initiating administrative enforcement proceedings that may result in the issuance of cease and desist orders reviewable by federal circuit courts of appeals, and by seeking civil remedies in court in certain instances.[27] The FTC also enforces, among other statutes, Section 7 of the Clayton Act and the Robinson-Patman Act.

State attorneys general may file actions under the federal antitrust laws as *parens patriae* on behalf of the state's consumers injured by the violation,[28] enforcement actions under their state antitrust laws (civil or criminal, depending on the particular state's laws), and civil actions for damages they suffer under their state antitrust laws.

In addition, any person (including federal and state governments) who is injured or threatened by a violation of federal antitrust law may bring a civil suit in federal court to enjoin particular conduct and, except for the federal government, to recover three times the party's actual damages.[29] The federal government may recover single damages.[30] A prevailing plaintiff in a civil action for damages under the federal (and most state) antitrust laws must be awarded its reasonable attorneys' fees and costs, but a prevailing defendant generally has no corresponding right. Private plaintiffs must satisfy the "antitrust standing" and "antitrust injury" requirements that are discussed later.[31]

Sections 1 and 2 of the Sherman Act are criminal as well as civil statutes. Violations are felonies and can result in incarceration of not more than three years for each criminal violation by an individual. The Sherman Act also

---

26. For discussions of enforcement by each of these parties, *see ALD V, supra* p. 9 n.23, at 725-96 (Antitrust Division enforcement); 603-16, 653-98 (FTC enforcement); 803-29 (state enforcement); 835-1028 (private enforcement).
27. 15 U.S.C. §§ 45(b), 45(m), 53(b), 57b.
28. *Id.* § 15c.
29. *Id.* §§ 15, 15a, 26.
30. *Id.* § 15a.
31. *See infra* pp. 52-57.

provides for per-violation fines of not more than $350,000 for individuals and $10 million for corporations. Much higher fines now can be imposed, equal to twice the defendant's gain or twice the loss suffered by victims.[32] Only the Antitrust Division has authority to prosecute Sherman Act violations criminally, but it has exercised that power against health-care providers only rarely.[33] How the Division proceeds depends on prosecutorial discretion, however, and Antitrust Division representatives have expressed interest in possible criminal prosecutions in the health-care sector.[34]

Both the FTC and Antitrust Division have formal procedures by which they issue advisory opinions with regard to proposed, but unimplemented, conduct. The FTC issues both full-Commission opinions and staff advisory opinions,[35] while the Antitrust Division issues "business review letters."[36] Under these procedures, parties planning to engage in specific types of conduct that may raise antitrust concern can write the agencies explaining their proposed conduct, and the agencies will respond stating whether, if the parties implement the conduct, the agency will challenge it. Both agencies have issued numerous advisory opinions discussing the proposed conduct of health-care

---

32. 18 U.S.C. § 3571(d).
33. *See* Am. Med. Ass'n v. United States, 317 U.S. 519 (1943); United States v. A. Lanoy Alston, D.M.D., P.C., 974 F.2d 1206 (9th Cir. 1992) (review of post-trial rulings following jury verdict for government in criminal price-fixing case against Arizona dentists; parties settled following remand and before retrial); United States v. Lake Country Optometric Soc'y, No. W95CR114 (W.D. Tex., Jul. 9, 1996) (guilty plea for fixing price of eye exams; $75,000 fine and five-year probation), *summarized at* [1988-1996 Transfer Binder] Trade Reg. Rep. (CCH) ¶ 45,095, at 44,781.
34. *See* Deborah Platt Majoras, Deputy Assistant Attorney General, Antitrust Division, Prepared Remarks Before the Federal Trade Commission Health Care and Competition Law and Policy Workshop (Sept. 9, 2002) (noting that "if, in our scrutiny of horizontal conduct, we discover health care businesses crossing the line to engage in explicit collusive arrangements regarding fees or market allocation, we will consider prosecuting criminally"), *at* http://www.usdoj.gov/atr/public/speeches/200195.pdf.
35. *See* 16 C.F.R. §§ 1.1-1.3. For helpful guidance regarding the FTC's advisory-opinion process, *see* Judith A. Moreland, Staff Attorney, Federal Trade Commission, "Overview of the Advisory Opinion Process at the Federal Trade Commission," Prepared Remarks Before the National Health Lawyers Association's Antitrust in the Healthcare Field Seminar (Feb. 13, 1997), *at* http://www.ftc.gov/bc/ speeches/speech2.htm.
36. *See* 28 C.F.R. § 50.6.

sector participants,[37] particularly the activities of provider-controlled contracting networks, such as physician-controlled independent practice associations (IPAs) and preferred provider organizations (PPOs).[38] Some state attorneys general also have advisory-opinion procedures as well.

In addition, the federal agencies have issued several sets of helpful antitrust guidelines, including guidelines for analyzing horizontal mergers,[39] other types of collaborative transactions among competitors,[40] and, perhaps most important here, particular actions undertaken by health-care providers.[41] These guidelines are extremely important in analyzing the types of conduct they cover and offer some of the most focused guidance available.

F. State Antitrust Statutes

Almost all states, as well as the District of Columbia, Puerto Rico, and the Virgin Islands, have some type of state antitrust statute. Most have provisions that parallel Sections 1 and 2 of the Sherman Act, and a number also have provisions similar to Sections 3 and 7 of the Clayton Act and the Robinson-

---

37. *E.g.,* FTC Staff Advisory Opinion to Bay Area Preferred Physicians (Sept. 23, 2003), *at* http://www.ftc.gov/bc/adops/bapp/030923.htm; Antitrust Division Business Review Letter to Washington State Medical Association (Sept. 23, 2002), *at* http://www.usdoj.gov/atr/public/busreview/200260.htm.

38. *E.g.,* FTC Staff Advisory Opinion to MedSouth, Inc. (Feb. 19, 2002), *at* http://www.ftc.gov/bc/ adops/medsouth.htm.

39. U.S. DEP'T OF JUSTICE & FEDERAL TRADE COMM'N, HORIZONTAL MERGER GUIDELINES (1992) (with April 8, 1997 revisions to Section 4 on efficiencies) [hereinafter *1992 Merger Guidelines*], *reprinted in* 4 Trade Reg. Rep. (CCH) ¶ 13,104.

40. FEDERAL TRADE COMM'N & U.S. DEP'T OF JUSTICE, ANTITRUST GUIDELINES FOR COLLABORATIONS AMONG COMPETITORS (2000) [hereinafter *Collaboration Guidelines*], *reprinted in* 4 Trade Reg. Rep. (CCH) ¶ 13,161.

41. U.S. DEP'T OF JUSTICE & FEDERAL TRADE COMM'N, STATEMENTS OF ANTITRUST ENFORCEMENT POLICY IN HEALTH CARE (1996) [hereinafter *Health Care Enforcement Statements*], *reprinted in* 4 Trade Reg. Rep. (CCH) ¶ 13,153. The statements discuss small hospital mergers, hospital joint ventures involving expensive equipment and high technology clinical services, provision of non-fee information by providers to payers, collective provision of fee information by providers to payers, the exchange of price and wage information, joint purchasing arrangements, physician-controlled contracting organizations, and multi-provider contracting organizations.

Patman Act.[42] Many state antitrust acts include a provision that interpretations of the federal antitrust laws should guide the courts' interpretation of the parallel state provisions.

Many state antitrust statutes have general exemptions for governmental regulation, insurance, and other matters, which may shield certain conduct of health-care providers or payers from claims under state antitrust law. Some states also have enacted "certificate of public advantage" statutes that establish a regulatory approval process for certain collaborative transactions and arrangements among health-care providers, such as mergers.[43] These statutes are intended to protect conduct approved by the state from federal antitrust claims by creating state procedures that attempt to meet the requirements of the state-action exemption doctrine discussed later.[44]

G. Government Enforcement in Health Care

Both state and federal antitrust agencies have been active enforcers of the antitrust laws in the health-care sector. The agencies have challenged, for example, a number of hospital mergers and provider price-fixing conduct directed at health plans.[45] The Antitrust Division has also examined allegedly anticompetitive conduct by health plans.[46] The agencies also have issued sig-

---

42. *See ABA State Antitrust Practice, supra* p. xiii n.8, for an in-depth analysis of state antitrust statutes and court decisions.
43. *See id.* App. C, which compiles and discusses these statutes. The state antitrust laws are also reproduced at 6 Trade Reg. Rep. (CCH) ¶¶ 30,201-602.
44. *See infra* pp. 44-45.
45. For compilations of health-care antitrust cases brought by the Antitrust Division, *see* U.S. Dep't of Justice, Antitrust Division, Health Care Task Force Recent Enforcement Actions (1999), *at* http://www.usdoj.gov/atr/public/health_care/2044.htm; U.S. Dep't of Justice, Antitrust Division, Summary of Antitrust Division Health Care Cases (since August 25, 1983) (undated), *at* http://www.usdoj.gov/atr/public/health_care/0000.pdf. For a compilation of FTC health-care cases, *see* Jeffrey W. Brennan, Assistant Director, David R. Pender, Deputy Assistant Director & Markus H. Meir, Deputy Assistant Director, Bureau of Competition, Federal Trade Commission, FTC Antitrust Actions in Health Care Services and Products (Oct. 24, 2003), *at* http://www.ftc.gov/bc/hcupdate031024.pdf.
46. *See* Deborah Platt Majoras, Deputy Assistant Attorney General, Antitrust Division, Prepared Remarks Before the FTC Health Care and Competition Law and Policy Workshop (Sept. 9, 2002) ("One area of primary concern for

nificant guidance through advisory opinions, explaining their general anti-trust enforcement policies in health care and analyzing numerous proposed health-care joint ventures and other collaborative arrangements.[47]

Federal and state enforcement authorities frequently cooperate in health-care antitrust investigations and enforcement actions, and the agencies have issued a protocol describing basic procedures for their coordinated enforcement.[48] States also coordinate antitrust enforcement among themselves through the Multistate Antitrust Task Force of the National Association of Attorneys General. These efforts serve important enforcement goals by permitting participants to share expertise and resources and affording greater certainty to health-care providers and payers seeking to resolve antitrust concerns in a consistent and expeditious manner. Federal and state enforcement authorities have overlapping jurisdiction with respect to most conduct,[49] and the states have enforced the antitrust laws in the health-care sector actively.[50]

[the] Litigation I [Section] will be the evaluation of mergers of, and unilateral or coordinated conduct by, health insurers."), *at* http://www.usdoj.gov/atr/public/speeches/ 200195.pdf.

47. The Antitrust Division business review letters and the FTC staff advisory opinion letters are available on their respective websites: http://www.usdoj.gov/atr/public/busreview/letters.htm and http://www.ftc.gov/bc/advisory.htm. In addition, all the agencies' advisory letters discussing health-care issues are gathered in 3 JOHN J. MILES, HEALTH CARE & ANTITRUST LAW, Apps. C & D (2003) [hereinafter *HCAL*]. Appendix E of that treatise collects significant speeches by agency officials discussing health-care antitrust issues. In addition, the Antitrust Division's business review letters relating to health care issued between September 28, 1993, and February 5, 2002 are summarized in U.S. Dep't of Justice, Antitrust Division, Health Care Business Review Letters Issued (Feb. 5, 2002), *at* http://www.usdoj.gov/atr/public/health_care/9950.pdf.

48. *See* U.S. DEP'T OF JUSTICE, FEDERAL TRADE COMM'N & NATIONAL ASS'N OF ATTOR-NEYS GENERAL, PROTOCOL FOR JOINT FEDERAL/STATE MERGER INVESTIGATIONS (1998), *reprinted in* 4 Trade Reg. Rep. (CCH) ¶ 13,420. For discussion of joint investigations, *see* ABA SECTION OF ANTITRUST LAW, STATE ANTITRUST ENFORCE-MENT HANDBOOK 42-44, 146-49 (2003) [hereinafter *ABA State Antitrust Handbook*].

49. *See generally* Robert Langer, *A Practitioner's Guide to State Antitrust Health Care Issues*, ANTITRUST, Fall 1995, at 32 (discussing examples of both joint and separate federal/state antitrust enforcement in health care).

50. *See ABA State Antitrust Handbook*, *supra* n.48, at 137-68 (discussing state antitrust enforcement in health-care markets).

CHAPTER 2

BASIC ANTITRUST CONCEPTS AND PRINCIPLES

A. Interstate Commerce

Federal antitrust statutes, by their terms, apply only to "trade or commerce among the several States, or with foreign nations."[1] In addition, because the antitrust laws were enacted pursuant to the congressional constitutional power over interstate and foreign commerce, a federal court would lack jurisdiction over the subject matter absent the requisite effect on interstate or foreign commerce. The interstate commerce requirement may be satisfied by showing that the challenged conduct directly interferes with the flow of goods or services in interstate commerce, or that the defendant's activities substantially affect interstate commerce.[2]

The Supreme Court, in *Summit Health, Ltd. v. Pinhas*,[3] established a low threshold for satisfying the interstate commerce requirement. In that case, the Court focused on the possible effect, if successful, of an alleged conspiracy to prevent the plaintiff physician from practicing at one hospital, and held that

---

1. *See* 15 U.S.C. §§ 1, 2. For discussion of the interstate-commerce requirement, *see ALD V*, *supra* p. 9 n.23, at 36-46.
2. *See* McLain v. Real Estate Bd., 444 U.S. 232 (1980); Hosp. Bldg. Co. v. Trs. of Rex Hosp., 425 U.S. 738 (1976); *see also* Freeman v. San Diego Ass'n of Realtors, 322 F.3d 1133, 1143 (9th Cir. 2003) ("Monopolizing the local lemonade stand doesn't get you into federal court. To make a federal case, a plaintiff must show that the activities in question, although conducted within a state, have a 'substantial effect on interstate commerce.'"), *cert denied,* 124 S.Ct. 355 (2003); Highmark, Inc. v. UPMC Health Plan, Inc., 276 F.3d 160 (3d Cir. 2001) (Lanham Act case explaining that "Congress's authority under the interstate commerce clause extends even to purely intrastate activity if that activity substantially affects interstate commerce.").
3. 500 U.S. 322 (1991).

the plaintiff sufficiently alleged that the conspiracy would reduce the amount of services provided in that market, that such services were delivered to out-of-state patients and generated revenue from out-of-state sources, and thus that the alleged conspiracy sufficiently affected interstate commerce. In recent years, courts rarely have dismissed federal antitrust claims based on lack of a sufficient nexus with interstate commerce.[4]

B. Relevant Market

Definition of relevant product and geographic markets is the starting point for analyzing many antitrust claims. As the Supreme Court has explained, "[w]ithout a definition of the market there is no way to measure [the defendants'] ability to lessen or destroy competition."[5] Thus, definition of the relevant market is necessary in assessing most rule-of-reason claims under Section 1 of the Sherman Act,[6] claims of monopolization and attempted mo-

---

4. *See, e.g.*, Carpet Group Int'l v. Oriental Rug Imps. Ass'n, Inc., 227 F.3d 62, 75 (3d Cir. 2000) ("a plaintiff's burden of establishing effects on commerce sufficient to confer jurisdiction is not great"); Brader v. Allegheny Gen. Hosp., 64 F.3d 869, 873-74 (3d Cir. 1995) (interstate commerce requirement satisfied where physician alleged that hospital unlawfully terminated his staff privileges and thus limited his ability to serve patients in the relevant market); BCB Anesthesia Care v. Passavant Mem'l Area Hosp. Ass'n, 36 F.3d 664, 666 (7th Cir. 1994) (reversing dismissal of antitrust claims on interstate commerce grounds, finding sufficient nexus with interstate commerce based on allegation that hospital's termination of contract with nurse anesthetists increased costs to out-of-state patients and payers). *But see* Nash v. N. Ark. Human Servs. Sys., 1997-1 Trade Cas. (CCH) ¶ 71,787 (E.D. Ark. 1997) (interstate commerce requirement not satisfied where former employee challenged agreement among local mental health centers not to hire each other's employees because plaintiff failed to allege how reimbursement from out-of-state payers would be affected by the agreement and a market-wide impact could not be presumed).
5. Walker Process Equip. Co. v. Food Mach. & Chem. Co., 382 U.S. 172, 177 (1965).
6. *See, e.g.*, Doctors Hosp. v. Southeast Med. Alliance, Inc., 123 F.3d 301, 310 (5th Cir. 1997); Oksanen v. Page Mem'l Hosp., 945 F.2d 696, 709 (4th Cir. 1991) (en banc).

nopolization under Section 2 of the Sherman Act,[7] and claims under Section 7 of the Clayton Act challenging mergers and acquisitions.[8]

The ultimate purpose for defining relevant markets is to identify other sellers who would constrain the ability of the defendants to raise their prices to supracompetitive levels—sellers to which customers of the defendants would turn to avoid the defendants' price increase because those sellers sell the same or similar product and are not too geographically distant from the customers. Thus, market definition has two dimensions—the products or services and the geographical area of competition affected by the conduct in question. More specifically, the relevant market includes all sellers whose participation in a price-fixing cartel would be necessary for the cartel to raise prices profitably because consumers would not switch to other sellers in sufficient numbers to force the cartel to rescind its price increase.

In general, the relevant product market consists of those products or services that are reasonably interchangeable by consumers for the same purpose—that is, products with a significant degree of price cross-elasticity of demand, meaning that an increase in the price of the product or service affected by the restraint results in a significant increase in the quantity demanded of a reasonably substitutable product or service.[9] The basic question

---

7. *See, e.g.*, Levine v. Cent. Fla. Med. Affiliates, Inc., 72 F.3d 1538, 1556 (11th Cir. 1996); M & M Med. Supplies & Serv., Inc. v. Pleasant Valley Hosp., 981 F.2d 160, 164 (4th Cir. 1992).

8. *See, e.g.*, United States v. Marine Bancorp., 418 U.S. 602, 618 (1974); FTC v. Freeman Hosp., 69 F.3d 260, 268 (8th Cir. 1995) ("The determination of the relevant market is a 'necessary predicate' to a finding of a Clayton Act violation. Without a well-defined relevant market, an examination of a transaction's competitive effect is without context or meaning."); FTC v. Cardinal Health, Inc., 12 F. Supp. 2d 34, 45 (D.D.C. 1998) ("Defining the relevant market is the starting point for any merger analysis.").

9. *See generally ALD V, supra* p. 9 n.23, at 532-77; *see, e.g.*, Brown Shoe Co. v. United States, 370 U.S. 294, 325 (1962) (explaining that "[t]he outer boundaries of a product market are determined by the reasonable interchangeability of use or the cross-elasticity of demand between the product itself and substitutes for it"); Am. Council of Certified Podiatric Physicians & Surgeons v. Am. Bd. of Podiatric Surgery, Inc., 185 F.3d 606, 622 (6th Cir. 1999); Brokerage Concepts, Inc. v. U.S. Healthcare, Inc., 140 F.3d 494, 513-14 (3d Cir. 1998) (noting that outer boundaries of the relevant product market are determined by evaluating which products would be reasonably interchangeable by consumers for the same purpose; interchangeability implies products are roughly equivalent for the use to which they are put).

in defining the relevant product market is whether a hypothetical monopolist selling the product in question (hospital services, for example) would be unable to increase its price profitably because too many customers would switch to alternative products. If so, those alternative products, because they are reasonably good substitutes for the hypothetical monopolist's product and thus constrain its ability to increase its price, are added to the relevant product market until a threshold is reached at which the hypothetical price increase would be profitable because consumers would not substitute even less interchangeable products for the product in question.[10]

Numerous decisions discuss definition of the relevant product market in different health-care contexts. The relevant product market for hospital services typically has been defined, often by stipulation of the parties, as the cluster of acute-care services typically provided only at inpatient hospitals;[11] that is, outpatient services are usually excluded and may constitute a separate relevant product market themselves. For physician services, product markets have been defined as primary care, or the distinct services of recognized medical specialties or subspecialties.[12] Relevant product markets for the services of payers typically have been defined broadly to include all forms of health-care financing,[13] but this question is quite fact-specific.

---

10. For a helpful discussion of this principle, *see* Gregory J. Werden, *The 1982 Merger Guidelines and the Ascent of the Hypothetical Monopolist Paradigm*, 71 ANTITRUST L. J. 253 (2003).
11. *See, e.g.*, FTC v. Tenet Health Care Corp., 186 F.3d 1045, 1051 (8th Cir. 1999) (agreement between the parties that the relevant product market was "delivery of primary and secondary inpatient hospital care services"); FTC v. Freeman Hosp., 69 F.3d 260, 268 (8th Cir. 1995) (agreement between parties that relevant product market was "acute care inpatient hospital services"); California v. Sutter Health Sys., 130 F. Supp. 2d 1109, 1119 (N.D. Cal. 2001) (parties agreed that relevant product market was composed of the "cluster of services comprising acute inpatient care").
12. *See, e.g.*, Morgenstern v. Wilson, 29 F.3d 1291, 1296 (8th Cir. 1994) (product market limited to heart surgery services); Antitrust Division Business Review Letter to Children's Healthcare, P.A. (Mar. 1, 1996) (market for pediatric services limited to pediatricians, excluding other types of primary care physicians), *at* http://www.usdoj.gov/atr/public/busreview/0555.htm.
13. *See, e.g.*, U.S. Healthcare, Inc. v. Healthsource, Inc., 986 F.2d 589, 598-99 (1st Cir. 1993) (rejecting product market limited to HMO-type health plans); Blue Cross & Blue Shield United v. Marshfield Clinic, 65 F.3d 1406, 1411 (7th Cir. 1995) (same); Ball Mem'l Hosp. v. Mut. Hosp. Ins., Inc., 784 F.2d

The relevant geographic market, broadly speaking, is "the area of effective competition . . . in which the seller operates, and to which the purchaser can practicably turn for supplies."[14] Similar to the methodology for defining relevant product markets, defining the relevant geographic market requires identifying those geographical areas and, in particular, the suppliers therein to which consumers would turn to defeat a hypothetical price increase by a hypothetical monopolist of the relevant product. Every relevant product market has its own relevant geographic market. With respect to health-care providers, relevant geographic markets typically are defined with reference to the distance patients would travel to receive particular types of services in response to a price increase by their current provider. They also might be defined by reference to which providers health plans could turn to to circumvent a price increase by more local providers. For the more complicated and sophisticated hospital or physician services, this geographical area is larger than in the case of primary-care hospital or physician services because patients are willing to travel greater distances for more complex services.[15] With respect to health-care financing,

---

1325, 1351 (7th Cir. 1986) (market included all forms of health-care financing); *cf.* Cont'l Orthopedic Appliances, Inc. v. Health Ins. Plan, 40 F. Supp. 2d 109 (E.D.N.Y. 1999) (refusing to dismiss claims by excluded suppliers of orthotic and prosthetic (O&P) products challenging health plans' contracts with rival suppliers; holding plaintiffs sufficiently alleged a relevant market limited to O&P health-care services sold to HMO patients in 11 counties in and around New York City); United States v. Aetna, Inc., 1999-2 Trade Cas. (CCH) ¶ 72,730 (N.D. Tex. 1999) (consent decree and competitive impact statement) (alleging relevant product market limited to HMO and HMO-based point-of-service health plans, excluding PPO and other types of plans).

14. Tampa Elec. Co. v. Nashville Coal Co., 365 U.S. 320, 327 (1961); *see generally ALD V, supra* p. 9 n.23, at 577-89; *see also Morgenstern*, 29 F.3d at 1296 (explaining that a relevant geographic market is "the area to which customers can practically turn for alternative sources of the product and in which the antitrust defendants face competition"); Ginzburg v. Mem'l Healthcare Sys., Inc., 993 F. Supp. 998, 1012 (S.D. Tex. 1997); FTC v. Butterworth Health Corp., 946 F. Supp. 1285, 1290 (W.D. Mich. 1996), *aff'd*, 121 F.3d 708 (6th Cir. 1997) (unpublished opinion reprinted at 1997-2 Trade Cas. (CCH) ¶ 71,863).

15. *See, e.g., Freeman Hosp.*, 69 F.3d at 268-72 (finding a regional market for acute-care hospital services); *Morgenstern*, 29 F.3d at 1296 (finding a regional market for heart-surgery services); Flegel v. Christian Hosp., 4 F.3d 682, 691 (8th Cir. 1993) (finding that a single county or a portion thereof was

such as the services of health-insurance plans, relevant geographic markets typically are broad, and may be regional or national.[16] On the other hand, if the concern is the health plan's market power as a purchaser of health-care services, then the relevant geographic market may be small because providers may not be able to sell their services to more distant purchasers.

The scope of relevant geographic markets for the same services can vary in different areas based on analysis of a range of actual market information, including statistics showing where patients travel to receive particular services, the locations of alternative providers, the types of providers patients use for particular services, opinions of providers and payers as to the identity of actual and potential competing providers or providers whom payers believe they must have in their networks, relative changes in prices between different providers, marketing and advertising strategies, and other factors. Courts have emphasized many times that, in defining a relevant geographic market, it is absolutely essential to evaluate where patients reasonably could and would turn in the face of increased prices or reduced quality and to include those suppliers in the relevant geographic market, rather than simply considering where patients currently obtain the service under existing competitive market conditions—that is, as a matter of law, the analysis must be dynamic, not static.[17]

---

the relevant geographic market for osteopathic physician services); Oltz v. St. Peter's Cmty. Hosp., 861 F.2d 1440, 1447-48 (9th Cir. 1988) (finding market for anesthesia services was a single city).

16. *See, e.g.*, Ball Mem'l Hosp. v. Mut. Hosp. Ins., 784 F.2d 1325, 1335-36 (7th Cir. 1986) (finding a regional or national relevant geographic market because money and the ability to spread risk, which have no geographical boundaries, are the productive assets in the insurance industry). *But cf.* United States v. Aetna, 1999-2 Trade Cas. (CCH) at 86,378-79 (competitive impact statement explaining that health-plan merger would threaten competition in relevant geographic markets limited to Dallas and Houston).

17. *See, e.g.*, FTC v. Tenet Health Care Corp., 186 F.3d 1045, 1052-55 (8th Cir. 1999) (noting that the plaintiff "must present evidence on the critical question of where consumers of hospital services could practically turn for alternative services should the merger be consummated and prices become anticompetitive. . . . This evidence must address where consumers could practically go, not where they actually go."); Doctor's Hosp. v. Southeast Med. Alliance, Inc., 123 F.3d 301, 311 (5th Cir. 1997) (same); FTC v. Freeman Hosp., 69 F.3d 260, 268-72 (8th Cir. 1995) (same); Gordon v. Lewistown Hosp., 272 F. Supp. 2d 393, 428 (M.D. Pa. 2003) (same).

C. Market Power

The concept of market power is one of the most important in antitrust analysis. To prove a violation of Section 1 of the Sherman Act, plaintiffs frequently must prove that the defendants have market power as sellers, or "the ability to raise prices above those that would be charged in a competitive market."[18] To prove monopolization or attempted monopolization in violation of Section 2 of the Sherman Act, a plaintiff must show that the defendant already has a substantial degree of market power; that is, monopoly power for a monopolization claim[19] and a dangerous probability of acquiring monopoly power for an attempted monopolization claim.[20] Under Section 7 of the Clayton Act, the concerns are that a merger may permit the merged firm itself to exercise market power or may result in a level of market concentration such that firms in the market will collectively exercise market power by engaging in tacit collusion or oligopolistic behavior.[21]

Market power, when the issue relates to the conduct of sellers, is the ability of a seller, or group of sellers acting in a concerted manner, to raise prices (or lower quality) significantly without losing so much business that it or they have to rescind the price increase. Firms lack market power if a sufficient number of consumers can substitute different products or purchase the same (or a reasonably substitutable) product from other sellers so that the price increase is unprofitable.[22] Market power is harmful because to raise its

---

18. NCAA v. Bd. of Regents, 468 U.S. 85, 109 n.38 (1984); *see also* Chicago Prof'l Sports Ltd. P'ship v. NBA, 95 F.3d 593, 600 (7th Cir. 1996) (explaining that "[s]ubstantial market power is an indispensable ingredient of every claim under the full Rule of Reason."); Levine v. Cent. Fla. Med. Affiliates, Inc., 73 F.3d 1538, 1552 (11th Cir. 1996) (requiring plaintiff to prove defendant's market power unless it can prove actual adverse effects on competition directly); Retina Assocs., P.A. v. S. Baptist Hosp., 105 F.3d 1376, 1384 (11th Cir. 1997) (finding that plaintiff failed to show market power and thus potential anticompetitive effects).

19. *E.g.,* United States v. AMR Corp., 335 F.3d 1109 (10th Cir. 2003).

20. *E.g.,* Am. Council of Certified Podiatric Physicians & Surgeons v. Am. Bd. of Podiatric Surgery, 185 F.3d 606, 622-23 (6th Cir. 1999). "Monopoly power" is merely a very high level of "market power." *See generally* Eastman Kodak Co. v. Image Technical Servs., 504 U.S. 451, 481 (1992).

21. *See infra* pp. 107-18, discussing the antitrust analysis of mergers.

22. *E.g.,* Brand Name Prescription Drugs Antitrust Litig., 123 F.3d 599, 603 (7th Cir. 1997) (explaining that market power is "the power to raise price above

price, the seller must restrict the amount of its output, and this both misallocates resources and redistributes income from consumers to sellers.[23]

A plaintiff may prove the existence of market power either directly—that is, by evidence of higher-than-competitive prices or lower-than-competitive quality or output—or indirectly through circumstantial evidence by defining the relevant market, and then proving that the defendants have a large market share and that barriers prevent or significantly hinder existing firms from expanding their output or deter new firms from entering the relevant market.[24] Evidence of the defendants' market share is important where there is insufficient direct evidence of the challenged conduct's actual detrimental effects on competition. A large market share may support an inference that the defendants' conduct is likely to have a substantial adverse effect on competition, but it is not sufficient, standing alone, to prove that conclusion.

Courts have set no definitive market-share thresholds that permit an inference of market power because other market characteristics must be considered, including particularly the degree of entry and expansion barriers, the relative size and number of competitors, the size and sophistication of purchasers, and trends in prices and market shares. The level of entry barriers is particularly important because, if entry into the market is quite easy, then

---

cost without losing so many sales as to make the price rise unsustainable"); *see also* AD/SAT v. Associated Press, 181 F.3d 216, 228-29 (2d Cir. 1999). For a general discussion of market power, *see ALD V, supra* p. 9 n.23, at 67-69. For a more detailed technical discussion of market power, *see* William H. Landes & Richard A. Posner, *Market Power in Antitrust Cases*, 94 Harv. L. Rev. 937 (1981).

23. *See generally* L.A.P.D., Inc. v. Gen. Elec. Co., 132 F.3d 402, 404 (7th Cir. 1997) (explaining that "[a]ntitrust law is designed to protect consumers from the higher prices—and society from the reduction in allocative efficiency when firms with market power curtail output.").

24. *E.g.,* United States v. Visa U.S.A., Inc., 344 F.3d 229, 239 (2d Cir. 2003) ("Such power may be proven through evidence of specific conduct undertaken by the defendant that indicates he has the power to affect price or exclude competition. . . . Alternatively, market power may be presumed if the defendant controls a large enough share of the relevant market."); Angelico v. Lehigh Valley Hosp., Inc., 184 F.3d 268, 276 (3d Cir. 1999); Levin v. Cent. Fla. Med. Affiliates, Inc., 72 F.3d 1538, 1555 (11th Cir. 1996); Flegel v. Christian Hosp., 4 F.3d 682, 688 (8th Cir. 1993).

even a seller with a very large market share has little, if any, market power.[25] Although most antitrust concerns focus on market power exercised by sellers, market power exercised by purchasers ("monopsony power") also raises antitrust concern. The purchaser with monopsony power decreases the price it pays for its inputs below the competitive level by restricting the amount of its purchases.[26] This action misallocates resources, redistributes income from the seller of the input to its purchaser, and ultimately can increase the price the purchaser of the input charges for its output, reduce the quality of its products or services, or reduce the quality of the input.[27] In health care, issues relating to monopsony arise most frequently between providers whose services are an input to managed-care organizations, whose output is health-care financing or different types of health plans.[28]

Frequently, antitrust analysis involves comparing the effects that particular conduct has on market power and the efficiencies the conduct generates. Broadly speaking, conduct enhances efficiency if it better satisfies the wants and desires of consumers or increases the ratio of a firm's outputs to its use of inputs. In general, indications of efficiencies include greater output, lower

---

25. *See, e.g.,* Am. *Council of Certified Podiatric Physicians & Surgeons,* 185 F.3d at 623 ("The difficulty of entry into the market is relevant because if entry is easy, even a firm holding a commanding percentage of the market cannot charge a price above the competitive price, for once it does, competitors will enter the market and undercut the firm's price."); Concord Boat Corp. v. Brunswick Corp., 207 F.3d 1039, 1059 (8th Cir. 2000) ("If entry barriers . . . are not significant, it may be difficult for even a monopoly company to control price . . . because a new firm can . . . easily enter the market to challenge it.").

26. *See generally* ROGER D. BLAIR & JEFFREY L. HARRISON, MONOPSONY: ANTITRUST LAW AND ECONOMICS (1993).

27. *See generally* United States v. Aetna, Inc., 1999-2 Trade Cas. (CCH) ¶ 72,730, at 86,380 (N.D. Tex. 1999) (competitive impact statement) (explaining that the merger of the Aetna and Prudential health plans would "give Aetna the ability to unduly depress physician reimbursement rates . . . , likely leading to a reduction in the quantity or degradation in the quality of physicians' services").

28. *See generally* Mark V. Pauly, *Managed Care, Market Power, and Monopsony,* 33 HEALTH SERVS. RESEARCH 1439 (1998); *see also* Thomas R. McCarthy & Scott J. Thomas, *Antitrust Issues Between Payers and Providers: The Monopsony Concern,* ABA ANTITRUST HEALTH CARE CHRONICLE, Summer 2002, at 3.

prices, lower costs, higher quality, better access, and increased choice resulting from the conduct under examination.[29]

D. Agreements Unreasonably Restraining Competition

1. *Concerted Action or Agreement*

Section 1 of the Sherman Act, which prohibits conspiracies or agreements (or
any type of concerted action) that unreasonably restrain competition, does
not apply to independent or unilateral conduct by a single entity. Rather, a
violation of Section 1 always requires proof of joint action by separate entities.[30] Thus, in analyzing a claim under Section 1, the conspiracy requirement
raises two broad questions: (1) whether the alleged conspirators have the
legal capacity to conspire; and if so, (2) whether, as a factual matter, the
challenged conduct resulted from concerted action or from unilateral action.

As to the first question—the legal capacity of parties to conspire—the
general principle is that the individual components of a single integrated
enterprise are incapable of conspiring. In *Copperweld Corp. v. Independence
Tube Corp.,* the seminal decision discussing this principle, the Supreme Court
held that a corporation and its wholly owned subsidiary are not capable of
conspiring for purposes of Section 1 because they always have a complete
unity of interests.[31] Based on the *Copperweld* holding and logic, lower courts
have also held that members of the same medical practice,[32] divisions of the

---

29. *See generally* HERBERT HOVENKAMP, FEDERAL ANTITRUST POLICY: THE LAW OF COM-
PETITION AND ITS PRACTICE § 2.3c at 74-76 (1999).
30. *See, e.g.,* Fisher v. City of Berkeley, 475 U.S. 260, 266-67 (1986) (explaining that absent concerted action, conduct cannot violate § 1 of the Sherman
Act); Am. Council of Certified Podiatric Physicians & Surgeons v. Am. Bd.
of Podiatric Surgery, 185 F.3d 606, 619 (6th Cir. 1999) (noting that "[i]n
order to have a § 1 violation, there must be an agreement, as § 1 does not
encompass unilateral conduct, no matter how anticompetitive"). For discussion of the concerted-action requirement, *see ALD V, supra* p. 9 n.23, at
3-36.
31. 467 U.S. 752, 777 (1984).
32. *See, e.g.,* Allen v. Washington Hosp., 34 F. Supp. 2d 958, 963 (W.D. Pa.
1999).

same corporation,[33] wholly owned subsidiaries of the same parent,[34] and different corporations controlled by the same persons[35] are legally incapable of conspiring. Courts also have held generally that shareholders, directors, officers, employees, and other agents of a firm cannot conspire with each other or with the firm absent proof that they had an "independent personal stake" in the result of the conspiracy different from that of the firm and, in participating in the conspiracy, were pursuing their own interests rather than those of the firm.[36] On the other hand, the actions of joint ventures[37] and health-care provider contracting networks comprised of otherwise separately practicing providers who control the organization[38] result from the joint action of their members and thus are subject to Section 1.

---

33. *E.g.*, Alvord-Polk, Inc. v. F. Schumacher & Co., 37 F.3d 996, 1000 (3d Cir. 1994).
34. *E.g.,* Advanced Health-Care Servs. v. Radford Cmty. Hosp., 910 F.2d 139, 145-46 (4th Cir. 1990).
35. *E.g.*, Century Oil Tool Corp. v. Prod. Specialties, Inc., 737 F.2d 1316 (5th Cir. 1984).
36. *See, e.g.*, Am. Council of Certified Podiatric Physicians & Surgeons v. Am. Bd. of Podiatric Surgery, 185 F.3d 606, 620-21 (6th Cir. 1999) (holding that a professional association and its members were incapable of conspiring for purposes of § 1, but that the members were capable of conspiring among themselves); St. Joseph's Hosp. v. Hosp. Corp. of Am., 795 F.2d 948, 956 (11th Cir. 1986) (holding that conspiracy between hospital and its manager was possible if the manager were acting in its own interests, outside the interests of the corporation); Poindexter v. Am. Bd. of Surgery, 911 F. Supp. 1510, 1519 (N.D. Ga. 1994) (holding that a board member was capable of conspiring with the board because the member and the plaintiff excluded from membership were competitors and thus the board member could have an independent interest in excluding him).
37. *See, e.g.*, Freeman v. San Diego Ass'n of Realtors, 322 F.3d 1133 (9th Cir.), *cert. denied*, 124 S.Ct. 355 (2003); Addamax Corp. v. Open Software Found., Inc., 152 F.3d 48, 52 (1st Cir. 1998) (explaining that "the operations of a joint venture represent collaboration of the separate entities that own or control it").
38. *See, e.g.*, Podiatrist Ass'n, Inc. v. La Cruz Azul, 332 F.3d 6, 14 (1st Cir. 2003) ("When competing health-care providers challenge an insurer's benefit policies . . . , those providers must make a threshold showing that the physicians effectively control the health-care plan."); Capital Imaging Assocs., P.C. v. Mohawk Valley Med. Assocs., Inc., 996 F.2d 537, 544 (2d Cir. 1993) (holding that an IPA constituted a combination subject to § 1 because its physician members were independent practitioners with separate economic interests).

Many antitrust claims have been asserted by physicians challenging adverse peer-review and staff-privilege decisions by hospitals, and courts have reached differing conclusions as to whether a hospital is capable of conspiring with the members of its medical staff involved in such decisions or whether the hospital and its medical staff constitute a single entity for purposes of Section 1.[39] The rule in most circuits is that hospitals and their medical staffs are incapable of conspiring when conducting peer-review activities because, when doing so, the medical staff is acting as the agent of the hospital.[40] A similar question is whether a hospital and an independent firm that manages it are capable of conspiring for purposes of Section 1, and courts have reached somewhat different conclusions on this issue.[41]

As to the second question—whether, as a factual matter, the conduct in question resulted from concerted or unilateral action—even where antitrust claims are asserted against health-care providers or payers that are capable of conspiring, significant issues frequently arise as to whether a plaintiff has adduced adequate proof that the conduct resulted from a conspiracy or understanding rather than from a defendant's unilateral action. Although the requisite conspiracy can be inferred from circumstantial evidence, the Supreme Court has warned that "conduct as consistent with permissible competition as with illegal conspiracy does not, standing alone, support an inference of antitrust conspiracy . . . [A plaintiff], in other words, must show that the inference of conspiracy is reasonable in light of the competing inferences of independent action or collusive action that could not have harmed [it]."[42] Thus, where circumstantial evidence that the conduct resulted from a con-

---

39. *Compare* Weiss v. York Hosp., 745 F.2d 786, 814-15 (3d Cir. 1984) (holding medical staff incapable of conspiring with hospital), *with* Bolt v. Halifax Hosp. Med. Ctr., 891 F.2d 810, 819 (11th Cir. 1990) (en banc) (holding that hospital and individual staff physicians are legally separate entities capable of conspiring); *see generally ALD V, supra* p. 9 n.23, at 31-33, 1330 for other cases on this point.

40. *E.g.*, Oksanen v. Page Mem'l Hosp., 945 F.2d 696, 702-05 (4th Cir. 1991) (en banc).

41. *Compare* Surgical Care Ctr. v. Hosp. Serv. Dist. No. 1, 309 F.3d 836 (5th Cir. 2002) (no conspiracy possible), *with St. Joseph's Hosp.*, 795 F.2d at 956 (conspiracy possible).

42. Matsushita Elec. Indus. Co. v. Zenith Radio Corp., 475 U.S. 574, 588 (1986); Viazis v. Am. Ass'n of Orthodontists, 314 F.3d 758, 762 (5th Cir. 2002).

spiracy is ambiguous, the plaintiff must adduce "evidence that tends to exclude the possibility of independent action . . . . [T]here must be direct or circumstantial evidence that reasonably tends to prove that [the parties] had a conscious commitment to a common scheme designed to achieve an unlawful objective."[43] For example, evidence that the defendants took the same action knowing that each would do so (so-called "conscious parallelism"), by itself, does not prove a conspiracy. In addition, the plaintiff must show that the action was not in each defendant's individual self-interest and would not have been expected absent concerted action.[44]

---

43. Monsanto Corp. v. Spray-Rite Serv. Corp., 465 U.S. 752, 768 (1984); *Matsushita*, 475 U.S. at 588; Am. Council of Certified Podiatric Physicians & Surgeons v. Am. Bd. of Podiatric Surgery, 185 F.3d 606, 620 (6th Cir. 1999); Stop & Shop Supermarket Co. v. Blue Cross & Blue Shield, 239 F. Supp. 2d 180, 187 (D.R.I. 2003) (explaining that "circumstantial evidence, alone, will not support a finding of conspiracy if that evidence is equally consistent with a finding that defendants did not conspire"); Merck-Medco Managed Care, LLC v. Rite Aid Corp., 22 F. Supp. 2d 447, 458 (D. Md. 1998) (same), *aff'd per curiam without published opinion*, 201 F.3d 436 (4th Cir. 1999) (opinion reprinted at 1999-2 Trade Cas. ¶ 72,640).

    See also DM Research, Inc. v. Coll. of Am. Pathologists, 170 F.3d 53, 56-57 (1st Cir. 1999) (rejecting inference of conspiracy between College and National Committee for Clinical Laboratory Standards to adopt scientifically unjustified laboratory standard because College and its members had no reason to adopt faulty standard that would raise costs for laboratories; also rejecting inference that the College and Committee each conspired with its own members because it is commonplace and useful for such organizations to adopt quality standards); Ostrzenski v. Columbia Hosp. for Women Found., 158 F.3d 1289 (D.C. Cir. 1998) (physician failed to show termination of staff privileges was not the result of a unilateral, legitimate peer-review decision); Willman v. Heartland Hosp., 34 F.3d 605, 611 (8th Cir. 1994) (rejecting inference of conspiracy based on peer-review proceeding concerning plaintiff because conduct was consistent with lawful motive of promoting quality health care); Minn. Ass'n of Nurse Anesthetists v. Unity Hosp., 5 F. Supp. 2d 694, 704-05 (D. Minn. 1998) (rejecting inference of conspiracy because hospitals' simultaneous termination of plaintiffs as employees in favor of exclusive contracts with rival anesthesiology practice group was consistent with each hospital's own self-interest and independent conduct), *aff'd*, 208 F.3d 655 (8th Cir. 2000).

44. *E.g.*, Williamson Oil Co. v. Philip Morris USA, 346 F.3d 1287, 1301-03 (11th Cir. 2003); InterVest, Inc. v. Bloomberg, L.P., 340 F.3d 144, 165-66 (3d Cir. 2003).

2. Proving an Unreasonable Restraint on Competition

If the challenged conduct resulted from concerted action, the analysis of its lawfulness under Section 1 of the Sherman Act turns to the question of whether that action unreasonably restrained (or would unreasonably restrain) competition. Although Section 1 literally prohibits "[e]very" agreement "in restraint of trade," the Supreme Court consistently has held that this provision outlaws only "unreasonable" restraints on competition.[45] In general, this means that the conduct must have a "substantial" or "significant" adverse effect on marketwide competition.[46] Depending on the nature and character of the challenged agreement, courts apply one of three analytical standards to determine whether it unreasonably restrains competition: (1) the rule of reason, (2) the per se rule, or (3) an intermediate standard usually referred to as the "quick look," "truncated" or "abbreviated," rule-of-reason standard. There are, however, no bright lines separating these modes of analysis; rather, they are a continuum, each intended to require only the amount of examination and proof necessary to determine or predict the challenged conduct's effect on competition.[47]

a. The Rule of Reason

Courts apply the "rule of reason" to evaluate the competitive consequences of most types of agreements challenged under Section 1 of the Sherman Act.[48] Rule-of-reason analysis requires consideration of a variety of factors, includ-

45. *See* NYNEX Corp. v. Discon, Inc., 525 U.S. 128, 133 (1998); State Oil Co. v. Kahn, 522 U.S. 3, 10 (1997); Arizona v. Maricopa County Med. Soc'y, 457 U.S. 332, 342-43 (1982); Standard Oil Co. v. United States, 221 U.S. 1, 60-70 (1911).
46. *E.g.*, Bhan v. NME Hosps., 929 F.2d 1404, 1413 (9th Cir. 1991) (noting that the requisite anticompetitive effect must be of "significant magnitude"). For discussion of the requirement that the agreement unreasonably restrain competition, *see ALD V, supra* p. 9 n.23, at 46-79.
47. For a helpful overview of the three standards, *see* Cont'l Airlines v. United Airlines, 277 F.3d 499 (4th Cir. 2002); Polygram Holding, Inc., Dkt. No. 9298 (FTC Jul. 28, 2003), *at* http://www.ftc.gov/ 03/2003/07/ polygramopinion.pdf.
48. For a thorough discussion of the rule of reason, *see* ABA ANTITRUST SECTION, MONOGRAPH NO. 23, THE RULE OF REASON (1999); *see also ALD V, supra* p. 9 n.23, at 58-79.

ing, most generally, specific information about the business or market in question; competitive conditions in the market before and after the restraint was imposed; and the restraint's history, nature, purpose, and effect.[49] A court's ultimate task under the rule of reason is to balance an agreement's procompetitive and anticompetitive effects.[50] The agreement is unlawful only if the latter predominate over the former.

To prove that the restraint has the requisite anticompetitive effect, the plaintiff must usually first show that the defendants have market power, a threshold screen that many courts apply to weed out unmeritorious cases relatively quickly.[51] The plaintiff may prove market power either by direct evidence that the challenged conduct resulted in higher prices or lower quality, or by circumstantial evidence of market power—that the defendants' market share is large and that entry and expansion barriers prevent other potential and actual competitors from constraining the defendants' anticompetitive conduct.[52] If the plaintiff meets that burden, the burden of going forward shifts to the defendants, to show procompetitive justifications for the restraint. Those justifications must relate to the restraint's effect on competition and not simply to a general public-welfare benefit unrelated to promoting a competitive market or greater efficiency.[53] If the defendants show that the restraint has procompetitive justifications, the burden shifts back to the plaintiff to show that the defendants could have achieved the

---

49. *See* Arizona v. Maricopa County Med. Soc'y, 457 U.S. 332, 343 n.13 (1982); Chicago Bd. of Trade v. United States, 246 U.S. 231, 238 (1918).

50. *See, e.g.,* Fraser v. Major League Soccer, L.L.C., 284 F.3d 47, 59 (1st Cir. 2002) (plaintiff must show, with regard to the challenged agreement, "that on balance the adverse effects on competition outweigh the competitive benefits").

51. *E.g.,* SCFC ILC, Inc. v. Visa U.S.A., Inc., 36 F.3d 958, 965 (10th Cir. 1994) ("Proof of market power . . . is a critical first-step, or 'screen,' or 'filter,' which is often dispositive of the case.").

52. *E.g.,* CDC Techs., Inc. v. IDEXX Labs, Inc., 186 F.3d 74, 80-81 (2d Cir. 1999); Doctor's Hosp. v. Southeast Med. Alliance, 123 F.3d 301, 310 (5th Cir. 1997); United States v. Brown Univ., 5 F.3d 658, 668 (3d Cir. 1993); Stop & Shop Supermarket Co. v. Blue Cross & Blue Shield, 239 F. Supp. 2d 180, 192 (D.R.I. 2003); Gateway Contracting Servs., LLC v. Sagamore Health Network, Inc., 2002-1 Trade Cas. (CCH) ¶ 73,640, at 93,180-81 (S.D. Ind. 2002).

53. *See generally* Nat'l Soc'y of Prof'l Eng'rs v. United States, 435 U.S. 679, 692 (1978).

procompetitive effects in a manner significantly less restrictive of competition or that the restraint's anticompetitive effects outweigh its procompetitive effects.[54]

b.   Per Se Rule

Some agreements are so obviously anticompetitive and so obviously lacking in procompetitive benefits that they are deemed to be unlawful automatically or "per se" under Section 1 of the Sherman Act. The per se unreasonable standard is, in effect, a conclusive presumption of unreasonableness that is appropriate "once experience with a particular kind of restraint enables the Court to predict with confidence that the rule of reason will condemn it."[55] Thus, to prove a violation of Section 1 under the per se standard, the plaintiff need only prove that the challenged conduct resulted from an agreement and that the agreement is of a character and nature or type that the courts have held is per se unlawful. The plaintiff need not prove a relevant market or that the defendants have market power, and the defendants are not permitted to offer procompetitive justifications for the agreement or to show that it actually has procompetitive effects.[56] As one court has explained, "The per se rule is the trump card of antitrust analysis. When the antitrust plaintiff successfully plays it, he need only tally his score."[57] In practice, successful invocation of the per se standard is a significant tactical advantage for a plaintiff, and thus the plaintiff will strain to fit the agreement within a per se unlawful category, while the defendants will strain to keep it out.

Courts are reluctant to apply the per se standard to "restraints imposed in the context of business relationships where the economic impact of certain

---

54. *E.g.*, Virgin Atl. Airways, Ltd. v. British Airways PLC, 257 F.3d 256, 264 (2d Cir. 2001); Law v. NCAA, 134 F.3d 1010, 1019 (10th Cir. 1998); Flegel v. Christian Hosp., 4 F.3d 682, 688 (8th Cir. 1993); Gordon v. Lewistown Hosp., 272 F. Supp. 2d 393, 416 (M.D. Pa. 2003); Ginzburg v. Mem'l Healthcare Sys., Inc., 993 F. Supp. 998, 1026 (S.D. Tex. 1997).
55. Arizona v. Maricopa County Med. Soc'y, 457 U.S. 332, 344 (1982).
56. *E.g.*, Nat'l Hockey League Players' Ass'n v. Plymouth Whalers Hockey Club, 325 F.3d 712, 718 (6th Cir. 2003) ("The *per se* rule identifies certain practices that 'are entirely devoid of redeeming competitive rationales. . . .' If a court determines that a practice is illegal *per se*, no examination of the practice's impact on the market or the procompetitive justifications for the practice is necessary for finding a violation of the antitrust laws.").
57. United States v. Realty Multi-List, Inc., 629 F.2d 1351, 1363 (5th Cir. 1980).

practices is not immediately obvious."[58] For this reason, many courts have hesitated to apply the per se rule to conduct in the health-care sector, particularly when the restraint implicates professional judgment or quality-of-care issues.[59]

c. "Quick Look" Rule of Reason

The Supreme Court and lower courts have applied an abbreviated or "quick-look" rule-of-reason analysis where the anticompetitive effects of the restraint are clear but there may be offsetting plausible procompetitive efficiencies or justifications.[60] Thus, there is no clear line of demarcation between per se analysis and rule-of-reason analysis.[61] The quick-look rule of reason comes into play particularly where the conduct entails concerted ac-

---

58. Ind. Fed'n of Dentists v. FTC, 476 U.S. 447, 458-59 (1986); *see also* NYNEX Corp. v. Discon, Inc., 525 U.S. 128, 135-37 (1998); State Oil Co. v. Kahn, 522 U.S. 3, 10, 18-19 (1997); Northwest Wholesale Stationers, Inc. v. Pac. Stationery & Printing Co., 472 U.S. 284, 295 (1985).

59. *E.g.*, *Ind. Fed'n of Dentists*, 476 U.S. at 458-59 (noting that courts are reluctant to condemn rules of professionals under the per se standard); Viazis v. Am. Ass'n of Orthodontists, 314 F.3d 758, 765 (5th Cir. 2003) ("The Supreme Court has been reluctant to apply the *per* se rule to standards promulgated by professional organizations."); Betkerur v. Aultman Hosp. Ass'n, 78 F.3d 1079, 1093 (6th Cir. 1996) (refusing to apply per se rule to hospital credentialing decision because decision resulted from professional judgment); Capital Imaging Assocs., P.C. v. Mohawk Valley Med. Assocs., Inc., 996 F.2d 537, 543 (2d Cir. 1993) (explaining that the Supreme Court "cautions against application of the per se rule against professional associations because the economic impact of professional activities is so difficult to track"); Wilk v. Am. Med. Ass'n, 719 F.2d 207, 221-22 (7th Cir. 1983).

60. *See* Cal. Dental Ass'n v. FTC, 526 U.S. 756, 770 (1999) (explaining that "quick look" rule-of-reason analysis is appropriate where "the great likelihood of anticompetitive effects can be easily ascertained" but that defendants' claims of procompetitive effects should be examined if plausible); Law v. NCAA, 34 F.3d 1010, 1020 (10th Cir. 1998) ("where a practice has obvious anticompetitive effects . . . there is no need to prove that that the defendant possesses market power. Rather, the court is justified in proceeding directly to the question of whether the procompetitive justifications advanced for the restraint outweigh the anticompetitive effects under a 'quick look' rule of reason.").

61. *See* NCAA v. Bd. of Regents, 468 U.S. 85, 104 n.26 (1984) ("there is often no bright line separating *per se* from Rule of Reason analysis").

tion among competitors that directly limits output or price competition—the type of agreements to which the per se rule would usually apply. The court will consider plausible procompetitive justifications for the conduct put forth by the defendants but, absent them, will condemn the agreement summarily. If plausible justifications relating to efficiencies do exist, then full-blown rule-of-reason analysis may be necessary.[62]

The Supreme Court has not clearly delineated the circumstances in which some form of abbreviated rule-of-reason analysis is appropriate or the necessary depth of that analysis. Rather:

> The truth is that our categories of analysis of anticompetitive effect are less fixed than terms like "per se," "quick look" and "rule of reason" tend to make them appear . . . [and] there is generally no categorical line to be drawn between restraints that give rise to an intuitively obvious inference of anticompetitive effect and those that call for more detailed treatment. What is required, rather, is an enquiry meet for the case, looking to the circumstances, details and logic of a restraint.[63]

As the Court explained, for application of the "quick look" standard rather than full rule-of-reason analysis, it must "obviously follow" that the restraint has a "net anticompetitive effect."[64]

d. The Role of Intent

In criminal antitrust cases, intent is an essential element of the offense.[65] In civil antitrust cases, the role of motive and intent in the antitrust analysis is

---

62. *See id.* at 103 (applying abbreviated analysis to NCAA's fixing of minimum prices and limiting number of college football games that could be televised); Ind. Fed. of Dentists v. FTC, 476 U.S. 447, 459 (1986) (applying abbreviated analysis to horizontal agreement among dentists to withhold x-rays that payers requested to review claims); Polygram Holding, Inc., Dkt. No. 9298 (FTC Jul. 28, 2003) (explaining FTC framework for analyzing horizontal agreements), *at* http://www.ftc.gov/03/2003/07/polygramopinion.pdf.
63. *Cal. Dental Ass'n*, 526 U.S. at 779 (1999).
64. *Id.* at 774.
65. *See generally* United States v. U.S. Gypsum Co., 438 U.S. 422 (1978).

less clear. Although the Supreme Court has said that a plaintiff may prove a violation of Section 1 of the Sherman Act in a civil case by proof of either an unlawful purpose or an anticompetitive effect,[66] most courts hold that proof of an anticompetitive motive or intent is not sufficient, standing alone, to prove a violation. Rather, a plaintiff must prove that the agreement resulted in an unreasonably anticompetitive effect—either through the presumption flowing from the per se rule or from proof of actual anticompetitive effect.[67]

The defendants' intent in entering into the agreement, however, is important because it can shed substantial light on the likely effect of their conduct; an anticompetitive effect would seem more likely if such were the defendants' intent than if it were not.[68] But benign intent is not a defense to an antitrust claim; as the Supreme Court has explained, "Good intentions will not save a plan otherwise objectionable."[69] If the agreement unreasonably restrains competition, it is no defense that the parties did not intend that result.[70]

---

66. *Id.* at 436 n.13.

67. *E.g.,* Schachar v. Am. Acad. of Ophthalmology, 870 F.2d 397, 400 (7th Cir. 1989) (explaining that proof of an anticompetitive intent without proof of an anticompetitive effect is not sufficient to prove a violation of § 1); *see also* All Care Nursing Serv., Inc. v. High Tech Staffing Servs., Inc., 135 F.3d 740, 747 (11th Cir. 1998); United States v. Dentsply Int'l, Inc., 277 F. Supp. 2d 387, 453 (D. Del. 2003) (noting that even the Department of Justice admitted that bad intent alone did not establish that conduct was anticompetitive), *appeal docketed,* No. 03-4097 (3d Cir., Oct. 14, 2003).

68. *E.g.,* Broad. Music, Inc. v. Columbia Broad. Sys., 441 U.S. 1, 19 (1979) (explaining that purpose tends to show effect); Appalachian Coals, Inc. v. United States, 288 U.S. 344, 372 (1933) (noting that while intent is not itself dispositive in a § 1 case, it helps the court interpret facts and predict consequences).

69. *Appalachian Coals,* 288 U.S. at 372; *see also* NCAA v. Bd. of Regents, 468 U.S. 85, 101 n.23 (1984) ("Good motives will not validate an otherwise anticompetitive practice.").

70. *E.g.,* Kreuzer v. Am. Acad. of Periodontology, 735 F.2d 1479, 1493 (D.C. Cir. 1984) (explaining that good intent is not a defense to a § 1 claim because the court must still assess the conduct's economic impact); White & White, Inc. v. Am. Hosp. Supply Corp., 540 F. Supp. 951, 1017 (W.D. Mich. 1982) (holding it irrelevant that defendant did not intend to restrain competition because defendant had entered an agreement that had such an effect), *rev'd on other grounds,* 723 F.2d 495 (6th Cir. 1983).

E. Monopolization and Other Section 2 Claims

Section 2 of the Sherman Act prohibits monopolization and attempted monopolization, as well as conspiracies to monopolize. The monopolization and attempted monopolization violations require no concerted action or agreement and generally apply to the exclusionary conduct of a single firm that already has, or would obtain through the challenged exclusionary conduct, a substantial degree of market power.

1. Monopolization

The monopolization violation of Section 2 requires proof of a defendant's (1) possession of monopoly power in the relevant market and (2) willful acquisition, maintenance, or expansion of that power by predatory or exclusionary conduct directed at deterring or preventing rivals from competing against it.[71] Importantly, monopoly power, by itself, is not unlawful; rather it is only the acquisition, maintenance, or expansion of monopoly power by improper means that results in unlawful monopolization violative of Section 2.[72]

Monopoly power, as defined by the courts, is "the power to control market price or exclude competition."[73] Monopoly power essentially is a greater degree of market power than required for a violation of Section 1,[74] although the courts have not established any precise threshold market share or other factors that distinguish monopoly power from market power. A market share in excess of 65 percent usually is necessary to establish an inference of mo-

---

71. United States v. Grinnell Corp., 384 U.S. 563, 570-71 (1966); *see also* Verizon Communications, Inc. v. Law Offices of Curtis V. Trinko, LLP, No. 02-682, slip op. at 7, 2004 WL 5101 at *6 (U.S. Jan. 13, 2004); Eastman Kodak Co. v. Image Technical Servs., 504 U.S. 451, 481 (1992). For discussion of the monopolization violation, *see ALD V, supra* p. 9 n.23, at 229-99.
72. *E.g.*, Goldwasser v. Ameritech, Inc., 222 F.3d 390, 397-98 (7th Cir. 2000).
73. United States v. E.I. duPont de Nemours & Co., 351 U.S. 377, 391 (1956). Significantly, the defendant need not actually exercise that power for the requirement to be met. *E.g.*, Conwood Co. v. U.S. Tobacco Co., 290 F.3d 768, 783 n.2 (6th Cir. 2002).
74. *See Kodak*, 504 U.S. at 481 ("Monopoly power under § 2 requires . . . something greater than market power under § 1.").

nopoly power, and courts frequently require a significantly higher share.[75] In addition to the defendant's market share, a number of other factors are relevant in determining whether it has monopoly power, particularly barriers to entry and barriers to the expansion of existing competitors (for example, certificate-of-need requirements or other governmental restrictions on entry), as well as other factors mentioned above with respect to market power.[76]

Because "monopolization," and not simply "monopoly" or monopoly power, is unlawful,[77] a firm does not violate Section 2 merely by charging a price in excess of the competitive price, or even the monopoly price.[78] Rather, monopolization entails "the willful acquisition or maintenance of [monopoly] power as distinguished from growth or development as a consequence of a superior product, business acumen, or historical accident."[79] Thus, only certain conduct, when combined with the market-structure requirement, results

---

75. *See, e.g., duPont*, 351 U.S. at 391 (75 percent share); *Kodak*, 504 U.S. at 481 (80 percent share); Blue Cross & Blue Shield United v. Marshfield Clinic, 65 F.3d 1406, 1411 (7th Cir. 1993) (noting that "50 percent is below any accepted benchmark for inferring monopoly power from market share"); *see generally* United States v. Aluminum Co. of Am., 148 F.2d 416, 424 (2d Cir. 1945) ("[O]ver ninety percent is enough to constitute a monopoly; it is doubtful whether sixty or sixty-four percent would be enough; and certainly thirty-three percent is not."); *see also ALD V, supra* p. 9 n.23, at 236-37 (citing market shares in various cases).

76. *See supra* pp. 20-21; *see also* Tops Mkts., Inc. v. Quality Mkts., Inc., 142 F.3d 90, 98 (2d Cir. 1998); Rebel Oil Co. v. Atl. Richfield Co., 51 F.3d 1421, 1439 (9th Cir. 1995); United States v. Dentsply Int'l, Inc., 277 F. Supp. 2d 387, 451-52 (D. Del. 2003) (rejecting government argument that defendant's 80 percent market share proved monopoly power; defendant could not exclude competitors from the market because, although defendant had exclusive arrangements with its distributors, defendant's competitors could use other distributors or distribute their product to customers directly), *appeal docketed*, No. 03-4097 (3d Cir. Oct. 14, 2003).

77. *See* United States v. Microsoft Corp., 253 F.3d 34, 51, 58 (D.C. Cir. 2001) (en banc) (per curiam).

78. *E.g.*, Verizon Communications, Inc. v. Law Offices of Curtis V. Trinko, LLP, No. 02-682, slip op. at 7, 2004 WL 51011, at *6 (U.S. Jan. 13, 2004) ("The mere possession of monopoly power, and the concomitant charging of monopoly prices, is not only not unlawful, it is an important element of the free-market system."); *Marshfield Clinic*, 65 F.3d at 1415 ("a lawful monopolist can charge any price it wants").

79. United States v. Grinnell Corp., 384 U.S. 563, 570-71 (1966).

in monopolization.[80] Courts have articulated the conduct requirement in various ways (for example, "unreasonably exclusionary," "predatory," or "anticompetitive" conduct), but the primary question generally is whether a defendant has taken deliberate steps to eliminate existing rivals or prevent new competition that are not based on efficiency or other valid business reasons, or that impair competition in an unnecessarily restrictive way.[81] In general, conduct is not predatory if the defendant has a valid business justification for engaging in it.[82] Conduct frequently challenged as the willful exer-

---

80. *E.g., Trinko,* slip op. at 7, 2004 WL 51011, at *6 ("the possession of monopoly power will not be found unlawful unless it is accompanied by an element of anticompetitive *conduct*").

81. *See, e.g.,* Aspen Skiing Co. v. Aspen Highlands Skiing Corp., 472 U.S. 585, 597, 605 (1985) (affirming judgment for plaintiff on monopolization claim based on jury instruction that a monopoly does not violate § 2 by refusing to deal with a competitor if valid business reasons exist for that refusal; also explaining that it is relevant to consider the conduct's impact on consumers and whether the defendant has impaired competition in an unnecessarily restrictive way, or has attempted to exclude rivals on some basis other than efficiency); *Microsoft,* 253 F.3d at 68 (attempting to define predatory or exclusionary conduct); Image Technical Servs. v. Eastman Kodak Co., 125 F.3d 1195, 1208-09 (9th Cir. 1997) (affirming judgment for plaintiff on monopolization claim based on jury instruction that it is unlawful for monopolist to engage in conduct, including refusals to deal, that unnecessarily excludes or handicaps competitors in order to maintain a monopoly); *Marshfield Clinic,* 65 F.3d at 1413-14 (expressing skepticism that defendant's conduct was exclusionary in an invidious sense because the practices were ambiguous from the standpoint of competition and efficiency).

   For the Antitrust Division's definition of exclusionary conduct, *see* R. Hewitt Pate, Assistant Attorney General, Antitrust Division, "The Common Law Approach and Improving Standards for Analyzing Single Firm Conduct," Prepared Remarks Before the Thirtieth Annual Conference on International Law and Policy, Fordham Corporate Law Institute (Oct. 23, 2003) at 10 ("whether the conduct would make economic sense but for its elimination or lessening of competition"), *at* http://www.usdoj.gov/atr/public/speeches/201847.pdf. For more in-depth discussions, *see* the series of articles in *The Section 2 Conundrum: Predatory Behavior in the Marketplace,* ANTITRUST, Fall 2003, at 7-59.

82. *See, e.g., Eastman Kodak Co. v. Image Technical Servs.,* 504 U.S. 451, 483 (1992); *Aspen Skiing,* 472 U.S. at 597, 604; ACT, Inc. v. Sylvan Learning Sys., Inc., 296 F.3d 657, 670-71 (8th Cir. 2002).

cise of monopoly power or predatory or unreasonably exclusionary conduct includes predatory pricing,[83] refusals to deal,[84] denials of access to an "essential facility" (a type of refusal to deal),[85] leveraging,[86] tying (a form of leveraging),[87] exclusive dealing agreements,[88] sham litigation,[89] and other exclusionary practices not constituting competition on the merits.[90]

2. *Attempted Monopolization*

Attempted monopolization in violation of Section 2 requires proof that (1) the defendant specifically intended to monopolize the relevant market; (2) the defendant engaged in predatory or unreasonably exclusionary conduct toward that end; and (3) a dangerous probability existed that the defendant would actually monopolize the relevant market if its exclusionary conduct continued.[91] Typically, a plaintiff alleges attempted monopolization when the defendant's market share is not sufficient to sustain a claim of monopolization, or when the defendant has monopoly power in one market and leverages that power toward achieving a monopoly in another market in which the defendant and plaintiff compete.

The plaintiff can prove the defendant's specific intent to monopolize by direct evidence or by inference from its anticompetitive conduct.[92] Many courts, however, have emphasized, especially with regard to subjective evidence of intent based on corporate documents, the importance of distinguish-

---

83. *See, e.g.*, Brooke Group, Ltd. v. Brown & Williamson Tobacco Co., 509 U.S. 209 (1993).

84. *See, e.g.*, *Aspen Skiing*, 472 U.S. at 601-02.

85. *See, e.g.*, McKenzie v. Mercy Hosp., 854 F.2d 365 (10th Cir. 1988); *but cf. Trinko*, slip op. at 11, 2004 WL 51011, at *7 (noting that Supreme Court has never recognized or repudiated the essential-facilities doctrine).

86. *See, e.g.*, M & M Med. Supplies & Serv., Inc. v. Pleasant Valley Hosp., 981 F.2d 160 (4th Cir. 1992) (en banc).

87. *See, e.g.,* Va. Panel Corp. v. MacPanel Co., 133 F.3d 860 (Fed. Cir. 1997).

88. *See, e.g.*, LePages v. 3M, 324 F.3d 141 (3d Cir. 2003) (en banc), *cert. filed*, 72 U.S.L.W. 3007 (U.S. June 20, 2003) (No. 01-1865).

89. *E.g.,* Intergraph Corp. v. Intel Corp., 195 F.3d 1346 (Fed. Cir. 1999).

90. *See ALD V*, *supra* p. 9 n.23, at 299-301, for a discussion of court decisions analyzing specific types of willful or predatory conduct.

91. Spectrum Sports, Inc. v. McQuillan, 506 U.S. 447, 456 (1993). For discussion of attempted monopolization, *see ALD V*, *supra* p. 9 n.23, at 299-308.

92. *Spectrum Sports*, 506 U.S at 459 (noting that "such conduct may be sufficient to prove the necessary intent to monopolize").

ing between a subjective intent merely to compete aggressively on the merits for as much business as possible and an intent to engage in predatory or unreasonably exclusionary conduct.[93] There is nothing sinister, for example, about a firm's documents expressing an intent merely to increase its market share or to obtain as much business as possible.[94]

A defendant's market share is usually the principal evidence used to show a dangerous probability of its achieving monopoly power, and courts typically require evidence of a market share of at least 40 percent.[95] Other market factors also are relevant to evaluating a dangerous probability of success, including ease of entry into the market, ease of expansion by existing competitors, the number and size of other competitors, and trends in market share and price.[96] Importantly, the plaintiff must show that the defendant was capable of achieving a monopoly-level market share.[97]

3. *Conspiracy to Monopolize*

A conspiracy to monopolize, the third of the Section 2 violations, requires proof of (1) a combination or conspiracy, (2) an overt act in furtherance of the conspiracy, and (3) a specific intent to monopolize.[98] This claim requires

---

93. *E.g.*, Olympia Equip. Leasing Co. v. Western Union Tel. Co., 797 F.2d 370, 379 (7th Cir. 1986) (noting that corporate documents stating that "these turkeys . . . ought to be flushed" provided little insight into the requisite intent to monopolize).

94. *E.g.*, Advanced Health-Care Servs. v. Giles Mem'l Hosp., 846 F. Supp. 488, 497 (W.D. Va. 1994).

95. *See ALD V, supra* p. 9 n.23, at 303-05, for a discussion of court decisions on this point.

96. *E.g.*, AD/SAT v. Associated Press, 181 F.3d 216, 226-27 (2d Cir. 1999); Rebel Oil Co. v. Atl. Richfield Co., 51 F.3d 1421, 1438 (9th Cir. 1995).

97. *E.g.*, Colo. Interstate Gas Co. v. Natural Gas Pipeline Co. of Am., 885 F.2d 683, 693-95 (10th Cir. 1998) (no attempted monopolization where defendant could not obtain monopoly power even if its predatory conduct continued); Surgical Care Ctr. v. Hosp. Serv. Dist. No. 1, 2001-1 Trade Cas. (CCH) ¶ 73,215, at 89,942 (E.D. La. 2001) (no dangerous probability of monopolization even if defendant drove plaintiff out of business because not all plaintiff's business would go to defendant, and plaintiff's expert testified that defendant's market share would only increase to between 50 and 60 percent), *aff'd*, 309 F.3d 836 (5th Cir. 2002).

98. *See* United States v. Yellow Cab Co., 332 U.S. 218, 225 (1947); Levine v. Cent. Fla. Med. Affiliates, Inc., 72 F.3d 1538, 1556 (11th Cir. 1996).

evidence of a common purpose of monopolizing among two or more parties,[99] although the conspirators need not be competitors.[100] Unlike other Section 2 claims, however, a conspiracy to monopolize claim may not require proof of the relevant market or the defendant's monopoly power, although such evidence may be relevant to whether the defendants had a specific intent to monopolize.[101] On the other hand, the Supreme Court has indicated that the plaintiff must prove that the conspiracy harmed competition,[102] which can be difficult absent proof of market power.

4. *"Monopsonization"*

Monopsony power is merely the mirror image of monopoly power on the buyer side—that is, a purchaser's market power in buying its inputs. Thus, it would appear that many of the general principles of monopolization and attempted monopolization would probably apply to alleged "monopsonization"

---

99. *See* Morgan, Strand, Wheeler & Biggs v. Radiology, Ltd., 924 F.2d 1484, 1488 (9th Cir. 1991) (conspiracy claim rejected because hospital decided independently to enter into exclusive agreement with radiologists); Geneva Pharms. Tech. Corp. v. Barr Labs., Inc., 201 F. Supp. 2d 236 (S.D.N.Y. 2002); United States v. Gen. Elec. Co., 1997-1 Trade Cas. (CCH) ¶ 71,765, at 79,410 (D. Mont. 1997) (dismissing conspiracy-to-monopolize claim challenging defendant's use of restrictive software licenses with hospitals because plaintiff did not allege that hospitals shared mutual goal with defendant of monopolizing the market for servicing hi-tech medical equipment); HTI Health Servs. v. Quorum Health Group, 960 F. Supp. 1104, 1140 (S. D. Miss. 1997) (rejecting conspiracy to monopolize claim challenging merger of physician groups because of lack of evidence of specific intent, noting that intent of groups was to provide better health care to their local community).
100. Discon, Inc. v. NYNEX Corp., 93 F.3d 1055, 1062 (2d Cir. 1996), *rev'd on other grounds*, 525 U.S. 128 (1998).
101. Freeman v. San Diego Ass'n of Realtors, 322 F.3d 1133, 1154 (9th Cir. 2003) (explaining that no particular level of power or dangerous probability of monopolization need be shown), *cert. denied*, 124 S.Ct. 355 (2003); *see ALD V, supra* p. 9 n.23, at 312, for further discussion of cases on this point.
102. NYNEX Corp. v. Discon, Inc., 525 U.S. 128, 139 (1998) (explaining that "[u]nless [the] agreements harmed the competitive process, they did not amount to a conspiracy to monopolize").

by a purchaser.[103] A plaintiff would need to (1) define the relevant market, (2) prove that the defendant buyer has substantial monopsony power, (3) show that the defendant engaged in predatory conduct excluding other purchasers from the market, and (4) prove the existence of entry and expansion barriers. It seems clear that just as a seller with legitimately obtained monopoly power may lawfully charge the monopoly price, a purchaser with legitimately obtained monopsony power would not violate the antitrust laws by paying suppliers only the below-competitive monopsony price.[104]

On the other hand, just as a firm with legitimately obtained monopoly power cannot lawfully maintain or expand its power by inappropriately anticompetitive conduct directed at its actual or potential rivals, the same is probably true of a firm with monopsony power. Thus, conduct other than competition on the merits that substantially harms other purchasers in the market or prevents the entry of new competing purchasers would raise concern absent a procompetitive justification for it.[105] Mergers among competing purchasers[106] and agreements among competing purchasers fixing the prices

---

103. Section 2 of the Sherman Act does not mention "monopsonization" as a violation but is probably sufficiently broad to prohibit it, even if under the rubric of "buyer monopolization." Moreover, monopsonization also could be the requisite predatory conduct for monopolization where it has the effect of excluding the monopsonist's competitors in the output market.

104. *See* Austin v. Blue Cross & Blue Shield, 903 F.2d 1385, 1390 (11th Cir. 1990) (holding that a third-party payer can use its market power to bargain for the lowest price it can get from providers); Ocean State Physicians Health Plan v. Blue Cross & Blue Shield, 883 F.2d 1101, 1111 (1st Cir. 1989) (same); Royal Drug Co. v. Group Life & Health Ins. Co., 737 F.2d 1433, 1438 (5th Cir. 1984) (same); Travelers Ins. Co. v. Blue Cross, 481 F.2d 80 (3d Cir. 1973) (same).

105. *Cf.* Telecor Communications, Inc. v. Southwestern Bell Tel. Co., 305 F.3d 1124 (10th Cir. 2002), *cert. denied,* 123 S. Ct. 2073 (2003), where the court appeared to hold that defendant, as part of a scheme to monopolize one market, monopsonized another by precluding other purchasers of the input from entering. *See also* DeLoach v. Philip Morris, Inc., 2001-2 Trade Cas. (CCH) ¶ 73,409, at 91,435 (M.D.N.C. 2001) (explaining that "antitrust law does not provide a remedy for '*nonabusive*' monopsony conduct," but rather "the Sherman Act offers protection only when a pure monopsonist . . . abuses its power").

106. *See* United States v. Aetna, Inc., 1999-2 Trade Cas. (CCH) ¶ 72,730 (N.D. Tex. 1999) (consent order and competitive impact statement) (merger of managed-care plans challenged in part because of alleged monopsony power by

they pay for their inputs[107] or allocating markets would likewise raise antitrust concern.[108]

F. Price Discrimination

Section 2(a) of the Clayton Act, as amended by the Robinson-Patman Act, prohibits a seller from selling commodities of "like grade and quality" to different purchasers at different prices, where the effect may injure competition. Under Section 2(f) of the Robinson-Patman Act, purchasers also may be liable if they knowingly receive or induce an unlawful discriminatory price.[109] Claims of price discrimination may arise with respect to the sale or purchase of commodities such as prescription drugs or medical equipment and supplies, but cannot arise with respect to physician and hospital services, or health-care financing, which are not commodities.[110]

"Primary-line" price discrimination occurs when the effect of the price discrimination on competition is at the level of the seller engaging in price discrimination—for example, where the seller engages in predatory pricing in one geographic area to drive its competitors there from the market while charging a higher price in another geographic area where it faces less competition.[111] "Secondary-line" price discrimination results where the effect of the price discrimination occurs at the level of the seller's customers—that is, where the seller discriminates in price between its customers who compete against one other,[112] providing one with a competitive cost advantage over the others.

---

health plan over physician suppliers of medical services resulting from proposed merger).
107. *E.g.,* Mandeville Island Farms v. Am. Crystal Sugar Co., 334 U.S. 219 (1948); Todd v. Exxon Corp., 275 F.3d 191 (2d Cir. 2001).
108. *See* Chester County Hosp. v. Independence Blue Cross, No. 02-2746 (E.D. Pa., filed Feb. 3, 2003) (amended complaint) (on file with editor) (alleging market-allocation agreement among health plans).
109. For discussion of the Robinson-Patman Act, *see ADL V, supra* p. 9 n.23, at 455-524.
110. *See* Ball Mem'l Hosp. v. Mut. Hosp. Ins., Inc., 784 F.2d 1325, 1340 (7th Cir. 1986) (medical services); Empire State Pharm. Soc'y v. Empire Blue Cross & Blue Shield, 778 F. Supp. 1253, 1258-59 (S.D.N.Y 1991) (health insurance).
111. *E.g.,* Brooke Group, Ltd. v. Brown & Williamson Tobacco Co., 509 U.S. 209 (1993); Bailey v. Allgas, Inc., 284 F.3d 1237 (11th Cir. 2002).
112. *E.g.,* Texaco v. Hasbrouck, 496 U.S. 543 (1990).

A seller's price discrimination is not unlawful if, in granting a lower price to a favored purchaser, the seller acts in "good faith to meet an equally low price of a competitor" (the "meeting competition" defense),[113] or if the price differential makes "only due allowance for differences in the cost of manufacture, sale or delivery resulting from the differing methods or quantities" in which the goods are "sold or delivered" (the "cost justification" defense).[114] In addition, some courts have applied the so-called "functional availability" defense, which provides that a price discrimination is not unlawful if the lower price is available to all buyers—that is, the buyers are aware of the lower price and, as a practical matter, meet the seller's requirements for obtaining it.[115] Purchases of commodities by nonprofit entities at discriminatory low prices may be exempt from the Robinson-Patman Act pursuant to the Nonprofit Institutions Act.[116]

G. Potentially Problematic Agreements

There are a number of frequently recurring types of agreements that typically warrant analysis for their potential antitrust ramifications. All else equal, horizontal agreements (that is, those among competitors) raise more potential concern than vertical agreements (that is, those between firms at different levels of the chain of distribution). Firms are "competitors" if they sell or purchase, or potentially sell or purchase, in the same relevant market.

1. Horizontal Price-Fixing Agreements

A horizontal price-fixing agreement is an agreement or understanding among competing sellers (or buyers) that directly affects the prices they charge (or pay) for their products (or inputs).[117] "Naked" horizontal price-fixing agree-

---

113. 15 U.S.C. § 13(b).

114. *Id.* § 13(a).

115. *See generally ALD V, supra* p. 9 n.23, at 493-94; *see also* FTC v. Morton Salt Co., 334 U.S. 37, 42 (1948).

116. *Id.* § 13c. The Nonprofit Institutions Act is discussed *infra* at p. 60.

117. *See* United States v. Socony-Vacuum Oil Co., 310 U.S. 150, 221 (1940) (explaining that "[a]ny combination which tampers with price structures is engaged in an unlawful activity"). For discussion of horizontal price-fixing agreements, *see ALD V, supra* p. 9 n.23, at 81-98.

ments (that is, those among non-integrated competitors or that are not reasonably necessary for the achievement of efficiencies), as opposed to "ancillary" price-fixing agreements,[118] are per se unlawful[119] and the Antitrust Division often prosecutes them criminally. Indeed, the Supreme Court has stated that "[n]o antitrust offense is more pernicious than price fixing."[120] Ancillary price-fixing agreements (or any type of ancillary agreement or restraint) are assessed under the rule of reason.[121]

---

118. In general, an agreement or restraint is ancillary if the parties have partially integrated their operations in an efficiency-enhancing manner and the agreement is reasonably necessary to achieve those efficiencies. For a more detailed discussion of the difference between naked and ancillary horizontal restraints, *see Collaboration Guidelines, supra* p. 12 n.40, §§ 1.2, 3.2; *see also* Rothery Storage & Van Co. v. Atlas Van Lines, Inc., 792 F.2d 210, 224 (D.C. Cir. 1986) (For a restraint to be ancillary, it must be "subordinate and collateral in the sense that it serves to make the main transaction more effective" and must be "related to the efficiency sought to be achieved.").

   Differentiating between naked and ancillary restraints often is difficult, but the issue arises frequently in health-care antitrust analysis—for example, in determining whether a provider contracting network's negotiating prices with payers is a naked or ancillary price-fixing agreement, *see infra* pp. 81-84; and in determining whether, in a joint venture among hospitals to provide particular services, an agreement among them not to offer the service individually is a naked or ancillary market-allocation agreement or agreement not to compete, *see infra* pp. 44, 119-20. Because the per se rule applies if the agreement is naked, an incorrect answer can have quite serious ramifications.

119. *E.g.*, Arizona v. Maricopa County Med. Soc'y, 457 U.S. 332 (1982) (sellers); All Care Nursing Serv., Inc. v. High Tech Staffing Servs., Inc., 135 F.3d 740, 747 (11th Cir. 1998) ("That price fixing is equally violative of antitrust laws whether it is done by buyers or sellers is also undisputed."); New York v. St. Francis Hosp., 94 F. Supp. 2d 399, 415 (S.D.N.Y. 2000); *see also* Todd v. Exxon Corp., 275 F.3d 191, 201 (2d Cir. 2001) ("a horizontal conspiracy among buyers to stifle competition is as unlawful as one among sellers").

120. FTC v. Ticor Title Ins. Co., 504 U.S. 621, 639 (1992); *see also* Freeman v. San Diego Ass'n of Realtors, 322 F.3d 1133, 1144 (9th Cir. 2003) (stating that "[n]o antitrust violation is more abominated than the agreement to fix prices"), *cert. denied*, 124 S.Ct. 355 (2003).

121. *E.g.*, Broad. Music, Inc. v. Columbia Broad. Sys., 441 U.S. 1 (1979).

2. Horizontal Agreements to Exchange Pricing Information

Although not per se unlawful, agreements among competitors by which they share or exchange pricing information may result in a violation of Section 1 of the Sherman Act when they increase prices or result in price stabilization.[122] Particularly important variables in determining their lawfulness are the number and relative sizes of competing firms participating in the exchange; whether the information is historical, current, or prospective; and the specificity of the price information exchanged. A problem can arise whether the exchange of prices is between sellers or buyers; an example of the latter would be a wage survey among employers.[123] A related problem is that exchanges of pricing information among competing sellers or buyers can facilitate price-fixing agreements that are per se unlawful.[124]

3. Horizontal Market-Allocation Agreements

Horizontal market-allocation agreements are agreements among competing sellers by which they agree about the geographical areas in which they will compete and not compete, the products or services they will offer, or the types of customers they will serve. Unless ancillary, such agreements are per se unlawful.[125] Because they prevent competition with regard to all competitive variables and not just price, horizontal market-allocation agreements are arguably more anticompetitive than price-fixing agreements.[126] The Antitrust Division frequently prosecutes market-allocation agreements criminally.

---

122. *See generally* United States v. U.S. Gypsum Co., 438 U.S. 422 (1978); United States v. Container Corp. of Am., 393 U.S. 333 (1969). For discussion of agreements among competitors to exchange price information, *see ALD V, supra* p. 9 n.23, at 93-98.

123. *E.g.*, Todd v. Exxon Corp., *supra* p. 43 n.119.

124. *See, e.g.*, Morton Salt Co. v. United States, 235 F.2d 573, 576-77 (10th Cir. 1953).

125. *E.g.*, Palmer v. BRG of Ga., 498 U.S. 46 (1990) (per curiam); United States v. Topco Assocs., 405 U.S. 596 (1972); New York v. St. Francis Hosp., 94 F. Supp. 2d 399, 415 (S.D.N.Y. 2000). For discussion of horizontal market-allocation agreements, *see ALD V, supra* p. 9 n.23, at 101-04.

126. *See* Blue Cross & Blue Shield United v. Marshfield Clinic, 65 F.3d 1406, 1415 (7th Cir. 1995) (stating that it would be illogical to prevent competitors from fixing prices, which destroys price competition, but permit them to divide markets, which eliminates all competition among them).

4. Bid-Rigging Agreements

Bid-rigging agreements are agreements among ostensibly competing bidders as to which bidder will win a contract put out to bid. The bidders agree that all except the predetermined winning bidder will provide the purchaser with higher, complementary bids (if the bidders are sellers rather than purchasers) to make the process appear competitive. Bid-rigging agreements are per se unlawful and usually prosecuted criminally, whether engaged in by sellers or purchasers.[127]

5. Group Boycotts or Concerted Refusals to Deal

In its broadest sense, a group boycott is an agreement among two or more entities not to deal in some respect with another party.[128] Typically, however, the agreement is among competitors. In what some courts refer to as a "classic group boycott," the target of the boycott is a competitor of the parties engaging in the boycott and the purpose for the boycott is to put the target at a competitive disadvantage vis-á-vis the boycotters.[129] Although older cases purportedly applied the per se rule to group boycotts, such arrangements are unlawful only if, at a minimum, the boycotting parties have market power or exclusive access to a trade relationship to which the target of the boycott must have access in order to compete effectively.[130]

---

127. United States v. Portac, 869 F.2d 1288 (9th Cir. 1989) (purchasers); United States v. Heffernan, 43 F.3d 1144 (7th Cir. 1994) (sellers).
128. For discussion of group boycotts or concerted refusals to deal, *see ALD V, supra* p. 9 n.23, at 104-25.
129. *See, e.g.* Bogan v. Hodgkins, 166 F.3d 509, 515 (2d Cir. 1999) (explaining that a "classic group boycott" is a "'concerted effort by a group of competitors . . . to protect themselves from competition from non-group members who seek to compete at that level'"); Armstrong Surgical Ctr., Inc. v. Armstrong County Mem'l Hosp., 185 F.3d 154, 157 (3d Cir. 1999); Disposable Contact Lens Antitrust Litig., 2001-1 Trade Cas. (CCH) ¶ 73,198, at 89,831 (M.D. Fla. 2001).
130. *See* Northwest Wholesale Stationers, Inc. v. Pac. Stationery & Printing Co., 472 U.S. 284 (1985). For a helpful discussion of the taxonomy of group boycotts and appropriate standards of analyses, *see* Kenneth L. Glazer, *Concerted Refusals to Deal Under Section 1 of the Sherman Act*, 70 ANTITRUST L.J. 1 (2002).

Some courts (and the enforcement agencies) sometimes use the term "group boycott" loosely to refer to an agreement among providers (or other types of sellers) not to deal with payers (or other types of purchasers) except at agreed-upon prices or other terms. These types of agreements are actually price-fixing agreements or agreements fixing other terms and conditions of sale.[131]

6. Horizontal Mergers

Horizontal mergers are mergers or other forms of total integration among competitors. The potential antitrust concerns they raise are (1) the creation of a relevant market so highly concentrated that participants behave interdependently as oligopolists (that is, engage in "coordinated interaction" or "tacit collusion"), or (2) the creation of a single post-merger firm able to exercise market power unilaterally.[132] The rule-of-reason standard applies to the analysis of all mergers.[133]

7. Vertical Mergers

Vertical mergers are mergers between firms at different levels in the chain of distribution, such as a firm and one of its suppliers (an "upstream" vertical merger) or one of its customers (a "downstream" vertical merger).[134] The primary antitrust concerns from vertical mergers are the creation of entry barriers, the necessity for competitors to enter both the upstream and downstream markets because of market foreclosure, and the increased probability of collusion at the downstream level.[135]

---

131. *See generally* Hartford Fire Ins. Co. v. California, 509 U.S. 764, 802 (1993) (noting that agreements on terms and conditions of sale, while sometimes referred to as group boycotts, are actually price-fixing agreements because otherwise, every price-fixing agreement would constitute a group boycott).
132. *See generally 1992 Merger Guidelines, supra* p. 12 n.39, §§ 2.1, 2.2. The state attorneys general also have issued enforcement guidelines discussing horizontal mergers. NATIONAL ASSOCIATION OF ATTORNEYS GENERAL, HORIZONTAL MERGER GUIDELINES (1993), *reprinted in* 4 Trade Reg. Rep. (CCH) ¶ 13,406. For discussion of horizontal mergers, *see ALD V, supra* p. 9 n.23, at 327-53.
133. Horizontal merger analysis is discussed *infra* at pp. 107-18.
134. For discussion of vertical mergers, *see ALD V, supra* p. 9 n.23, at 362-68.
135. *See generally* U.S. DEP'T OF JUSTICE, MERGER GUIDELINES (1984), *reprinted in* 4 Trade Reg. Rep. (CCH) ¶ 13,103; Ford Motor Co. v. United States, 405 U.S. 562, 570-71 (1972); Brown Shoe Co. v. United States, 370 U.S. 294, 323-24 (1962).

8. *Vertical Price-Fixing Agreements*

Vertical price-fixing agreements (or "resale price maintenance" agreements) are agreements between sellers and their customers who resell the product that establish the price or price level at which the product must be resold.[136] Vertical price-fixing agreements establishing maximum resale prices are analyzed under the rule of reason, while those setting minimum resale prices are per se unlawful.[137]

9. *Tying Agreements*

A tying arrangement is an agreement between a seller and buyer by which the seller agrees to sell the buyer one product or service (the "tying product") only on the condition that the buyer agree to purchase a second product or service (the "tied product") from the seller or from another seller it designates.[138] Tying agreements are usually tested under an abbreviated form of the rule of reason: the plaintiff must show, at a minimum, that the seller has market power in the market for the tying product.[139] In addition, the plaintiff must prove that the seller was coerced to purchase the separate tied product or service and that the arrangement affected a significant volume of interstate commerce.[140] In most circuits, the plaintiff must also prove that the seller has an economic interest in the sale of the tied product when the seller forces the buyer to purchase the tied product from a source other than itself.[141]

---

136. *E.g.*, Bus. Elecs. Corp. v. Sharp Elecs. Corp., 485 U.S. 717, 723-36 (1988).
137. State Oil Co. v. Khan, 522 U.S. 3 (1997). The state attorneys general have issued enforcement guidelines discussing vertical price-fixing agreements and other restraints resulting from vertical agreements. *See* NATIONAL ASSO-CIATION OF ATTORNEYS GENERAL, VERTICAL RESTRAINTS GUIDELINES (1995), *reprinted in* 4 Trade Reg. Rep. (CCH) ¶ 13,400.
138. *E.g.*, Eastman Kodak Co. v. Image Technical Servs., Inc., 504 U.S. 451, 462 (1992). For discussion of tying arrangements, *see ALD V*, *supra* p. 9 n.23, at 175-214.
139. *E.g.*, Jefferson Parish Hosp. Dist. No. 2 v. Hyde, 466 U.S. 2, 14 (1984).
140. *E.g.*, Palladin Assocs., Inc. v. Mont. Power Co., 328 U.S. 1145, 1159 (9th Cir. 2003); Gordon v. Lewistown Hosp., 272 F. Supp. 2d 393, 446 (M.D. Pa. 2003).
141. *E.g.*, Beard v. Parkview Hosp., 912 F.2d 138, 141-42 (6th Cir. 1990).

10. Exclusive Dealing Agreements

An exclusive dealing agreement is an agreement between a seller and purchaser obligating the purchaser to buy a particular product or service only from the seller (sometimes called a "requirements contract") or the seller to sell a product or service only to that purchaser.[142] Because "[a]ll contracts are by their very nature exclusionary"[143] and because exclusive contracts can generate significant efficiencies, exclusive dealing agreements are always tested under the rule of reason[144] and require analysis of whether the agreement will result in the seller or buyer obtaining, maintaining, or increasing market power.[145] In making this determination, courts examine numerous variables, the most important of which are the percentage of the market foreclosed to competitors of the buyer or seller because of the agreement and the duration of the exclusive arrangement.[146]

---

142. For discussion of exclusive dealing agreements, *see ALD V, supra* p. 9 n.23, at 214-26.
143. Foto USA, Inc. v. Bd. of Regents, 141 F.3d 1032, 1037 (11th Cir. 1998).
144. *See generally* Tampa Elec. Co. v. Nashville Coal Co., 365 U.S. 320 (1961); *see also* Jefferson Parish Hosp. Dist. No. 2 v. Hyde, 466 U.S. 2, 29 (1984); Woman's Clinic, Inc. v. St. John's Health Sys., Inc., 252 F. Supp. 2d 857, 865 (W.D. Mo. 2002).
145. *E.g.*, Minn. Ass'n of Nurse Anesthetists v. Unity Hosp., 208 F.3d 655, 662 (8th Cir. 2000) (explaining that plaintiff must show either an adverse effect on competition such as higher prices or lower quality or that defendant had market power in the relevant market). For a helpful discussion of the analysis of exclusive dealing agreements, *see* Jonathan M. Jacobson, *Exclusive Dealing, "Foreclosure," and Consumer Harm*, 70 ANTITRUST L.J. 311 (2002).
146. *E.g.*, United States v. Microsoft Corp., 253 F.3d 34, 69 (D.C. Cir. 2001) (en banc) (per curiam) (exclusive contracts are not unlawful unless they foreclose a substantial percentage of the market to defendant's competitors); Omega Envtl., Inc. v. Gilbarco, Inc., 127 F.3d 1157, 1163 (9th Cir. 1997) ("the short duration and easy terminability of these agreements negate substantially their potential to foreclose competition"); U.S. Healthcare, Inc. v. Healthsource, Inc., 986 F.2d 589, 596 (1st Cir. 1993) (absent proof of substantial market foreclosure, further analysis is unnecessary); United States v. Dentsply Int'l, Inc., 277 F. Supp. 2d 387, 450 (D. Del. 2003) (short duration and easy terminability of agreements argued against anticompetitive effects), *appeal docketed*, No. 30-4097 (3d Cir. Oct. 14, 2003); Minn. Mining & Mfg. Co. v. Appleton Papers, Inc., 35 F. Supp. 2d 1138, 1143 (D. Minn. 1999).

H. Antitrust Exemptions, Immunities, and Coverage

There are a number of antitrust exemptions or immunities that apply to particular types of parties or conduct that can arise in health-care antitrust cases. Where an exemption applies, the antitrust laws do not apply to the parties or conduct in question. The more important exemptions are discussed below. For the most part, these doctrines are affirmative defenses that should be pled in response to a complaint. A cardinal principle of antitrust jurisprudence, however, is that antitrust exemptions are disfavored and thus that courts construe them strictly.[147]

1. Nonprofit Entities and Non-Commercial Conduct

The courts have made it clear that there is no general exemption from the antitrust laws for nonprofit entities.[148] On the other hand, several courts have held that because noncommercial activities do not constitute "trade or commerce," the antitrust laws do not apply to them.[149] The courts, however, have not clearly delineated the types of conduct that are non-commercial rather than commercial. Some suggest that if the conduct provides the organization with a "commercial advantage,"[150] if the entity "received pecuniary benefit from the transaction"[151] or a "direct economic benefit,"[152] or if the conduct involves the "exchange of money for services,[153] it is commercial conduct.

In addition, Section 4 of the FTC Act[154] provides the FTC with jurisdic-

---

147. *See, e.g.*, FTC v. Ticor Title Ins. Co., 504 U.S. 621, 636 (1992).
148. NCAA v. Bd. of Regents, 468 U.S. 85, 105 (1984); Eleven Line, Inc. v. N. Tex. State Soccer Ass'n, Inc., 213 F.3d 198, 205-06 (5th Cir. 2000).
149. *E.g.*, Smith v. NCAA, 139 F.3d 180, 185 (3d Cir. 1998); Hamilton Chapter of Alpha Delta Psi, Inc. v. Hamilton Coll., 128 F.3d 59, 63 (2d Cir. 1997) ("there is no blanket exemption from the antitrust laws based on an organization's non-profit status," but "noncommercial activities of certain organizations have been found outside the scope of the antitrust laws" because they are not trade or commerce).
150. Smith v. NCAA, 139 F.3d at 185.
151. Va. Vermiculite, Ltd. v. W.R. Grace & Co., 108 F. Supp. 2d 549, 604 (W.D. Va. 2000).
152. Adidas Am., Inc. v. NCAA, 40 F. Supp. 2d 1275, 1286 (D. Kan. 1999).
153. Bronx Legal Servs v. Legal Servs. for N.Y. City, 2003-1 Trade Cas. (CCH) ¶ 73,954, at 95,720 (S.D.N.Y. 2003).
154. 15 U.S.C § 44.

tion under Section 5 of that Act over entities "organized to carry on business for [their] own profit or that of [their] members." In the health-care sector, this standard has led to litigation over whether the FTC has Section 5 jurisdiction over the activities of professional associations. The FTC has argued successfully that such associations, even if nonprofit entities, carry on business for the profit of their members[155] and thus fall within the FTC's Section 5 jurisdiction. In *California Dental Association v. FTC*,[156] the Supreme Court held that the FTC had jurisdiction over the association because its contributions to the profits of its members were "proximate and apparent."[157]

2. State-Action Immunity

The state-action immunity doctrine is premised on our federal system of dual sovereignty and thus the principle that the federal antitrust laws do not apply to actions taken by the states, even if anticompetitive.[158] The conduct of sovereign branches of state governments is absolutely immune from successful antitrust challenge.[159] The conduct of state agencies and subordinate state and local entities and agencies is immune only if the action in question is clearly articulated and affirmatively expressed by the state as state policy.[160] To sustain this requirement, the state need not mandate the challenged conduct, but there must be evidence that the state intended to replace competition with regulation, that the conduct was authorized by the state, and that the challenged anticompetitive effects were contemplated or reasonably foreseeable by the state.[161] Under this standard, for example, the peer-review activities of

---

155. *See* Am. Med. Ass'n v. FTC, 638 F.2d 443 (2d Cir. 1980), *aff'd by an equally divided court*, 455 U.S. 676 (1982).
156. 526 U.S. 756 (1999).
157. *Id*. at 767.
158. *See* Parker v. Brown, 317 U.S. 341, 350-51 (1943). For discussion of the state-action exemption, *see ALD V, supra* p. 9 n.23, at 1213-22.
159. Hoover v. Ronwin, 466 U.S. 558 (1984).
160. *E.g.*, Town of Hallie v. City of Eau Claire, 471 U.S. 34 (1985).
161. *E.g.*, City of Columbia v. Omni Outdoor Adver., Inc., 499 U.S. 365 (1991); Surgical Care Ctr. v. Hosp. Serv. Dist. No. 1, 171 F.3d 231 (5th Cir. 1999) (en banc); Daniels v. Am. Bd. of Emergency Med., 235 F. Supp. 2d 194, 205 (W.D. N.Y. 2002).

governmental hospitals, such as county or special-district hospitals, frequently enjoy antitrust immunity.[162]

Finally, the conduct of private parties may enjoy state-action immunity where the conduct is both clearly articulated and affirmatively expressed by the state as state policy and is actively supervised by the state.[163] The "active state supervision" requirement has been interpreted rather strictly, requiring that state officials actually exercise their power to review and approve or disapprove the challenged action to ensure that it accords with the state's policy.[164] The mere potential for state supervision—by a regulatory scheme in place but not operating, for example—is insufficient to sustain the exemption.[165]

The state-action doctrine may apply to bar claims asserted against health-care providers or payers that are governmental entities.[166] The doctrine also has been applied to bar antitrust claims against private health-care providers that obtain exclusive contracts from public hospitals and other local governmental entities.[167] The state-action doctrine generally has not barred antitrust claims challenging peer-review decisions by private hospitals because states

---

162. *E.g.*, Crosby v. Hosp. Auth., 93 F.3d 1515 (11th Cir. 1996); Martin v. Mem'l Hosp., 86 F.3d 1391 (5th Cir. 1996); Wee v. Rome Hosp., 1996-1 Trade Cas. (CCH) ¶ 71,429 (N.D.N.Y. 1996).
163. Cal. Retail Liquor Dealers Ass'n v. Midcal Aluminum, Inc., 445 U.S. 97, 105 (1980).
164. *E.g.*, Patrick v. Burget, 486 U.S. 94, 101 (1988).
165. FTC v. Ticor Title Ins. Co., 504 U.S. 621, 634 (1992).
166. *See, e.g.*, Martin v. Mem'l Hosp., 86 F.3d at 1397 (municipal hospital granting exclusive contract for end-stage renal disease services need only show it acted pursuant to a clearly articulated and affirmatively expressed state policy); *cf. Surgical Care Ctr.*, 171 F.3d at 235 (state-action exemption inapplicable because state statute authorizing hospital district to form joint ventures was intended only to level playing field between governmental and private hospitals, not to displace competition).
167. *See, e.g.*, Neo Gen Screening, Inc. v. New Eng. Newborn Screening Program, 187 F.3d 24 (1st Cir. 1999) (doctrine applied to state's exclusive contract with provider of blood screening services); A-1 Ambulance Serv. v. County of Monterey, 90 F.3d 333 (9th Cir. 1996) (doctrine applied to county's grant of exclusive operating areas for non-emergency ambulance services); Martin v. Mem'l Hosp., 86 F.3d at 1398-1400 (doctrine applied to municipal hospital's exclusive contract with provider of end-stage renal disease services).

typically do not actively supervise hospital peer-review proceedings and their results.[168]

The state action doctrine also may apply to conduct approved under state health-care "certificate of public advantage" (COPA) statutes. These statutes are intended to shield collaborative conduct among health-care providers, such as hospital mergers, approved by the state through its COPA procedure from federal antitrust claims. Courts, however, have not yet addressed whether the approval and oversight procedures established and carried out under COPA statutes satisfy the active state supervision requirement.[169] Courts have declined to apply the state-action doctrine to bar antitrust claims challenging hospital mergers that were subject to state certificate-of-need review because of a lack of continuing state supervision over the hospital's conduct follow-

---

168. *See, e.g.*, Patrick v. Burget, 486 U.S. at 1664 (declining to apply state-action doctrine to a hospital peer-review credentialing decision after holding that the active supervision requirement mandates that the state exercise ultimate control over the challenged anticompetitive conduct); Miller v. Ind. Hosp., 930 F.2d 334, 337-39 (3d Cir. 1991) (finding administrative procedures for evaluating peer-review process insufficient to constitute active state supervision).

    For an extensive discussion of the FTC's views about the state-action exemption, *see* Federal Trade Commission, *Report of the State Action Task Force* (Sept. 2003), *at* http://www.ftc.gov/05/2003/ 09/stateactionreport.pdf; Alabama Trucking Ass'n, Dkt. No. 9307 (FTC Oct. 30, 2003) (Analysis of Proposed Consent Order to Aid Public Comment), *at* http://www.ftc.gov/ os/2003/10/alabamaana.pdf; Indiana Household Movers Warehousemen, Dkt. No. C-4077 (FTC Apr. 29, 2003) (Analysis of Proposed Consent Order to Aid Public Comment), *at* http://www/ftc.gov/05/2003/03/ indianahouseholdmoversanalysis.pdf. Through its report on the state-action exemption and recent enforcement actions, the FTC is attempting to narrow the scope of the exemption from that in recent court decisions.

169. *See ABA State Antitrust Practice, supra* p. xiii n.8, App. C, which compiles state COPA statutes; *see also* Sarah Vance, *Immunity for State-Sanctioned Provider Collaboration After* Ticor, 62 ANTITRUST L.J. 409 (1994) (analyzing extent of supervision provided in state COPA statutes); FTC Staff Letter to Columbus Hospital and Montana Deaconess Hospital (June 28, 1996) (stating that staff had not determined whether state-action immunity applied to the hospitals' merger under the state's COPA procedure, but that staff had decided not to recommend a challenge to the transaction), *reprinted in* 3 *HCAL, supra* p. 14 n.47, App. D65.

ing the merger.[170] But mergers by governmental hospitals may enjoy the exemption depending on their authority to participate in such mergers under state law.[171]

3. Soliciting Governmental Action

The so-called *Noerr-Pennington* (or "solicitation of governmental action") exemption doctrine provides immunity from antitrust claims for petitioning the government to act, even when the petitioning is undertaken concertedly and even if the intent or effect of the petitioning is anticompetitive.[172] Thus, for example, no antitrust liability can attach when a firm or group of firms requests a governmental agency to take action that would seriously harm competition or a competitor and the government takes that action.

The *Noerr-Pennington* doctrine applies to a broad range of conduct, including lobbying regarding legislation or regulation, and the initiation of, or participation in, judicial or administrative proceedings. The doctrine does not apply to solicitation activities directed at private standard-setting bodies or the general public,[173] to boycotts or coercion of the government to force it to act, or to other private marketplace conduct directed at inducing governmental action.[174] Nor does the doctrine protect "sham" petitioning activities—that is, direct interference with a rival's business relationships by using the governmental process itself, rather than the outcome of that process, as an

---

170. *See* FTC v. Univ. Health, Inc., 938 F.2d 1206, 1213 (11th Cir. 1991); North Carolina v. P.I.A. Asheville, Inc., 740 F.2d 274, 277 (4th Cir. 1984).
171. *See* FTC v. Hosp. Bd., 38 F.3d 1184 (11th Cir. 1994).
172. *See* UMW v. Pennington, 381 U.S. 657 (1965); E. R.R. Presidents Conf. v. Noerr Motor Freight, Inc., 365 U.S. 127 (1961); Marian v. Fisher, 338 F.3d 189, 197 (3d Cir. 2003) ("That immunity is so potent that it protects petitioning notwithstanding an improper purpose or motive."). For discussion of the *Noerr-Pennington* doctrine, *see ALD V, supra* p. 9 n.23, at 1223-37.
173. *See* Allied Tube & Conduit Corp. v. Indian Head, Inc., 486 U.S. 492 (1988); Warfarin Sodium Antitrust Litig., 1999-1 Trade Cas. (CCH) ¶ 72,457 (D. Del. 1998), *rev'd on other grounds*, 214 F.3d 395 (3d Cir. 2000).
174. *See* FTC v. Superior Court Trial Lawyers Ass'n, 493 U.S. 411, 425 (1990) (no immunity for trial lawyers' boycott aimed at inducing higher fees for court-assigned counsel for indigent criminal defendants); Sandy River Nursing Care v. Aetna Cas., 985 F.2d 1138, 1142-43 (1st Cir. 1993) (no immunity where private-party defendants imposed a boycott, even though their purpose was to induce favorable governmental action).

anticompetitive weapon.[175] For example, a party's filing of litigation, which is usually protected by the doctrine, is not protected if it is "sham" litigation—that is, objectively baseless in the sense that no reasonable litigant could expect to win, and subjectively baseless in the sense that the plaintiff's intent was not to win the litigation but instead to use the litigation process itself to harm its competitor.[176]

Courts have reached different conclusions as to whether the doctrine protects petitioning of a governmental entity that is acting in a purely commercial or proprietary capacity (where, for example, the government is acting merely as a seller or purchaser in the market),[177] but the majority view appears to be that there is no commercial exception to the doctrine.[178] In addition, there is some confusion about whether the doctrine applies to misrepresentations made to administrative agencies (such as a state agency reviewing a certificate-of-need application) in the context of petitioning for or against administrative action.[179] The emerging view appears to be that mis-

---

175. *See* Prof'l Real Estate Investors, Inc. v. Columbia Pictures Indus., 508 U.S. 49 (1993); City of Columbia v. Omni Outdoor Adver., Inc., 499 U.S. 365 (1991); Cal. Motor Transp. Co. v. Trucking Unlimited, 404 U.S. 508 (1972).

176. *Prof'l Real Estate Investors,* 508 U.S. at 51.

177. *See, e.g., City of Columbia,* 499 U.S. at 379 (recognizing possibility of exception but not deciding the issue); Cont'l Ore Co. v. Union Carbide & Carbon Corp., 370 U.S. 690, 707-08 (1962) (suggesting a commercial exception); George R. Whitten Jr., Inc. v. Paddock Pool Bldrs., Inc., 424 F.2d 25, 33 (1st Cir. 1970) (recognizing commercial exception).

178. *E.g., Sandy River Nursing Care,* 985 F.2d at 1142-43; Greenwood Util. Comm'n v. Miss. Power Co., 751 F.2d 1484, 1499-1500 (5th Cir. 1983); *In re* Airport Car Rental Antitrust Litig., 693 F.2d 84, 87-88 (9th Cir. 1982); Total Benefit Servs. v. Group Ins. Adm'rs, 875 F. Supp. 1228, 1241-42 (E.D. La. 1995).

179. *See, e.g., Prof'l Real Estate Investors,* 508 U.S. at 57 (leaving question open); Davic Maine Corp. v. Rancourt, 216 F.3d 143, 147 (1st Cir. 2000) (holding that even false statements are protected); Armstrong Surgical Ctr., Inc. v. Armstrong County Mem'l Hosp., 185 F.3d 154, 158 (3d Cir. 1999) (misrepresentations protected); Kottle v. Northwest Kidney Ctrs., 146 F.3d 1056, 1060 (9th Cir. 1998) (misrepresentations can constitute sham petitioning); St. Joseph's Hosp. v. Hosp. Corp. of Am., 795 F.2d 948, 955 (11th Cir. 1986) (misrepresentations in adjudicative hearings can constitute sham petitioning); Potters Med. Ctr. v. City Hosp. Ass'n, 800 F.2d 568, 578 (6th Cir. 1986) (providing knowingly false information can constitute sham petitioning); Hosp. Bldg. Co. v. Trs. of Rex Hosp., 691 F.2d 678, 687 (4th Cir. 1982) (same).

representations do not destroy the exemption unless they are "material" and go to the "core" or "legitimacy" of the government's decision. [180]

4. Business of Insurance

The McCarran-Ferguson Act[181] provides the "business of insurance" with a limited exemption from federal antitrust law to the extent the conduct in question is regulated by state law and is not an "agreement to boycott, coerce, or intimidate, or an act of boycott, coercion, or intimidation."[182]

The Supreme Court has held that in determining whether particular conduct constitutes the business of insurance, courts should consider whether (1) it spreads or transfers policyholder risk; (2) it constitutes an integral part of the policy relationship between the insurer and insured; and (3) participation in the conduct is limited to entities within the insurance industry. None of the factors, however, is determinative by itself.[183] In general, courts have held that a payer's contracts with, and its conduct toward, its participating providers are not the business of insurance but that its conduct toward its insureds is.[184] The exemption does apply to the concerted fixing of insurance premi-

---

180. *See* Cheminor Drugs, Ltd. v. Ethyl Corp., 168 F.3d 119, 124 (3d Cir. 1999) (holding that "a *material* misrepresentation that affects the very core of a litigant's case will preclude *Noerr-Pennington* immunity"); *Kottle*, 146 F.3d at 1063 (fraud or intentional misrepresentations can constitute a sham if they deprive the proceeding of "its legitimacy").

181. 15 U.S.C. §§ 1011-1015.

182. Hartford Fire Ins. Co. v. California, 509 U.S. 764, 780 (1993); *see* St. Paul Fire & Marine Ins. Co. v. Barry, 438 U.S. 531 (1978). For discussion of the McCarran-Ferguson Act, *see ALD V, supra* p. 9 n.23, at 1369-75.

183. Union Labor Life Ins. Co. v. Pireno, 458 U.S. 119, 129-34 (1982).

184. *See, e.g., id.* (use of peer-review committee to determine reasonableness of chiropractic charges not the business of insurance); Group Life & Health Ins. Co. v. Royal Drug Co., 440 U.S. 205 (1979) (payer's agreement with its participating pharmacists to offer low-cost drugs to policyholders not the business of insurance because it was aimed solely at cutting the payer's costs and did not spread or transfer health-insurance risk); Ocean State Physicians Health Plan v. Blue Cross & Blue Shield, 883 F.2d 1101, 1110 (1st Cir. 1989) (most-favored-nation pricing provisions in payer's contracts with providers not the business of insurance); Rozema v. Marshfield Clinic, 1997-1 Trade Cas. (CCH) ¶ 71,796 (W.D. Wis. 1997) (health plan's refusal to contract with provider not protected by McCarran Act because refusal related to relationship between insurer and provider rather than the relationship between insurer and insured).

ums[185] but would not protect a price-fixing agreement among insurers with regard to their reimbursement of providers. Thus, while providers sometimes argue that insurers enjoy an antitrust exemption providing them with advantageous bargaining leverage in contract negotiations, the exemption has little, if any, effect on the relative bargaining power of providers and payers. Courts have not yet addressed whether a payer's risk-sharing agreements with healthcare providers constitute the business of insurance.

The term "boycott" has a different and narrower meaning for purposes of the McCarran Act than for purposes of Section 1 of the Sherman Act. In *Hartford Fire Insurance Company v. California*, the Supreme Court appeared to limit the meaning of "boycott" in the McCarran Act context to refusals to deal in order to achieve an object collateral to the main transaction, explaining that conduct constitutes a "boycott" where, in order to coerce a target into certain terms on one transaction, parties refuse to engage in other unrelated or collateral transactions with the target.[186]

5. Labor Unions

The statutory and nonstatutory labor exemptions shield certain conduct by employees and their labor organizations, as well as employers, from antitrust claims. The statutory labor exemption flows from Section 6 of the Clayton Act,[187] which declares that "the labor of a human being is not a commodity or article of commerce"; Section 20 of the Clayton Act;[188] and Sections 1, 4, 5, and 13 of the Norris-LaGuardia Act,[189] which prohibit federal courts from issuing injunctions growing out of labor disputes. The statutory exemption protects unilateral union conduct—that is, conduct by a bona fide labor organization acting in its own self-interest to further a labor objective, where the union has not combined with a non-labor group.[190]

---

185. SEC v. Nat'l Secs., Inc., 393 U.S. 453, 460 (1969) ("Certainly, the fixing of rates is part of [the business of insurance]."); Slagle v. ITT Hartford, 102 F.3d 494, 498 (11th Cir. 1996); Bristol Hotel Mgmt. Corp. v. Aetna Cas. & Sur. Co., 20 F. Supp. 2d 1345 (S.D. Fla. 1998).
186. *See Hartford Fire Ins. Co.,* 509 U.S. at 803.
187. 15 U.S.C. § 17.
188. *Id.* § 52 .
189. 29 U.S.C. §§ 101, 104, 105, 113.
190. *See, e.g.,* United States v. Hutcheson, 312 U.S. 219, 236 (1941). For discussion of the labor exemption, *see ALD V, supra* p. 9 n.23, at 1375-82.

The nonstatutory labor exemption is an implied antitrust immunity created by the courts. It protects from successful antitrust challenge a labor union's collective bargaining with an employer over wages, hours, and other terms and conditions of employment, as well as the resulting agreements between labor and management covering these matters. Courts have extended the nonstatutory exemption to other concerted activities and agreements between labor groups and other parties that arise in a collective-bargaining setting, are intimately related to a mandatory subject of bargaining, and lack the potential to restrain competition in business markets in ways not flowing naturally from eliminating competition over wages and working conditions.[191] The exemption also protects multi-employer agreements in the context of collective bargaining between employers and their employees.[192]

The statutory and nonstatutory labor exemptions can apply to physicians (including medical residents and fellows) and other health-care practitioners who are employees of, for example, hospitals or HMOs, and bargain collectively with their employer. But the relationship between a health insurer and its participating physicians who have their own independent practices is an independent-contractor relationship rather than one of employment,[193] and independent businesspersons cannot immunize themselves from the antitrust laws by forming an association, labeling it a labor union, and then fixing the prices they charge their customers.[194] This limitation, as a practical matter, has foreclosed application of the labor exemption to health-care practitioners' collective negotiations with health plans.

---

191. *See, e.g.,* Connell Constr. Co. v. Plumbers & Steamfitters Local Union No. 100, 421 U.S. 616, 635 (1975); Sheet Metal Div. of Capital Dist. Sheet Metal, Roofing & Air Conditioning Contractors Ass'n v. Local 38, Sheet Metal Workers Int'l Ass'n, 208 F.3d 18, 26 (2d Cir. 2000).
192. *See, e.g.,* Brown v. Pro Football, Inc., 518 U.S. 231 (1996).
193. *See* 29 U.S.C. § 152(3), providing that the term "employee," as used in the National Labor Relations Act, does not include independent contractors; *see also* AmeriHealth, Inc., Case 4-RC (NLRB Reg'l Director Dec.) (May 24, 1999) (holding that independently practicing physicians were not employees of an HMO with which they contracted to provide services and thus could not be certified as a bargaining unit).
194. *See, e.g.,* Los Angeles Meat & Provisions Drivers Union, Local 626 v. United States, 371 U.S. 94, 101 (1962); Spence v. Southeastern Alaska Pilots Ass'n, 1991-1 Trade Cas. (CCH) ¶ 69,453 (D. Alaska 1990) (holding that an association of independent contractors cannot sustain the labor exemption).

6. *Local Government Antitrust Act*

The Local Government Antitrust Act of 1984[195] provides that antitrust plaintiffs may not recover damages in actions under the federal antitrust laws from any local government or its officials or employees acting in an official capacity. The Act also bars damage claims against private parties based on any official action by a local government or its officials.[196] Claims for injunctive relief, however, are not barred.[197] The courts have applied the Act to dismiss antitrust damage claims challenging a public hospital's denial of staff privileges or grant of exclusive contracts.[198] Courts have reached differing conclusions, however, as to whether the Act bars damage claims against hospital districts created pursuant to state law, depending on the relationship between the district and the state.[199]

---

195. 15 U.S.C. §§ 34-36.
196. *Id.* § 36(a); *see* Patel v. Midland Mem'l Hosp., 298 F.3d 333, 346 (5th Cir. 2002).
197. *See, e.g.,* Daniel v. Am. Bd. of Emergency Med., 988 F. Supp. 127, 192 (W.D.N.Y. 1997).
198. *See, e.g.,* Cohn v. Bond, 953 F.2d 154, 158 (4th Cir. 1991) (holding that physicians who made peer-review decisions at the behest of, or by delegation from, the local governmental hospital's board of trustees were protected from damages under the Act); Sandcrest Outpatient Servs., P.A. v. Cumberland County Hosp. Sys., 853 F.2d 1139, 1145 (4th Cir. 1988) (members of governmental hospital's medical staff protected as long as they acted in an official capacity and were directed by government officials who were acting in their official capacities); Fremaux v. Bd. of Comm'rs, 1997-1 Trade Cas. (CCH) ¶ 71,852 (E.D. La. 1997) (hospital district's grant of exclusive contract for radiology services covered by Act).
199. *Compare* Crosby v. Hosp. Auth., 93 F.3d 1515 (11th Cir. 1996) (hospital authority, board members, and committee members who made peer-review recommendations were immune from damages under the Act); *Cohn v. Bond,* 953 F.2d at 158-59 (members of medical staff of municipal hospital who recommended denial of staff privileges acted as agents of hospital and were immune from damages under the Act), *with* Tarabishi v. McAlester Reg'l Hosp., 951 F.2d 1558 (10th Cir. 1991) (public trust hospital was not a special function governmental unit, and thus hospital and members of its medical staff were not immune under Act for claim based on revocation of physician's staff privileges).

7. Health Care Quality Improvement Act

The Health Care Quality Improvement Act of 1986[200] (HCQIA) provides immunity from federal antitrust damage claims, but not liability, for professional review actions by health-care entities conducted in accordance with the Act's requirements. HCQIA does not bar claims for injunctive relief. A professional review action is an action or recommendation made in the course of professional review activity that is based on a physician's competence or professional conduct and that may adversely affect the physician's clinical privileges or membership in a professional society.[201]

For HCQIA's damage immunity to apply, the professional review action must have been taken (1) in the reasonable belief that it would further quality health care, (2) after a reasonable effort to obtain the facts, (3) after adequate notice and a hearing or other "fair" procedures, and (4) in the reasonable belief that the action was warranted by the facts known after reasonable efforts to obtain them. Professional review actions are presumed to meet HCQIA's standards, although the presumption may be rebutted by a preponderance of the evidence.[202] Thus, the burden is on the plaintiff to prove that the immunity does not apply.[203]

In determining whether a professional review action meets the four requirements, courts apply an objective standard of review based on the totality of circumstances. They generally have found HCQIA immunity to apply to professional review actions challenged under the antitrust laws.[204] A substan-

---

200. 42 U.S.C. §§ 11,101-11,152.
201. *Id.* § 11,151(9). For discussion of the Health Care Quality Improvement Act, *see ALD V, supra* p. 9 n.23, at 1333-35.
202. 42 U.S.C. § 11,112(a). *See, e.g.*, Singh v. Blue Cross/Blue Shield, 308 F.3d 25, 32 (1st Cir. 2003) ("With the benefit of the statutory presumption, the [defendant] is relieved of the initial burden of providing evidentiary support for its contention at summary judgment that there is no genuine issue of material fact on its compliance with the HCQIA standards.").
203. *See, e.g.*, Sugarbaker v. SSM Health Care, 190 F.3d 905, 912 (8th Cir. 1999) ("The court must ask whether a reasonable jury . . . could conclude that plaintiff has shown, by a preponderance of the evidence, that the hospital's actions were outside the scope of the statutory standards."); Brader v. Allegheny Gen. Hosp., 167 F.3d 832, 839 (3d Cir. 1999).
204. *See, e.g.*, Mathews v. Lancaster Gen. Hosp., 87 F.3d 624, 638 (3d Cir. 1996); Smith v. Ricks, 31 F.3d 1478, 1485 (9th Cir. 1994); Bryan v. James E. Holmes Reg'l Med. Ctr., 33 F.3d 1318, 1335 (11th Cir. 1994); Poliner v. Texas Health Sys., 2003-2 Trade Cas. (CCH) ¶ 74,174, at 97,512 (N.D. Tex. 2003).

tially prevailing defendant may recover its attorney's fees if an antitrust claim challenging a professional review action is shown to be frivolous, unreasonable, without foundation, or in bad faith.[205] There is no private right of action under HCQIA,[206] and the Act has been adjudged constitutional.[207]

8. *Nonprofit Institutions Act*

The Nonprofit Institutions Act[208] provides an exemption from the Robinson-Patman Act for the sale of supplies to nonprofit and charitable institutions, including hospitals, as long as the supplies are for their "own use." In *Abbott Laboratories, Inc. v. Portland Retail Druggists Association*, the Supreme Court explained that a hospital's "own use" of a commodity is "what reasonably may be regarded as use by the hospital in the sense that such use is part of and promotes the hospital's intended institutional operation in the care of persons who are its patients."[209] For example, the Court held that the hospital's resales of prescription drugs, purchased at prices below those charged area community pharmacies, for outpatient treatment at the hospital were exempt from the Robinson-Patman Act, while sales of prescription refills to former patients or walk-in customers were not. Likewise, a nonprofit HMO's sales of prescription drugs to its members are for its "own use" because part of its institutional operation is the provision of continuing and preventive care.[210] The FTC has issued numerous advisory opinions discussing the Act's applicability to health-care sector transactions.[211]

205. 42 U.S.C. § 11,113; *see, e.g.*, Addis v. Holy Cross Health Sys., 88 F.3d 482, 486-87 (7th Cir. 1996) (remanding for consideration of defendants' entitlement to attorneys fees under HCQIA, even though summary judgment was entered for defendants on other grounds).
206. *See, e.g.*, Wayne v. Genesis Med. Ctr., 140 F.3d 1145, 1147 (8th Cir. 1998); Canady v. Providence Hosp., 903 F. Supp. 125, 126 (D.D.C. 1995).
207. Linda Frelich, M.D., P.A. v. Upper Chesapeake Health, Inc., 313 F.3d 205, 214 (4th Cir. 2002).
208. 15 U.S.C. § 13c.
209. 425 U.S. 1, 14 (1976).
210. DeModena v. Kaiser Found. Health Plan, 743 F.2d 1388, 1393 (9th Cir. 1984).
211. *E.g.*, FTC Staff Advisory Opinion to Dunlap Memorial Hospital (Jan. 6, 2004), *at* http://www.ftc.gov/os/2004/01/040106dunlapet.pdf; FTC Staff Advisory Opinion to Valley Baptist Medical Center (Mar. 13, 2003), *at* http://www.ftc.gov/os/2003/03/030313vbmc.htm; FTC Staff Advisory Opinion to

I. Antitrust Standing and Injury; Statute of Limitations

Section 4(a) of the Clayton Act[212] provides a treble-damage remedy for "any person who shall be injured in its business or property by reason of anything forbidden in the antitrust laws." Section 16 of the Clayton Act[213] authorizes injunctive relief "against threatened loss or damage by a violation of the antitrust laws." Court decisions interpreting these provisions have established important requirements for such relief in addition to proof of a violation.

A plaintiff seeking damages under Section 4 must allege and prove (1) an actual injury to itself for which the antitrust violation is a material and direct cause; (2) that the injury is to its "business or property";[214] (3) that it suffered "antitrust injury"; (4) antitrust standing—that its injury is not too remote or subject to other complicating factors (that is, overlapping claims by others and the risk of inconsistent or duplicative damage awards); and (5) in damage actions, the amount of its damages.[215] The antitrust standing and antitrust injury requirements are related and particularly important in the health-care field.

Antitrust standing is narrower than constitutional standing under Article III of the U.S. Constitution.[216] The antitrust standing requirement focuses on whether a plaintiff is an appropriate party to assert antitrust claims challenging the conduct in question. The Supreme Court has outlined several factors for determining whether a plaintiff has antitrust standing: (1) the causal connection between the antitrust violation and the harm to the plaintiff, and whether the harm was intentional; (2) the nature of the plaintiff's injury, including whether the plaintiff is a consumer or competitor in the relevant market; (3) the directness of the plaintiff's injury and whether its damages are speculative; (4) the potential for duplicative recoveries and whether ap-

---

Arkansas Children's Hospital (Mar. 13, 2003), *at* http://www.ftc.gov/os/ 2003/03/ 030313ach.htms; FTC Staff Advisory Opinion to Health Access, Inc. (Mar. 8, 2002), *at* http://www.ftc. gov/bc/adops/viquestet.htm.

212. 15 U.S.C § 15(a).

213. *Id.* § 21.

214. *See* Reiter v. Sonotone Corp., 442 U.S. 330, 337-38 (1979) ("business or property" means anything of material value that is owned or possessed).

215. *See ALD V, supra* p. 9 n.23, at 838-82, for a discussion of each of these requirements.

216. *E.g., id.; see also* Am. Adver. Mgmt., Inc. v. Gen. Tel. Co., 190 F.3d 1051, 1054 n.3 (9th Cir. 1999).

portionment of damages would be complex; and (5) the existence of more direct victims of the challenged conduct.[217] If the plaintiff is not yet a participant in the relevant market, it must show that it intended to enter the market and was prepared to do so.[218] Where the plaintiff is suing to recover overcharges, as in a case challenging a horizontal price-fixing agreement, only direct purchasers from the conspirators may recover damages,[219] although many state antitrust laws permit indirect purchasers from the conspirators to recover.[220]

Courts have sometimes applied these standards to deny antitrust standing to physicians challenging adverse peer-review actions, denial of staff privileges, and loss of exclusive hospital contracts on the ground that consumers or payers would suffer the direct consequences of a loss of competition in the market for the physician's services and thus are more appropriate plaintiffs.[221]

---

217. Associated Gen. Contractors v. Cal. State Council of Carpenters, 459 U.S. 519, 537-44 (1983).

218. *E.g.*, Xechem, Inc. v. Bristol-Myers Squibb Co., 274 F. Supp. 2d 937, 943 (N.D. Ill. 2003).

219. Ill. Brick Co. v. Illinois, 431 U.S. 720 (1977); *see also* Kansas v. Utilicorp United, Inc., 497 U.S. 199 (1990).

220. *See* California v. ARC Am. Corp., 490 U.S. 93 (1990) (holding that such state laws are not preempted by the federal antitrust laws).

221. *See, e.g.*, Todorov v. DCH Healthcare Auth., 921 F.2d 1438, 1452-54 (11th Cir. 1991) (physician's interests were not aligned with those of patients because he would benefit from high prices); Park Ave. Radiology Assocs. v. Methodist Health Sys., 198 F.3d 246 (6th Cir. 1999) (unpublished opinion reprinted at 1999-2 Trade Cas. (CCH) ¶ 72,712) (affirming summary judgment for defendants, based on lack of standing, on radiologists' challenge to exclusive contract and referral arrangements with hospital and affiliated preferred provider organization); Marshall v. Americus-Sumter County Hosp. Auth., 2003-2 Trade Cas. (CCH) ¶ 74,122, at 97,140 (M.D. Ga. 2002) ("Other district and circuit courts have also found that physicians who are denied staff privileges at hospitals do not have standing to bring an antitrust claim."); Feldman v. Palmetto Gen. Hosp., 1997-2 Trade Cas. (CCH) ¶ 71,978 (S.D. Fla. 1997) (holding that podiatrist lacked standing to challenge alleged boycott by hospital and surgeons to deny him referrals because patients would be more appropriate plaintiffs). *But cf.* Verizon Communications, Inc. v. Law Offices of Curtis V. Trinko, LLP, No. 02-682, slip op. at 1-2, 2004 WL 51011 at *11 (U.S. Jan. 13, 2004) (Stevens, Souter & Thomas, JJ., concurring) (indicating, by analogy, that physician, but not payers or consumers, would have standing in staff-privilege case).

Other courts, however, have held that health-care providers have standing to assert such claims.[222] Courts also have applied these standards to other types of antitrust claims and claimants.[223]

　　To recover damages in an antitrust case, a plaintiff must also prove that its injury constitutes "antitrust injury." To sustain the antitrust-injury requirement, a plaintiff must show that its injury "reflects the anticompetitive effect either of the violation or of anticompetitive acts made possible by the violation."[224] In general, to constitute antitrust injury, the injury must result from the competition-reducing effects of the violation.[225] For example, if a hospi-

---

222. *See, e.g.*, Doctors Hosp. v. Southeast Med. Alliance, Inc., 123 F.3d 301, 305-06 (5th Cir. 1997) (holding that hospital had standing to challenge exclusion from preferred provider organization); Ertag v. Naples Cmty. Hosp., 121 F.3d 721 (11th Cir. 1997) (per curiam opinion reprinted at 1997-2 Trade Cas. (CCH) ¶ 71,966) (reversing summary judgment for defendants and finding that physicians had standing to challenge denial of staff privileges, noting that plaintiffs need not be the "most" efficient antitrust enforcers).

223. *See, e.g.*, Serv. Employees Int'l Union Health & Welfare Fund v. Philip Morris, Inc., 249 F.3d 1068 (D.C. Cir. 2001) (finding that union's costs in paying for treatment of smokers was too indirect an injury for standing); Simon v. Value Behavioral Health, Inc., 208 F.3d 1073 (9th Cir. 2000) (affirming dismissal, because of plaintiff's lack of standing, of antitrust claims challenging insurers' and employers' alleged exclusion of non-network providers from market, where the claim was asserted by assignee of benefits claims of mental health providers who themselves were assigned the claims by patients); Ore. Laborers-Employers Health & Welfare Fund v. Philip Morris, Inc., 185 F.3d 957 (9th Cir. 1999) (holding that plaintiffs lacked standing to assert claims challenging alleged conspiracy among tobacco companies to suppress competition in making safer cigarettes or alternative products because plaintiffs' alleged harm was too remote and merely derivative of the harm suffered by smokers); Int'l Bhd. of Teamsters v. Philip Morris, Inc., 196 F.3d 818 (7th Cir. 1999) (same; also applying indirect-purchaser doctrine to bar health plans' damages claims); Steamfitters Local Union No. 420 Welfare Fund v. Philip Morris, Inc., 171 F.3d 912 (3d Cir. 1999) (same); Laborers Local 17 Health & Benefit Fund v. Philip Morris, Inc., 191 F.3d 229 (2d Cir. 1999) (same).

224. Brunswick Corp. v. Pueblo Bowl-O-Mat, Inc., 429 U.S. 477, 489 (1977); *see also* Montfort of Colo., Inc. v. Cargill, Inc., 479 U.S. 104 (1986) (also holding that plaintiff must prove threatened antitrust injury to obtain injunctive relief); Glen Holly Entm't, Inc. v. Tektronix, Inc., 343 F.3d 1000, 1008 (9th Cir. 2003) ("loss or damage to a competitor due merely to increased competition, such as a diminution of profits due to price competition following a merger by other competitors, is not antitrust injury").

tal grants staff privileges to the plaintiff physician's competitor, thus diverting patients from plaintiff to the competitor, the conduct might injure the plaintiff, but the injury, even if resulting from an antitrust violation, would not constitute antitrust injury because it would increase, rather than decrease, competition.[226]

Conduct that increases competition does not result in antitrust injury,[227] even if it constitutes "unfair competition."[228] Similarly, a number of courts, perhaps confusing the antitrust-injury requirement with that of whether the conduct unreasonably restrains competition and is thus unlawful, have held that a plaintiff suffers no antitrust injury when the challenged conduct is not capable of injuring competition in the market.[229] In assessing whether a plain-

---

225. Atl. Richfield Co. v. USA Petroleum, Inc., 495 U.S. 328, 343 (1990); *see also* U.S. Gypsum Co. v. Ind. Gas Co., 350 F.3d 623, 627 (7th Cir. 2003) (antitrust injury is injury from "those things that make the practice unlawful, such as reduced output or higher prices"); Giampollo v. Somerset Hosp. Ctr. for Health, 189 F.3d 464 (3d Cir. 1999) (finding no antitrust injury where hospital allowed several physicians, rather than only plaintiff, to interpret tests; hospital's action may have harmed plaintiff, but it increased patient choice).

226. *E.g.*, Angelico v. Lehigh Valley Hosp., Inc., 184 F.3d 268, 273-74 (3d Cir. 1999) (explaining that district court erred by basing antitrust-injury assessment on whether plaintiff proved an adverse effect on competition).

227. *E.g.*, *Glen Holly*, 343 F.3d at 1008 ("loss or damage to a competitor due merely to increased competition such as a possible diminution of profits due to price competition . . . is not antitrust injury").

228. *E.g.*, Phillips Getschow Co. v. Green Bay Brown County Prof'l Football Stadium Dist., 270 F. Supp. 2d 1043, 1046, 1048 (E.D. Wis. 2003).

229. *See, e.g.*, Doctor's Hosp. v. Southeast Med. Alliance, 123 F.3d 301, 305-06 (5th Cir. 1997) (holding that hospital excluded from preferred provider organization need not demonstrate injury to competition in the market merely to establish antitrust injury for standing purposes); Mathews v. Lancaster Gen. Hosp., 87 F.3d 624, 641 (3d Cir. 1996) (holding that plaintiff failed to show antitrust injury from loss of staff privileges because his claim alleged injury only to an individual competitor, not to competition in the market as a whole); Brader v. Allegheny Gen. Hosp., 64 F.3d 869, 876 (3d Cir. 1995) (explaining that whether defendant's conduct adversely affected competition should be decided after discovery, not pursuant to a motion to dismiss for failure to allege antitrust injury); Parks v. Hillsdale Cmty. Health Ctr., 1999-1 Trade Cas. (CCH) ¶ 72,555 (W.D. Mich. 1999) (granting defendants summary judgment because orthopedic surgeons lacked stand-

tiff has alleged antitrust injury, some courts hold that the court should assume that the plaintiff has alleged a violation and then determine whether the injury the plaintiff would suffer from that violation would flow from any competition-reducing effects of that violation.[230] Normally, for antitrust injury to result, the plaintiff must be either a customer or competitor in the relevant market affected by the restraint.[231] Antitrust injury is a requirement for recovery of damages or injunctive relief, even for parties challenging conduct that is unlawful per se and thus for which no anticompetitive effect need actually be shown for a violation.[232]

Issues about antitrust injury frequently arise with respect to antitrust claims asserted by a firm against its competitors. As one court has explained, "[B]ecause antitrust law aims to protect competition, not competitors, a court must analyze the antitrust injury question from the viewpoint of the consumer. An antitrust plaintiff must prove that the challenged conduct affected the prices, quantity or quality of goods or services, not just his own welfare."[233] Thus, a health-care provider challenging a price-fixing agreement among its rivals may not suffer antitrust injury (or even injury-in-fact) if the provider would benefit from the agreement by being able to raise its own prices (or when the collusive price undercut plaintiff's price).[234] A payer or consumer, in contrast, suffers antitrust injury if it will have to pay higher prices because of the

---

ing to challenge referral practices favoring rival surgery group's "clinically-aggressive practice style" absent evidence of anticompetitive effects); Wagner v. Magellan Health Servs., 121 F. Supp. 2d 673 (N.D. Ill. 2000) (granting defendants judgment on the pleadings because of lack of antitrust injury where psychiatrist claimed that payer and hospital staff conspired to keep him from receiving emergency room patients; plaintiff did not allege prices increased or output decreased.)

230. *See, e.g., Angelico,* 184 F.3d at 275 n.2 (explaining that district court erred by conflating the antitrust-injury inquiry under § 4 of the Clayton Act with that of effect on competition, which is an element of a § 1 claim); *see also Doctor's Hosp.,* 123 F.3d at 305-06 (explaining that court, in determining whether plaintiff suffered antitrust injury, should assume that defendants violated the Sherman Act and then determine whether that violation would cause plaintiff antitrust injury).

231. *E.g.,* Barton & Pittinos, Inc. v. SmithKline Beecham Corp., 118 F.3d 178, 182 (3d Cir. 1997).

232. Atl. Richfield Co. v. USA Petroleum Co., 495 U.S. 528, 332 (1990).

233. *Lancaster Gen. Hosp.,* 87 F.3d at 641.

234. *See Atl. Richfield,* 495 U.S. at 337 (noting a competing dealer would not suffer antitrust injury from a conspiracy to fix minimum resale prices, but

price-fixing agreement.[235] Courts have reached differing conclusions as to whether a provider has sufficiently alleged or shown the requisite antitrust injury based on its exclusion from a market (or from certain opportunities in the market) because of conduct by rivals (for example, denial or termination of staff privileges, loss of an exclusive contract, or exclusion from a preferred provider organization).[236] The better view would seem to be that the competitor's exclusion from the market constitutes antitrust injury but does

rather would benefit from defendant's higher prices); Retina Assocs. v. S. Baptist Hosp., 105 F.3d 1376, 1383 (11th Cir. 1997) (per curiam) (adopting district court opinion that plaintiff's rule-of-reason claim was deficient as a matter of law because rival's exclusive referral arrangement – which allegedly increased costs to consumers – would allow plaintiff to increase his own fees or gain more business with lower fees); J. Allen Ramey, M.D., Inc. v. Pac. Found. for Med. Care, 999 F. Supp. 1355, 1361 (S.D. Cal. 1998).

235. *See, e.g.*, Blue Cross & Blue Shield United v. Marshfield Clinic, 152 F.3d 588, 592 (7th Cir. 1998).

236. *See, e.g.*, Angelico v. Lehigh Valley Hosp., Inc., 184 F.3d 268 (3d Cir. 1999) (reversing summary judgment for defendant and holding that physician challenging adverse staff-privilege decision alleged antitrust injury); Johnson v. Univ. Health Servs., Inc., 161 F.3d 1334 (11th Cir. 1998) (affirming summary judgment for defendant because plaintiff had not suffered antitrust injury resulting from hospital affiliate's withdrawal of financial support for plaintiff's medical practice; noting plaintiff retained hospital privileges and was not restricted from competing in the market); BCB Anesthesia Care, Ltd. v. Passavant Mem'l Area Hosp. Ass'n, 36 F.3d 664, 667-69 (7th Cir. 1994) (affirming dismissal of provider's challenge to hospital's adverse staffing decision because of lack of antitrust injury; collecting numerous other cases rejecting similar claims); Balaklaw v. Lovell, 14 F.3d 793, 797-98 (2d Cir. 1994) (affirming summary judgment for defendants and holding that physician failed to show antitrust injury from loss of exclusive contract with hospital in competitive-bidding process); Levine v. Cent. Fla. Med. Affiliates, Inc., 864 F. Supp. 1175, 1179-80 (M.D. Fla. 1994) (granting summary judgment for defendants because physician failed to show antitrust injury from suspension of staff privileges and exclusion from exclusive referral arrangement; plaintiff was able to compete successfully exercising privileges at other area hospitals), *aff'd on other grounds*, 72 F.3d 1538 (11th Cir. 1996); Todorov v. DCH Healthcare Auth., 921 F.2d 1438, 1452-54 (11th Cir. 1991) (affirming summary judgment for defendants and holding that physician failed to show antitrust injury resulting from denial of staff privileges).

not constitute an antitrust violation absent a significant adverse effect on market-wide competition.[237]

The antitrust standing requirements for injunctive relief under Section 16 of the Clayton Act are more lenient than those applicable to claims for damages under Section 4.[238] A party seeking injunctive relief is only required to show threatened injury, but that injury still must be antitrust injury.[239] Also, because issues of duplicative damage recoveries and apportionment of damages do not arise when only injunctive relief is demanded, indirect purchasers from those engaging in the antitrust violation may seek injunctive relief.[240]

The statute of limitations under Section 4 of the Clayton Act for recovering damages in federal antitrust cases is four years.[241] Fraudulent concealment of the violation may toll the running of the statute.[242] In addition, the statute of limitations is tolled during the pendency of an action by the government and for one year thereafter.[243]

---

237. *See, e.g.,* Doctor's Hosp. v. Southeast Med. Alliance, Inc., 123 F.3d 301, 307 (5th Cir. 1997).
238. *See, e.g., Marshfield Clinic,* 152 F.3d at 590-92 (affirming denial of damages but reversing denial of injunctive relief, holding that payer showed threatened loss or damage by evidence that it purchased services from a participant in an antitrust conspiracy to divide markets).
239. Cargill, Inc. v. Montford of Colo., Inc., 479 U.S. 104, 111 (1986).
240. *See, e.g.,* Freeman v. San Diego Ass'n of Realtors, 322 F.3d 1133, 1145 (9th Cir. 2003) (indirect purchaser doctrine does not apply to claims for injunctive relief), *cert. denied,* 124 S.Ct. 355 (2003); Warfarin Sodium Antitrust Litig., 214 F.3d 395, 401 (3d Cir. 2000) (reversing dismissal of indirect purchasers' claim for injunctive relief for lack of standing because direct-purchaser status is not required for injunctive relief, there was no risk of duplicative damages, plaintiffs were foreseeable and necessary victims of the violation, and plaintiffs' alleged injury was inextricably intertwined with that of direct purchasers); McCarthy v. Recordex Serv., 80 F.3d 842, 856 (3d Cir. 1996).
241. 15 U.S.C. § 15b.
242. *See generally* Supermarkets of Marlington, Inc. v. Meadow Gold Dairies, Inc., 71 F.3d 119 (4th Cir. 1995); *In re* Monosodium Glutamate Antitrust Litig., 2003-1 Trade Cas. (CCH) ¶ 73,963 (D. Minn. 2003).
243. 15 U.S.C. § 16(i).

CHAPTER 3

SIGNIFICANT ANTITRUST ISSUES
IN HEALTH CARE

Antitrust cases in the health-care sector have involved a wide array of conduct in many varied settings.[1] This section discusses a number of recurring health-care antitrust issues, as well as some issues likely to arise in the future. The same antitrust analysis applies in health-care antitrust cases as in cases arising in other sectors of the economy, but the courts, in deciding health-care antitrust cases, have taken into consideration the sometimes unusual characteristics of health-care industries that may affect whether particular conduct will result in anticompetitive effects.

A. Staff-Privilege Determinations: Peer-Review Decisions and Exclusive Contracts

Conduct relating to medical-staff privileges, other forms of provider credentialing, and exclusive contracting for hospital-based physician services has been perhaps the most frequent target of private antitrust claims in health care. Although courts and the enforcement agencies have recognized that decisions whether to grant a physician staff privileges at the hospital may enhance competition and benefit consumers by promoting higher quality and more efficient delivery of services,[2] the refusal by hospitals to grant practitioners staff privileges is inherently exclusionary in that some practitioners

---

1. A number of the practices in the health-care sector discussed here are also discussed in *ALD V, supra* p. 9 n.23, at 1326-69.
2. *See, e.g.*, Ostrzenski v. Columbia Hosp. for Women, 158 F.3d 1289, 1291 (D.C. Cir. 1998) ("no reasonable jury could find plaintiff was denied hospital staff privileges as the result of an unlawful conspiracy, rather than because of concern about his medical competence"); Willman v. Heartland Hosp., 34 F.3d 605, 610-11 (8th Cir. 1994) (exclusion through the peer-review process is lawful if the hospital had legitimate reasons to believe plaintiff provided substandard care); Marshall v. Planz, 13 F. Supp. 2d 1231, 1243 (M.D. Ala. 1998); Antitrust Division Business Review Letter to American Medical Association (Dec. 2, 1986), *reprinted in* 3 *HCAL, supra* p. 14 n.47, App. C20.

may be denied access to facilities they claim are necessary to their ability to compete. Moreover, physicians who are actual or potential competitors of those adversely affected by an adverse privilege determination frequently participate in the decision-making process, thereby raising possible issues of anticompetitive motive and intent.

Staff-privilege antitrust claims of exclusion typically have been asserted by practitioners who were subjected to an adverse staff-privilege peer-review action,[3] or who were prevented from practicing at the hospital because of an exclusive contract between the hospital and another group of physicians providing a hospital-based physician service such as anesthesia, radiology, or pathology.[4] Courts, almost always applying the rule of reason, have rejected the overwhelming majority of these claims, usually at the summary-judgment stage, for failure to prove the requisite conspiracy or the requisite adverse effect on competition. Many staff-privilege cases have been dismissed for failure to state a claim on standing or antitrust-injury grounds because the plaintiff, although alleging injury to himself or herself, failed to allege the requisite adverse effect on market-wide competition.[5] Courts also have rejected several claims challenging peer-review actions and seeking damages because of several of the antitrust-immunity principles discussed before, such as the Health Care Quality Improvement Act.

1. Staff-Privilege Restrictions Based on Peer-Review Actions

Individual health-care practitioners frequently have asserted antitrust claims

---

3. *E.g.*, Vakaria v. Swedish Covenant Hosp., 190 F.3d 799 (7th Cir. 1999); Gordon v. Lewistown Hosp., 272 F. Supp. 2d 393 (M.D. Pa. 2003).
4. *E.g.*, Jefferson Parish Hosp. Dist. No. 2 v. Hyde, 466 U.S. 2 (1984).
5. Patel v. Midland Mem'l Hosp., 298 F.3d 333 (5th Cir. 2002), *cert. denied*, 537 U.S. 1108 (2003); Samuel v. Herrick Mem'l Hosp., 201 F.3d 830 (6th Cir. 2000); Chalal v. Northwest Med. Ctr., 147 F. Supp. 2d 1160 (N.D. Ala. 2000); Korshin v. Benedictine Hosp., 34 F. Supp. 2d 133 (N.D.N.Y. 1999); Parks v. Hillsdale Cmty. Health Ctr., 1999-1 Trade Cas. (CCH) ¶ 72,555 (W.D. Mich. 1999); Alpern v. Cavarocchi, 1999-1 Trade Cas. (CCH) ¶ 72,514 (E.D. Pa. 1999); Ginzburg v. Mem'l Healthcare Sys., Inc., 993 F. Supp. 998 (S.D. Tex. 1997). *But see* Nilivar v. Mercy Health Sys., 142 F. Supp. 2d 859, 874 (S.D. Ohio 2000) (plaintiff's allegations that restraint not only affected him but resulted in higher prices, lower quality, and less choice sufficiently alleged antitrust injury).

challenging adverse staff-privilege and peer-review decisions denying, limiting, suspending, revoking, or otherwise adversely affecting their access to hospital facilities. In many markets, there are numerous competing practitioners, and a decision denying one practitioner hospital staff privileges will not significantly harm competition, even if the action completely excludes the practitioner from the relevant market or substantially limits his or her ability to compete.[6] Moreover, in many cases, plaintiffs are unable to show that the hospital or other credentialing body acted pursuant to an agreement or conspiracy with others as Section 1 of the Sherman Act requires,[7] or possessed or threatened to obtain substantial market power in the relevant market of the affected practitioner as required for a claim of monopolization or attempted monopolization under Section 2.[8]

The staff-privilege determination or credentialing procedure at most hospitals involves several levels of review, including a recommendation regarding the affected practitioner's privileges from the medical staff's credentialing committee to its executive committee, a recommendation from that committee to the hospital's board of directors or trustees, a hearing for the affected practitioner before a medical-staff hearing committee if the recommendation is adverse to him or her, a recommendation by the hearing committee to the board, a meeting between the affected practitioner and the board or a committee of the board if that recommendation is adverse, and a final decision by the board.

Parties challenging an adverse staff-privilege peer-review action under Section 1 typically seek to show an agreement or conspiracy between the hospital and the physicians on its medical staff participating in the decision. Therefore, a threshold question is whether these parties are legally capable of

---

6. *E.g.*, Mathews v. Lancaster Gen. Hosp., 87 F.3d 624, 642 (3d Cir. 1996) (noting that while plaintiff was excluded from defendant hospital, the same services were available from a large and increasing number of providers); Anesthesia Advantage, Inc. v. Metz Group, 759 F. Supp. 638, 648 (D. Colo. 1991) (explaining that "'[t]he consumer does not care how many sellers of a particular good or service there are; he cares only that there be enough to assure him a competitive price and quality'").

7. County of Tuolumne v. Sonora Cmty. Hosp., 236 F.3d 1148, 1156 (9th Cir. 2001); *Lancaster Gen. Hosp.*, 87 F.3d at 640; Nurse Midwifery Assocs. v. Hibbett, 918 F.2d 605, 611-12 (6th Cir. 1990).

8. *E.g.*, Beard v. Parkview Hosp., 912 F.2d 138, 144 (6th Cir. 1990) (dismissing plaintiff's case because plaintiff and defendant were not competitors).

conspiring with one another or whether they constitute a single entity. Courts have ruled, in general, that a corporation is not capable of conspiring with its own officers, employees, or agents because the corporation is deemed to control their actions, and collectively they are deemed to have a complete unity of economic interests.[9] Based on this principle, most courts have held that when engaging in peer review and credentialing, the medical staff acts as an agent of the hospital, and thus that it and the hospital constitute a single entity incapable of conspiring for purposes of Section 1.[10] There are decisions to the contrary, however.[11]

Even where such a conspiracy is deemed legally possible, a plaintiff still must have direct or circumstantial evidence that the decision adversely affecting him or her resulted from a conspiracy—that is, a conscious commitment to a common scheme designed to achieve an unlawful objective—rather than from the hospital's unilateral action.[12] The typical role of the medical staff in the credentialing process is to make a recommendation to the hospital's board about the action it should take with regard to the practitioner in question. One party's merely making a recommendation that another party can accept or reject, standing alone and absent any coercion, however, does not result in a conspiracy between the parties.[13] Hospitals typically adhere to

---

9. *See generally supra* pp. 24-25.
10. *E.g.*, Muzquiz v. W.A. Foote Mem'l Hosp., 70 F.3d 422, 429 (6th Cir. 1995); Oksanen v. Page Mem'l Hosp., 945 F.2d 696, 699 (4th Cir. 1991) (en banc); Nanavati v. Burdette Tomlin Mem'l Hosp., 857 F.2d 96, 117-18 (3d Cir. 1988).
11. *E.g.*, Crosby v. Hosp. Auth., 93 F.3d 1515, 1528-29 (11th Cir. 1996) (hospital and staff may be capable of conspiring); Bolt v. Halifax Hosp. Med. Ctr., 891 F.2d 810, 818-19 (11th Cir. 1990). For a circuit-by-circuit analysis of this issue, *see* 2 *HCAL, supra* p. 14 n.47, ¶ 10:10, at 10-70 through 10-73.
12. *See generally* Monsanto Co. v. Spray-Rite Serv. Corp., 465 U.S. 752, 786 (1984) (general conspiracy principle); *see also* Mathews v. Lancaster Gen. Hosp., 87 F.3d 624, 639 (3d Cir. 1996) (finding insufficient evidence from which to infer conspiracy). *But see* Boczar v. Manatee Hosp. & Health Sys., 993 F.2d 1514, 1517-19 (11th Cir. 1993) (finding sufficient circumstantial evidence of conspiracy).
13. *E.g.*, County of Toulumne v. Sonora Cmty. Hosp., 236 F.3d 1148, 1156 (9th Cir. 2001) (explaining that "simply because the 'board is likely to follow the recommendation of the medical staff does not establish, or even reasonably suggest, the existence of a conspiracy'"); *Lancaster Gen. Hosp.*, 87 F.3d at 639; Willman v. Heartland Hosp., 34 F.3d 605, 612 (8th Cir. 1994) (noting

procedures whereby final decisions are made unilaterally by the hospital board rather than by physicians who serve on credentialing or peer-review committees, but a court might find a conspiracy between them where the plaintiff's competitors actually controlled the decision-making process[14] or coerced the board.[15] Numerous courts, however, have held that the plaintiff practitioner failed to prove the requisite concerted action for purposes of a Section 1 claim.[16]

If the plaintiff proves that the peer-review decision resulted from an agreement, he or she still must prove that the decision unreasonably restrained competition. The courts have held almost universally that the competitive effects of adverse peer-review decisions are analyzed under the rule of reason[17] and thus that the plaintiff must not only prove injury to himself or

---

that the fact that the hospital board, rather than competing physicians, made the final decision about plaintiff's privileges undermined plaintiff's conspiracy claim); *Page Mem'l Hosp.*, 945 F.2d at 706 ("making a peer review recommendation does not prove the existence of a conspiracy; there must be something more"); Todorov v. DCH Healthcare Auth., 921 F.2d 1438, 1458-59 (11th Cir. 1991); Gordon v. Lewistown Hosp., 272 F. Supp. 2d 393, 419 (M.D. Pa. 2003); Chalal v. Northwest Med. Ctr., 147 F. Supp. 2d 1160, 1182 (N.D. Ala. 2000) (noting that board made credentialing decision and there was no evidence it "perfunctorily approved the recommendations of the medical staff committees").

14. *See* Brown v. Presbyterian Healthcare Servs., 101 F.3d 1324, 1335 (10th Cir. 1996).

15. *See* Oltz v. St. Peter's Cmty. Hosp., 861 F.2d 1440, 1451 (9th Cir. 1988).

16. *E.g.*, Ostrzenski v. Columbia Hosp. for Women Found., 158 F.3d 1289 (D.C. Cir. 1998); *Lancaster Gen. Hosp.*, 87 F.3d at 639; Nurse Midwifery Assocs. v. Hibbitt, 918 F.2d 605 (6th Cir. 1990); *DCH Healthcare Auth.*, 921 F.2d at 1459; Maric v. St. Agnes Hosp. Corp., 65 F.3d 310 (2d Cir. 1995); *Northwest Med. Ctr.*, 147 F. Supp. 2d at 1183; Alpern v. Cavarocchi, 1999-1 Trade Cas. (CCH) ¶ 72,514 (E.D. Pa. 1999); Marshall v. Planz, 13 F. Supp. 2d 1231 (M.D. Ala. 1998); Ginzburg v. Mem'l Healthcare Sys., Inc., 993 F. Supp. 998 (S.D. Tex. 1997).

17. *E.g.*, Diaz v. Farley, 215 F.3d 1175, 1184 (10th Cir. 2000) ("the fact that the conduct at issue . . . concerns decisions relating to health care presents a further reason why we should be cautious in applying a *per se* test"); Angelico v. Lehigh Valley Hosp., Inc., 184 F.3d 268, 276 (3d Cir. 1999); Oksanen v. Page Mem'l Hosp., 945 F.2d 696, 709 (4th Cir. 1991) (en banc); Tarabishi v. McAlester Reg'l Hosp., 951 F.2d 1558, 1571 (10th Cir. 1991); Pfenninger v. Exempla, Inc., 116 F. Supp. 2d 1184, 1194 (D. Colo. 2000). *But see* Weiss v.

herself but must prove a market-wide, significantly adverse effect on competition.[18] If the relevant market for the types of medical services provided by the plaintiff is unconcentrated or the plaintiff has privileges at other facilities in the relevant market, then the plaintiff's exclusion is not likely to have any significant anticompetitive effect.[19] In addition, a number of courts have found that a hospital's protection of high-quality medical services through the credentialing process is a strong procompetitive justification for its action.[20]

A number of plaintiffs in staff-privilege antitrust cases have included a claim against the hospital for monopolization or attempted monopolization. Such claims should fail to survive a motion to dismiss, however, because, unless the hospital employs physicians who compete with the plaintiff, the hospital is not a competitor in the relevant market and thus cannot monopolize or attempt to monopolize it.[21]

York Hosp., 745 F.2d 786, 820 (3d Cir. 1984) (purporting to apply the per se rule); Sweeney v. Athens Reg'l Med. Ctr., 709 F. Supp. 1563, 1573 (M.D. Ga. 1989) (same); Vuciecevic v. MacNeal Mem'l Hosp., 572 F. Supp. 1424, 1429 (N.D. Ill. 1983) (same).

18. *E.g.*, Giampolo v. Somerset Hosp. Ctr. for Health, 189 F.3d 464 (3d Cir. 1999) (unpublished opinion reprinted at 1999-2 Trade Cas. (CCH) ¶ 72,574); Lie v. St. Joseph Hosp., 964 F.2d 567, 569 (6th Cir. 1992).

19. *E.g.*, Poliner v. Texas Health Sys., 2003-2 Trade Cas. (CCH) ¶ 74,174, at 97,509 (N.D. Tex. 2003) (no effect on competition because plaintiff had privileges at seven other hospitals); Jackson v. Radcliffe, 1992-1 Trade Cas. (CCH) ¶ 69,808, at 67,755 (S.D. Tex. 1992) (no significant adverse effect on competition where excluded radiologist was one of 250 in the area).

20. *E.g.*, Patel v. Midland Mem'l Hosp., 298 F.3d 333, 345-46 (5th Cir. 2002), *cert. denied*, 537 U.S. 1108 (2003); Vakaria v. Swedish Covenant Hosp., 190 F.3d 799, 810-11 (7th Cir. 1999); Willman v. Heartland Hosp., 34 F.3d 605, 610-11 (8th Cir. 1994); Poliner v. Texas Health Sys., 2003-2 Trade Cas. (CCH) ¶ 74,174 (N.D. Tex. 2003) ("Monitoring the competence of physicians through peer review is clearly in the public interest, and revocation or suspension of a physician's privileges because of legitimate concerns about the quality of patient care that he rendered is obviously a lawful objective."); Marshall v. Planz, 13 F. Supp. 2d at 1243 (noting that "[m]any courts have recognized that by imposing sanctions on physicians who do not satisfy their patient-care requirements, hospitals do indeed take steps to enhance, rather than restrict, competition"); *Mem'l Healthcare Sys.*, 993 F. Supp. at 1025.

21. *See generally* Discon, Inc v. NYNEX Corp., 93 F.3d 1055, 1062 (2d Cir. 1996) ("it is axiomatic that a firm cannot monopolize a market in which it does not

Finally, an antitrust exemption doctrine may apply to the peer-review credentialing process. For example, especially if the hospital is a governmental facility, the state-action exemption may protect the peer-review decision from successful antitrust challenge.[22] Similarly, if the hospital is a local governmental entity such as a county or special-district hospital, the Local Government Antitrust Act may protect it from damages even if the plaintiff establishes liability.[23] Assuming the peer-review proceeding met its requirements, the Health Care Quality Improvement Act of 1986 will protect even private hospitals from damages (although not from liability).[24]

Several antitrust cases have involved refusals by hospitals to grant staff privileges to allied health practitioners, such as nurse midwives or nurse anesthetists.[25] The antitrust framework for analyzing adverse credentialing decisions affecting allied practitioners is the same as that for analyzing refusals to grant staff privileges to physicians. The exclusion of an entire class of practitioners, all else equal, however, can have a greater adverse effect on competition than the exclusion of one of many competing physicians, especially if the allied health practitioner is a lower-cost alternative to physicians.

2. Exclusive Contracts Between Hospitals and Hospital-Based Physicians

Hospitals and other health-care facilities frequently use exclusive contract arrangements with a single physician group for anesthesia, radiology, pathology, and other specialized physician services that are integral to the hospital's delivery of its health-care services. These hospital-based medical services also typically entail use of equipment based at and owned by the facility. In some cases, staff privileges are conditioned on the practitioner's having an exclusive contract with the facility to provide services there, such that termination or expiration of the group's exclusive contract will result in automatic termination of the group members' medical-staff privileges as well. Disappointed rivals also wishing to provide those services at the hospital frequently

---

compete"), *rev'd on other grounds*, 525 U.S. 128 (1999); *see also* Beard v. Parkview Hosp., 912 F.2d 138, 144-45 (6th Cir. 1990); White v. Rockingham Radiologists, Ltd., 820 F.2d 98, 104 (4th Cir. 1987).

22. *See supra* pp. 43-45, discussing state-action immunity.
23. *See supra* pp. 49-50, discussing the Local Government Antitrust Act.
24. *See supra* pp. 50-51, discussing the Health Care Quality Improvement Act.

assert antitrust claims challenging the exclusive contract and the denial or termination of related medical-staff privileges as an unlawful tying or exclusive dealing arrangement, a group boycott, or monopolization or attempted monopolization. These claims, for the most part, have failed for several reasons.

Although exclusive contracts inherently foreclose other practitioners from serving patients at a given facility, such arrangements may be an effective means of maintaining efficiency and quality of patient care.[26] Hospital-based services typically entail use of the facility's own medical equipment and close interaction with that facility's nursing and technical staff, and an exclusive arrangement may facilitate scheduling and full-time coverage, permit better departmental management, improve resource utilization and quality assurance, promote teamwork, and control costs. These benefits promote both higher-quality care and greater efficiencies in the delivery of services.

Exclusive contracts between hospitals and hospital-based physicians have been challenged most often as tying arrangements in which the hospital ties the purchase of physician services from the group to the sale of some type of hospital service—for example, requiring a patient to use the hospital's exclusive radiology group to interpret radiological tests as a condition to the hospital's selling the patient the technical component of radiology services. Here, a plaintiff must prove that the two services are separate and distinct rather than a single service;[27] that the hospital has market power in the rel-

---

25. *E.g.*, Minn. Ass'n of Nurse Anesthetists v. Unity Hosp., 208 F.3d 655 (8th Cir. 2000) (nurse anesthetists); BCB Anesthesia Care, Ltd. v. Passavant Mem'l Area Hosp. Ass'n, 36 F.3d 664 (7th Cir. 1994) (same); Cohn v. Bond, 953 F.2d 154 (4th Cir. 1992) (chiropractors); Cooper v. Forsyth County Hosp. Auth., 789 F.2d 278 (4th Cir. 1986) (podiatrists).

26. *See, e.g.*, Jefferson Parish Hosp. Dist. No. 2 v. Hyde, 466 U.S. 2, 43-44 (1984) (O'Connor, Burger, Powell & Rehnquist, JJ., concurring) (listing procompetitive benefits of exclusive contracts between hospitals and hospital-based physicians); Burnham Hosp., 101 F.T.C. 991 (1983) (FTC advisory opinion).

27. *See, e.g.*, *Jefferson Parish Hosp.*, 466 U.S. at 18-25 (anesthesia services and hospital operating rooms); Collins v. Associated Pathologists, Ltd., 844 F.2d 473, 477-78 (7th Cir. 1988) (pathology services and hospital services); Drs. Steuer & Latham, P.A. v. Nat'l Med. Enters., 672 F. Supp. 1489, 1505-08 (D.S.C. 1987), *aff'd per curiam without published op.*, 846 F.2d 70 (4th Cir. 1988) (pathology services).

evant market for the service it sells—the tying product or service;[28] and, in most circuits, that the hospital has a direct economic interest in the sale of the physicians' services. For example, a plaintiff must show that the hospital shared in the radiologists' fees for the professional component of the services.[29] In addition, although tying arrangements are often said to be per se unlawful, many cases permit the defendant to present procompetitive justifications for the arrangement, thus requiring an almost full-blown rule-of-reason analysis.[30] Rarely have plaintiffs been able to meet all these burdens.[31]

The plaintiff also may challenge the contract simply as an unlawful exclusive-dealing agreement. Here, rule-of-reason analysis clearly applies; the plaintiff, as a threshold matter, must usually define the relevant market and show that the contract forecloses a substantial share of the market to competitors of the group with the exclusive contract.[32] If the plaintiff sustains that initial burden, it must still show that the contract is likely to lead to higher prices, lower quality, or some other adverse effect on market-wide competition for the physician services in question. The contract's procompetitive

---

28. *E.g., Jefferson Parish Hosp.*, 466 U.S. at 16-17 (1984); McMorris v. Williamsport Hosp., 597 F. 2d 899, 912 (M.D. Pa. 1984); Burnham Hosp., 101 F.T.C. 991 (1983) (FTC advisory opinion).

29. *E.g.*, County of Toulumne v. Sonora Cmty. Hosp., 236 F.3d 1148, 1158 (9th Cir. 2001); Beard v. Parkview Hosp., 912 F.2d 138, 141-43 (6th Cir. 1990); White v. Rockingham Radiologists, Ltd., 820 F.2d 98, 104 (4th Cir. 1987); Nilivar v. Mercy Health Sys., 142 F. Supp. 859, 880 (S.D. Ohio 2000).

30. *See generally* PSI Repair Servs. v. Honeywell, Inc., 104 F.3d 811, 815 (6th Cir. 1997).

31. *See* BCB Anesthesia Care Ltd. v. Passavant Mem'l Hosp. Ass'n, 36 F.3d 664, 667 (7th Cir. 1994) ("thousands of pages" discussing physician exclusions from hospitals "almost always came to the same conclusion: the staffing decision at a single hospital was not a violation of Section 1 of the Sherman Act"); Hager v. Venice Hosp., 944 F. Supp. 1530, 1537 (M.D. Fla. 1996) ("Courts throughout the country have interpreted the federal antitrust laws as allowing hospitals to enter into exclusive service provider agreements. A staffing decision at a single hospital based on an exclusive contract is not violative of the antitrust laws.").

32. *See, e.g.*, Morales-Villalobos v. Garcia-Llorens, 316 F.3d 51, 55 (1st Cir. 2003) (noting, in hospital-physician exclusive contract challenge, that "substantial foreclosure is ordinarily a *requirement* for a seller arguing that she or he has been unreasonably excluded from opportunities to sell").

effects, if any, are relevant and must be balanced against any anticompetitive effects in determining the overall effect of the contract on competition.[33]

An important question when defining the relevant geographic market in hospital-physician exclusive contract cases is whether the purchaser under such contracts is the hospital contracting with the physician group or area patients. If the hospital is deemed to be the purchaser, the relevant geographic market is quite large, perhaps the entire United States, because hospitals attempting to recruit a group typically would do so on a nationwide basis, and hospital-based physicians are quite mobile and search for positions over a large geographic area.[34] If, on the other hand, the patient is the purchaser, the relevant geographic market is probably local, because patients typically would not be willing to travel long distances for such services in light of a price increase by local providers.[35] Several decisions have held that both markets must be analyzed.[36]

After defining the relevant market, the court examines the usual factors important in antitrust exclusive-dealing analysis: (1) the percentage of the market that the contract forecloses, (2) the duration of the contract (including

---

33. *See generally* Drs. Steuer & Latham, P.A. v. Nat'l Med. Enters., 672 F. Supp. 1489, 1503 (D.S.C. 1987), *aff'd per curiam without published op.*, 846 F.2d 70 (4th Cir. 1988).

34. *E.g.*, Minn. Ass'n of Nurse Anesthetists v. Unity Hosp., 208 F.3d 655, 661 (8th Cir. 2000) (emphasizing the mobility of physicians and thus finding a national market); Collins v. Associated Pathologists, Ltd., 844 F.2d 473, 479 (7th Cir. 1988) (national market for pathologists); Reddy v. Good Samaritan Hosp. & Health Ctr., 137 F. Supp. 2d 948, 969 (S.D. Ohio 2000) (explaining that "courts have concluded, in the context of a hospital entering into an exclusive contract with a group of physicians . . . that the relevant . . . market is the market in which physicians compete for jobs," a national market).

35. *Cf. Morales-Villalobos* (reversing district court decision dismissing case because relevant geographic market could not be decided on a motion to dismiss); *see* Pilch v. French Hosp., 2000-1 Trade Cas. (CCH) ¶ 72,935 (C.D. Cal. 2000).

36. *E.g.*, Balaklaw v. Lovell, 14 F.3d 793, 799 (2d Cir. 1994); Oltz v. St. Peter's Cmty. Hosp., 861 F.2d 1440, 1446-47 (9th Cir. 1988); Burnham Hosp., 101 F.T.C. 991 (1983); *cf.* Jefferson Parish Hosp. Dist. No. 2 v. Hyde, 466 U.S. 2, 29-30 (1984) (recognizing but not deciding the issue).

whether the hospital can terminate the contract on short notice without cause,[37] (3) the extent and coverage of other exclusive contracts in the market that would prohibit the plaintiff from practicing[38] and thus whether the plaintiff could compete from other facilities,[39] (4) the level of market concentration, (5) the physician group's market power[40] (and particularly the likely effect of the contract on its market power), (6) entry barriers, (7) whether there was competition for the contract,[41] and (8) any procompetitive effects resulting from the arrangement.[42] The ultimate question is always whether the contract has resulted (or is likely to result) in higher prices or lower quality for consumers.[43] Courts typically find no anticompetitive effects where the hospital merely substitutes one exclusive group for another.[44]

---

37. *E.g.*, Balaklaw v. Lovell, 14 F.3d at 798; Konik v. Champlain Valley Physicians Hosp. Med. Ctr., 733 F.2d 1007, 1017 (2d Cir. 1985); Nilivar v. Mercy Health Sys., 142 F. Supp. 2d 859 (S.D. Ohio 2000); Burnham Hosp., 101 F.T.C. 991 (1983).

38. *See Good Samaritan Hosp. & Health Ctr.*, 137 F. Supp. 2d at 969 (noting that "[p]reventing the plaintiff from practicing . . . at one hospital cannot have anti-competitive effects in that market").

39. *E.g.*, Korshin v. Benedictine Hosp., 34 F. Supp. 2d 133, 138 (N.D.N.Y. 1999).

40. *E.g.*, Reddy v. Good Samaritan Hosp. & Health Ctr., 137 F. Supp. 2d 948, 969 (S.D. Ohio 2000); Minn. Ass'n of Nurse Anesthetists v. Unity Hosp., 5 F. Supp. 2d 694, 707-08 (D. Minn. 1998), *aff'd*, 208 F.3d 655 (8th Cir. 2000).

41. *E.g.*, Smith v. N. Mich. Hosps., 703 F.2d 942, 955 (6th Cir. 1983); *Nilivar*, 142 F. Supp. 2d at 876-77.

42. *E.g.*, Parikh v. Franklin Med. Ctr., 940 F. Supp. 395, 405 (D. Mass. 1996); Balaklaw v. Lovell, 822 F. Supp. 892, 904 (N.D.N.Y. 1993), *aff'd*, 14 F.3d 793 (2d Cir. 1984).

43. *See, e.g.*, *Minn. Ass'n of Nurse Anesthetists*, 208 F.3d at 662 (explaining that "plaintiffs have failed to prove actual adverse effects on competition . . . such as increased prices for anesthesia services, or a decline in either the quality or quantity of such services available to surgery patients"); *cf.* Jefferson Parish Hosp. Dist. No. 2. v. Hyde, 466 U.S. 2, 31 & n.52 (1984) (indicating that plaintiff must show an actual adverse effect on competition and that plaintiff failed to prove an adverse effect on quality or price).

44. *E.g.*, Nilivar v. Mercy Health Sys., 142 F. Supp. 2d 859, 876 (S.D. Ohio 2000); Mid-Mich. Radiology Assocs., P.C. v. Cent. Mich. Cmty. Hosp., 1995-1 Trade Cas. (CCH) ¶ 70,943, 74,250 (E.D. Mich. 1995).

B. Pricing Conduct: Horizontal, Vertical, and Unilateral

"Pricing conduct" covers a broad range of activities. One of the major purposes of the antitrust laws is to prevent many types of conduct that directly or indirectly affect prices as a result of market power. This subsection outlines several types of collusive or exclusionary conduct arising in the health-care sector that can have a direct or relatively direct effect on prices and thus might violate the antitrust laws. The remaining subsections discuss conduct with more indirect effects on prices.

1. Horizontal Price-Fixing Agreements Among Providers

a. In General

As noted before, "naked" price-fixing agreements among competing sellers or buyers are per se unlawful.[45] In the health-care sector, horizontal price-fixing agreements among providers can arise in a number of contexts and forms. For example, members of a medical society might simply agree on the prices at which they will offer their services;[46] a group of providers might agree to refuse to contract with a payer unless it increases reimbursement[47] or co-payment amounts;[48] or the group might develop a schedule of minimum

---

45. *See supra* p. 44.

46. *E.g.*, United States v. Lake Country Optometric Soc'y, No. W95CR114 (W.D. Tex., Jul. 9, 1996) (guilty plea for fixing price of eye exams; $75,000 fine and five-year probation), *summarized at* [1988-1996 Transfer Binder] Trade Reg. Rep. (CCH) ¶ 45,095, at 44,781; society pled guilty and paid $75,000 fine); United States v. Mass. Allergy Soc'y, 1992-1 Trade Cas. (CCH) ¶ 69,846 (D. Mass. 1992) (consent decree) (allegation that defendant forced HMO to increase reimbursement).

47. *E.g.*, Baltimore Metro. Pharm. Ass'n, 117 F.T.C. 95 (1994) (consent order); Mich. State Med. Soc'y, 101 F.T.C. 191 (1983) ("boycott" of Blue Cross and Medicaid to increase reimbursement); United States v. Mont. Nursing Home Ass'n, 1982-2 Trade Cas. (CCH) ¶ 64,852 (D. Mont. 1982) (consent decree) (settling case alleging agreement among nursing homes not to participate in Medicaid absent increased reimbursement); DeGregorio v. Segal, 443 F. Supp. 1257 (E.D. Pa. 1978) (same).

48. United States v. A. Lanoy Alston, D.M.D., P.C., 974 F.2d 1206 (9th Cir. 1992).

fees,[49] an "advisory" or "suggested" fee schedule,[50] or a relative-value guide including suggested relative values for different medical services but not the conversion-dollar values by which the relative values are multiplied to turn them into a fee schedule.[51] Or, as discussed next, providers may encounter antitrust problems when they form provider-controlled contracting networks to jointly negotiate prices and other aspects of contracts with third-party payers.

b.   Provider-Controlled Contracting Networks

In recent years, health-care providers, particularly physicians, have created and participated in a variety of different types of organizations to market and deliver their services in a coordinated manner as a group, such as physician organizations (POs), independent practice associations (IPAs), preferred provider organizations (PPOs), and physician-hospital organizations (PHOs). To the extent that pricing decisions of these organizations are controlled by competing providers, those networks (and their directors, employees, and consultants engaging in price negotiations with payers) have been a frequent price-fixing target of both state and federal governmental antitrust enforcement.[52] The network's actions are deemed to result from the concerted action

---

49. *E.g.*, N. Cal. Pharm. Ass'n v. United States, 306 F.2d 379 (9th Cir. 1962).

50. *See, e.g., Alston,* 974 F.2d at 1214 ("adoption of suggested . . . fee schedules will run afoul of Section One's per se rule as a thinly veiled attempt at price fixing"). *But see* United States v. Am. Soc'y of Anesthesiologists, 473 F. Supp. 147 (S.D.N.Y. 1979) (upholding defendant's advisory fee schedule).

51. *E.g.*, Am. Coll. of Obstetricians & Gynecologists, 88 F.T.C. 955 (1976), *modified*, 104 F.T.C. 524 (1984). For an extended discussion of the development, dissemination, and use of such schedules, *see* Am. Soc'y of Internal Med., 105 F.T.C. 505 (1985) (FTC Advisory Opinion).

52. *See, e.g.*, Piedmont Health Alliance, Inc., Dkt. No. 9314 (FTC Dec. 24, 2003) (administrative complaint), *at* http://www.ftc.gov/os/caselist/0210119/ 031222comp0210119.pdf; United States v. Mountain Health Care, P.A., 2003-2 Trade Cas. (CCH) ¶ 74,162 (W.D.N.C. 2003) (consent decree and competitive impact statement) (provider-controlled network fee schedule); N. Tex. Specialty Physicians, Dkt. No. 9312 (FTC Sept. 17, 2003) (complaint), *at* http://www.ftc.gov/05/2003/09/ntexasphysicianscomp.pdf; Physician Network Consulting, L.L.C., Dkt. No. C-4094 (FTC Aug. 29, 2003) (consent order) (naming consultant as respondent), *at* http://www.ftc.gov/05/2003/ 08/physnetwork.do.pdf.; R.T. Welter & Assocs., Inc., Dkt. No. C-4063 (FTC

of its members; as the FTC noted some years ago, "[a]ntitrust law considers the actions and decisions of an organization . . . controlled by a group of competitors to be the joint action of the group's members."[53]Although most of the enforcement actions have challenged physician networks, the agencies have not hesitated to challenge networks or other organizations negotiating prices on behalf of competing hospitals, dentists, and pharmacies.[54] In one case, the FTC brought an enforcement action against a hospital, alleging it

---

Oct. 11, 2002) (consent order) (agent negotiating on behalf of provider-controlled network), *at* http://www.ftc.gov/05/2002/10/piwcdo.pdf; United States v. Federation of Certified Surgeons & Specialists, Inc., 1999-1 Trade Cas. (CCH) ¶ 72,549 (M.D. Fla. 1999) (consent decree and competitive impact statement) (naming consultant firm as a defendant); Virginia v. Physicians Group, Inc., 1995-2 Trade Cas. (CCH) ¶ 71,236 (W.D. Va. 1995) (consent decree) (requiring payment of $170,000 to state).

The applicable antitrust principles are very different where the network or health plan is not controlled by competing providers but rather by, for example, a large managed-care plan. Commercial insurers may unilaterally "fix" the amounts they will pay their participating providers because their doing so does not result from any agreement among competitors. Ensuring that physicians understand this distinction is frequently difficult. On the other hand, if commercial insurers who compete to enter into participation agreements with providers agreed on the level of provider reimbursement they would pay, a serious price-fixing issue would arise. The McCarran Act's limited exemption for the business of insurance, *see supra*, pp. 47-48, would not protect such an agreement. *See, e.g.*, Ohio v. Ohio Med. Indem., Inc., 1978-2 Trade Cas. (CCH) ¶ 62,154 (S.D. Ohio 1978); *see generally* Group Life & Health Ins. Co. v. Royal Drug Co., 440 U.S. 205 (1979) (relationships between health insurers and their participating providers do not constitute the business of insurance because they do not spread or transfer risk).

53. Federal Trade Commission, *Enforcement Policy with Respect to Physician Agreements to Control Medical Prepayment Plans*, 46 Fed. Reg. 48,982 (Oct. 5, 1981); *see also* Va. Acad. of Clinical Psychologists v. Blue Shield, 624 F.2d 476, 481 (4th Cir. 1980) (physician-controlled Blue Shield plan constituted combination among physicians).

54. *See, e.g.*, S. Ga. Health Partners, L.L.C., Dkt. No. C-4100 (FTC Oct. 31, 2003) (hospitals and physicians) (consent order), *at* http://www.ftc.gov/os/ 2003/11/sgeorgiado.pdf; Me. Health Alliance, Dkt. No. C-4095 (FTC Aug. 27, 2003) (same) (consent order), *at* http://www.ftc.gov/os/2003/08/ mainehealthdo.pdf; Colegio de Cirujanos Dentistas, Dkt. No. C-3953 (FTC June 12, 2000) (dentists), *at* http://www.ftc.gov/os/2000/06/collegio.do. ntm; Associacion de Farmacias, 127 F.T.C. 266 (1999) (pharmacies).

was a co-conspirator in an alleged agreement among physicians to negotiate jointly with payers.[55] The agencies, in bringing enforcement actions, have not only named the networks as respondents or defendants but have also named individual physician members of the networks, the networks' executive directors, and the networks' consultants, depending on the role of each. In addition, both the Antitrust Division and FTC have conducted investigations of the networks' or providers' attorneys or law firm when, for example, they believed the attorney participated in negotiating price terms on behalf of the network or on behalf of provider clients who were competitors.

In *Arizona v. Maricopa County Medical Society*,[56] the Supreme Court held that a physician-controlled network's creation and use of a maximum fee schedule "fit squarely into the horizontal price-fixing mold"[57] and were per se unlawful. The Court found that the network, a medical foundation, was not offering a new service in the market but rather that its physicians were using the organization to sell their existing services to certain customers at fixed prices. The Court declined to treat the foundation as an integrated joint venture, which would justify rule-of-reason analysis of the physicians' joint pricing, in part because the participating physicians had not pooled their capital or otherwise shared the risk of loss and opportunity for profit. The Court also rejected the foundation's arguments that its maximum fee schedules were lawful, or at least deserved analysis under the rule of reason, because they were reasonable and because the organization intended to contain costs and provide a competitive alternative to existing health plans. The enforcement agencies, in distinguishing legitimate joint-pricing conduct of provider contracting organizations from naked price-fixing conspiracies among their participating providers, continue to examine whether the organization offers a new and different product or whether participants share risks and opportunities.[58]

---

55. Tenet Healthcare Corp., Dkt. No. C-4106 (FTC Feb. 3, 2004) (consent order), *at* http://www.ftc.gov/os/caselist/0210119/040203dotenet0210119.pdf. For a discussion, *see* Vince Galloro, *Equal Opportunity: FTC Proves Price-Fixing Not Just for Docs Anymore*, MOD. HEALTHCARE, Jan. 5, 2004, at 14.

56. 457 U.S. 332 (1982).

57. *Id.* at 357.

58. *See Health Care Enforcement Statements, supra* p. 12 n.41, Statement 8.A.4 (explaining that "normally [the sharing of substantial risk] is a clear and reliable indicator that a physician network involves sufficient integration by physician participants to achieve significant efficiencies").

Since *Maricopa*, the courts have not squarely addressed in any detail the extent of economic integration or level of shared risk necessary for competing providers to engage in joint pricing without running afoul of the per se rule condemning naked horizontal price-fixing agreements. The enforcement agencies, however, have offered substantial guidance on their policies regarding such conduct through their *Health Care Enforcement Statements*, speeches, and enforcement actions.[59] Many of the consent decrees and orders resulting from these actions provide further guidance on the agencies' views about the antitrust ramifications of joint pricing or price negotiations and actual or threatened "boycotts" (which, in actuality, are price-fixing agreements) by providers to increase prices.[60] The enforcement agencies also have issued numerous advisory opinions discussing proposed pricing conduct of provider contracting networks based on the agencies' enforcement policies.[61]

---

59. See Robert F. Leibenluft, Assistant Director, Bureau of Competition, Federal Trade Commission, "Antitrust Issues Raised by Rural Health Care Networks," Prepared Remarks Before the U.S. Department of Health and Human Services (Feb. 20, 1998), *reprinted in* 4 *HCAL, supra* p. 14 n.47, App. E80. For a listing of FTC health-care cases brought through September 2003, *see* Jeffrey W. Brennan, Assistant Director, David R. Pender, Deputy Assistant Director & Markus H. Meir, Deputy Assistant Director, Bureau of Competition, Federal Trade Commission, "FTC Antitrust Actions in Health Care Services and Products" (Oct. 24, 2003), *at* http://www.ftc.gov/bc/hcupdate031024.pdf. For Antitrust Division health-care enforcement actions, *see* Antitrust Division, "Summary of Antitrust Division Health Care Cases Since August 25, 1983" (1999), *at* http://www.usdoj.gov/atr/public/health_care/0000.htm.

60. *See, e.g.*, Me. Health Alliance, Dkt. No. C-4095 (FTC Aug. 29, 2003) (consent order), *at* http://www.ftc.gov/05/2003/08/mainehealthdo.pdf; Physicians Integrated Servs., Dkt. No. C-4054 (FTC Jul. 19, 2002) (consent order), *at* http://www.ftc.gov/05/2002/07/pisddo.pdf; Alaska Healthcare Network, Dkt. No. C-4007 (FTC Apr. 25, 2001) (consent order), *at* http://www.ftc.gov/05/2001/04/alaskodo.htm; United States v. Mountain Health Care, P.A., 2003-2 Trade Cas. (CCH) ¶ 74,162 (W.D.N.C. 2003) (consent decree and competitive impact statement); United States v. Health Choice, 1996-2 Trade Cas. (CCH) ¶ 71,065 (W.D. Mo. 1996) (consent decree and competitive impact statement); United States v. HealthCare Ptrs., Inc., 1996-1 Trade Cas. (CCH) ¶ 71,337 (D. Conn. 1996) (consent decree).

61. *See, e.g.*, Antitrust Division Business Review Letter to Michigan Hospital Group (Apr. 2, 2002) (discussing a contracting network of non-competing hospitals), *at* http://www.usdoj.gov/atr/ public/busreview/10933.pdf; Anti-

The Antitrust Division and FTC *Health Care Enforcement Statements,* last revised in 1996, are the most comprehensive explanation of the federal antitrust enforcement agencies' enforcement policies with respect to joint pricing conduct by provider-controlled contracting organizations.[62] Statement 8, which discusses "physician network joint ventures," describes two "Antitrust Safety Zones" for physician networks engaged in joint-pricing activities, explains the circumstances under which rule-of-reason analysis of such conduct is appropriate, and discusses the steps in that analysis. Statement 8 applies to physician-controlled organizations that include only physicians and negotiate prices on their behalf. Statement 9 discusses "multiprovider networks," that is, provider contracting organizations consisting of physicians that do not establish prices, or contracting organizations that include providers other than, or in addition to, physicians, such as physician-hospital organizations (PHOs). In both statements, the agencies emphasize that when competitors economically integrate into a joint venture, their agreements on prices (or allocations of services or markets) will be analyzed under the rule of reason if the agreements are reasonably necessary to accomplish the procompetitive benefits of the integration.[63]

trust Division Business Review Letter to Rio Grande Eye Associates (Aug. 19, 2001) (discussing a network of ophthalmologists), *at* http://www.usdojgov/atr/public /busreview/8973.pdf; FTC Staff Advisory Opinion to Northeast Pharmacy Service Corp. (Jul. 27, 2000) (discussing pharmacy services network), *at* http://www.ftc.gov/bc/adops/neletfi5.htm; Antitrust Division Business Review Letter to Midwest Behavioral Health, LLC (Feb. 4, 2000) (discussing network of behavioral health providers), *at* http://www.usdoj.gov/atr/public/busreview/4120.pdf; FTC Staff Advisory Opinion to Associates in Neurology (Aug. 13, 1998) (discussing neurology network), *at* http://www.ftc.gov/bc/adops/ainlet.fin.htm.

62. Also helpful are the more recently issued *Collaboration Guidelines, supra* p. 12 n.40. The *Collaboration Guidelines,* while not directed at the health-care sector specifically, discuss the analysis of all types of collaborative arrangements among competitors, including joint ventures, except mergers.

63. For a discussion of the joint-venture analysis applicable to provider contracting organizations, *see* John J. Miles, *Joint Venture Analysis and Provider-Controlled Health Care Networks,* 66 ANTITRUST L.J. 127 (1997); *cf.* Augusta News Co. v. Hudson News Co., 269 F.3d 41, 48 (1st Cir. 2001) (explaining that "it is a standard form of joint venture for local firms to combine to provide offerings—here, one-stop service for large buyers—that none could as easily provide by itself, and a joint venture often entails setting a single price for the joint offering").

Where participants in a network have agreed to share financial risk, the risk-sharing arrangement itself, if sufficient to improve resource utilization, is deemed to establish both an overall efficiency goal for the venture and the incentives for its members to achieve that goal. In addition, because the risk of the venture is shared among member providers, it is reasonably necessary for them to agree on the prices they will charge for their services.[64] Accordingly, in such situations, the agencies will apply the rule of reason to evaluate joint pricing by participants. Statements 8 and 9 describe several types of arrangements through which participants in provider contracting networks might establish the necessary sharing of financial risk. These include (1) offering capitated prices for the venture's services (that is, a fixed, predetermined periodic payment for each covered life, regardless of the amount of services actually provided); (2) accepting payment for the network's services based on a predetermined percentage of a health plan's premium or revenue; (3) creating significant financial incentives (such as a fee withhold, bonus, or penalty) to induce network participants as a group to achieve specified cost-containment goals; and (4) accepting a global fee or all-inclusive case rate to provide a complex or extended course of treatment to patients. The agencies explain that they will consider, on a case-by-case basis, other types of substantial financial risk-sharing mechanisms that provide the same procompetitive incentives as those enumerated above to reduce utilization and costs.

Additionally, Statements 8 and 9 explain that a provider organization, even absent substantial shared financial risk, might develop and implement a "clinical-integration" program among the participating providers to achieve procompetitive efficiencies. To the extent that an agreement among the providers on prices for the venture's integrated services is reasonably necessary to achieve these efficiencies, the agencies will evaluate the agreement under the rule of reason. The agencies describe clinical integration as an active and ongoing program to evaluate and modify the practice patterns of participants and to create a high degree of interdependence and cooperation among them to control costs and ensure quality. Indicia of clinical integration may include

---

64. *See generally* Mark D. Whitener, Deputy Director, Bureau of Competition, Federal Trade Commission, "Antitrust, Medicare Reform and Health Care Competition," Prepared Remarks (Dec. 5, 1995) ("The emphasis on risk sharing is designed to assure that the elimination of price competition among network participants that inevitably results from common terms is related to functional integration that is likely to achieve efficiencies."), *reprinted in* 4 *HCAL, supra* p. 14 n.47, App. E60.

utilization management, selective credentialing geared toward efficiency objectives, and significant investment of capital and other resources necessary to implement the programs. Even where a network implements an efficiency-enhancing clinical-integration program, the question remains whether the network's joint negotiations are reasonably necessary for achievement of those benefits. One FTC staff advisory opinion discusses clinical integration in some detail,[65] and Statement 8 presents one hypothetical example.[66] Otherwise, there is very little guidance available to provider groups about clinical integration.[67]

Although the negotiation of price terms by insufficiently integrated provider-controlled contracting networks clearly raises serious antitrust concern, the Ninth Circuit's *International Healthcare Management* decision indicates that they may be able to negotiate non-price terms. The decision, however, does not sanction concerted refusals to participate in health plans if the plans reject the network's demands.[68]

Whether it consists of hospitals,[69] physicians, or other types of providers, absent integration, joint-pricing activities by a provider contracting organization including competitors are per se unlawful. Statement 9, however, describes acceptable "messenger" arrangements that non-integrated provider

---

65. FTC Staff Advisory Opinion to MedSouth, Inc. (Feb. 19, 2002), *at* http://www.ftc.gov.bc.adops/medsouth.htm.
66. *Health Care Enforcement Statements, supra* p. 12 n.41, Statement 8, Example 1.
67. *See* Thomas B. Leary, *The Antitrust Implications of "Clinical Integration": An Analysis of the FTC Staff's Advisory Opinion to MedSouth*, 47 St. Louis L.J. 1 (2003); Scott D. Danzis, Note, *Revising the Revised Guidelines: Incentives, Clinically Integrated Physician Networks and the Antitrust Laws*, 87 Va. L. Rev. 531 (2001).
68. Int'l Healthcare Mgmt. v. Hawaii Coalition for Health, 332 F.3d 600 (9th Cir. 2003); *see also Health Care Enforcement Statements*, Statement 4, *supra* p. 12 n.41 (discussing providers' collective provision of non-fee-related information to purchasers of health-care services and noting that "[p]roviders who collectively threaten to or actually refuse to deal with a purchaser because they object to the purchaser's administrative, clinical, or other terms governing the provision of services run a substantial antitrust risk").
69. United States v. Classic Care Network, Inc., 1995-1 Trade Cas. (CCH) ¶ 70,997 (E.D.N.Y. 1995) (consent decree) (alleging that hospital contracting network members agreed, through the network, not to grant discounts to health plans).

organizations can use to facilitate contracting by their participants without engaging in price-fixing agreements.[70] A messenger-arrangement network may convey to health plans information obtained individually from participating providers about the price terms each will accept. The messenger also may convey to participating providers the contract proposals of health plans, and convey back to the health plans the independent and unilateral responses of each provider (or each fully integrated provider practice) as to whether it will participate in the plan at that price. The messenger also may provide objective or empirical information to both providers and payers to assist them in their assessment of a contract proposal.

The purpose for using a messenger arrangement is to prevent the network and its participants from entering into price-fixing agreements through the network. The key requirement of a messenger arrangement is that it not create or facilitate an agreement among competing providers through the network on price terms by using a network-developed fee schedule, coordinating the providers' responses, disseminating among the providers the views of their rivals with respect to contract terms or acceptable prices, expressing opinions on proposed contract terms, collectively negotiating offers from payers for participants, or refusing to transmit contract proposals to provider members of the network for their individual decision based on the messenger's judgment about the attractiveness of contract offers. Most frequently, messenger-arrangement networks encounter problems because the network believes it may lawfully negotiate price offers if it then messengers the negotiated offers to its participating providers for their individual decision. The agencies reject this position.[71]

The federal agencies have issued numerous advisory opinions discussing messenger-arrangement networks.[72] Both agencies, however, have also filed numerous enforcement actions against provider-controlled networks for price-fixing, alleging that networks claiming to be only messenger net-

---

70. *Health Care Enforcement Statements, supra* p. 12 n.41, Statement 9.C & Example 4.
71. *See id.*, Statement 9.C n.65.
72. *E.g.*, FTC Staff Advisory Opinion to Bay Area Preferred Physicians (Sept. 23, 2003), *at* http://www.ftc.gov/bc/adops/bapp030923.htm; FTC Staff Advisory Opinion to Alliance of Independent Medical Services, LLC (Dec. 22, 1997) (discussing an ambulance network), *at* http://www.ftc.gov.bc/ adops/ aims.fin.htm; Antitrust Division Business Review Letter to Home Care Alliance, Inc. (Oct. 4, 1996) (discussing a home-care contracting organization),

works were actually negotiating price offers on behalf of their members with payers.[73] The conduct in which the network and messenger may law-

---

at *h*ttp://www.usdoj.gov/atr/public/busreview/ 0942.htm. For a more complete list of agency advice about messenger-arrangement networks, *see* 2 *HCAL, supra* p. 13 n.47, at p. 15-135 n.5.

73. The FTC's Analysis of Agreement Containing Consent Order to Aid Public Comment in its *Memorial Hermann Health Network Providers* case is instructive:

The messenger may not . . . negotiate fees and other competitively significant terms on behalf of the participating physicians, nor facilitate the physicians' coordinated responses to contract offers, for example, by electing not to convey a payor's offer to the physicians based on the messenger's opinion of the acceptability or appropriateness of the offer.

Rather than acting simply acting as a "messenger," [respondent] engaged in collective negotiations on its members' behalf with third-party payors. [Respondent's] improper collective negotiations included actively bargaining with third-party payors by proposing and counter-proposing fee schedules (among other terms), gathering fee information from its members and using that information to negotiate prices, refusing to messenger proposals it deemed unacceptable on price and other terms, and, to maintain its bargaining power, on occasion, discouraging its participating physicians from entering into unilateral agreements with third-party payors. For example, [respondent] periodically polled its physician members, asking each to disclose the minimum fee that he or she would accept in return for providing medical services pursuant to future [network] payor agreements. [Respondent] would then calculate minimum acceptable fees for use in payor negotiations, based in part on the information received from physician members concerning their future pricing intentions, and would often begin discussions regarding a possible contract for physician services by informing the payor of these minimum fees and stating that it would not enter into or otherwise forward to its physician members any payor offer that did not satisfy those fee minimums.

. . . [Respondent] in fact often did not convey to its physician members payor offers that provided for fees that did not satisfy [respondent's] Board of Directors. . . . Only after the third-party payor acceded to fee and other contract terms acceptable to [respondent], would [respondent] convey the payor's proposed contract to [respondent's] participating physicians for their consideration. For example, in one instance [respondent] refused a payor's request to messenger an offer [respondent's] Board deemed unacceptable. Instead, [respondent] notified its members that it had rejected the offer because it was below the minimum acceptable fee level previously set pursuant to physician member surveys, and then

fully engage while representing provider members of the network in dealing with payers is quite limited.[74]

Finally, horizontal price-fixing concerns can arise when competing physician groups agree among themselves on the terms by which they will provide services to hospitals and their patients. In one case, for example, the FTC challenged an agreement among two anesthesiology practices in which they agreed on the price they would charge a hospital to provide coverage and refused to negotiate with the hospital separately.[75]

"polled" its members to determine whether or not they agreed with the Board's decision to reject the offer. A majority of physician members voted to agree with the Board's decision, and [respondent] then again rejected the payor's offer and explicitly refused to forward the offer to any of its physician members. Subsequently, the payor increased its proposed fees to [respondent's] fee minimums, and [respondent] then entered into a contract with the payor and messengered the agreement to its physician members, affording them the option to participate (or not) in the payor's offer.

Mem'l Hermann Health Network Providers, File No. 031 0001 (FTC Nov. 25, 2003) (Analysis of Agreement Containing Consent Order to Aid Public Comment), *at* http://www.ftc.gov/os/caselist/ 0310001/031125 anl0310001.pdf.; *see also id.*, Dkt No. C-4104 (FTC Jan. 8, 2004) (consent order) *at* http://www.ftc.gov/os/caselist/031001/040113do0310001.pdf.

Other challenges to purported messenger arrangements include Piedmont Health Alliance, Inc., Dkt. No. 9134 (FTC Dec. 24, 2003) (administrative complaint), *at* http://www.ftc.gov/os/caselist/ 0210119/031222/ comp0210119.pdf; System Health Providers, Dkt. No. C-4064 (FTC Aug. 20, 2002) (consent order), *at* http://www.ftc.gov/os/2002/08/shpds.pdf; Aurora Associated Primary Care Physicians, L.L.C., Dkt. No. C-4055 (FTC Jul. 19, 2002) (consent order), *at* http://www.ftc/gov/03/2002/07/ aurorado.pdf; United States v. Fed'n of Physicians & Dentists, Inc., 2002-2 Trade Cas. (CCH) ¶ 73,868 (D. Del. 2002) (consent decree and competitive impact statement); United States v. Fed'n of Certified Surgeons & Specialists, Inc., 1999-1 Trade Cas. (CCH) ¶ 72,549 (M.D. Fla. 1999) (consent decree and competitive impact statement).

74. For a list and overview of the types of messenger-arrangement conduct that can raise antitrust concern, *see* Jeff Miles, *Ticking Antitrust Time Bombs: A Message to Messed-Up Messenger Models,* AHLA HEALTH LAWYERS NEWS, Nov. 2002, at 5.

75. Grossmont Anesthesia Servs. Med. Group, Inc., Dkt. No. C-4086 (FTC Jul. 15, 2003) (consent order), *at* http://www.ftc.gov/os/2003/gasdo.pdf.

Thus far, all of the agencies' enforcement actions against provider contracting networks have terminated by consent orders and decrees without litigation. In general, the orders and decrees enjoin the unlawful conduct; include some "fencing in" injunctive provisions that go beyond the unlawful conduct itself; permit the networks to reform their contracting methodology to operate lawfully as legitimate messenger arrangements, "qualified risk-sharing joint arrangements," or "qualified clinically-integrated joint arrangements"; require the networks to notify and provide copies of the order to various parties; require the networks to terminate their payer contracts (or provide payers with the option to terminate the contracts); and require the respondents to file periodic compliance reports. In several cases, however, the order or decree has required the network to cease doing business or dissolve.[76] The term of FTC consent orders is 20 years, while that of Antitrust Division consent decrees is typically 10 years.

It always bears remembering that naked horizontal price-fixing agreements are subject to criminal prosecution by the Antitrust Division.[77] Thus, regardless of the context in which they arise, their antitrust ramifications can be particularly serious.

2. *Competitor Exchanges of Pricing Information and Price Surveys*

Competing health-care providers sometimes participate in surveys concerning their prices or may otherwise exchange or share competitively sensitive

---

76. *See* United States v. Mountain Health Care, P.A., 2003-2 Trade Cas. (CCH) ¶ 74,162 (W.D.N.C. 2003) (consent decree requiring defendant to dissolve and competitive impact statement); Carlsbad Physicians Ass'n, Inc., Dkt. No. C-4081 (FTC June 13, 2003) (consent order requiring respondent to "cease and desist from all business and all other activities of any nature whatsoever"), *at* http://www.ftc.gov/os/2003/06/carlsbaddo.htm; Obstetrics and Gynecology Med. Corp., Dkt. No. C-4048 (FTC May 14, 2002) (consent order requiring respondents to cease business), *at* http://www.ftc.gov/os/ 2002/05/obgyndo.pdf.

77. *See, e.g.*, United States v. Rhone-Poulenc Biochimie, S.A., Cr. No. 4:03CR567RWS (E.D. Mo., filed Sept. 18, 2003) (criminal information alleging price-fixing conspiracy among producers of chemical to decrease rate at which x-ray contrast media disperses in the body during imaging procedures; guilty plea and $5 million fine), *at* http://www.usdoj.gov/atr/ public/press_releases/2003/201284.htm.

information, such as the wages they pay or their strategic plans. Although most are lawful, some information exchanges, especially those that disclose prices or pricing formulas, such as relative-value scales[78] or wages paid to employees, can raise significant antitrust concerns.[79] In general, competitively sensitive information such as information relating to current or future prices, current or future costs, projected services, or planned entry into or exit from markets can present antitrust risk if shared with competitors, particularly if the relevant market that would be affected by the exchange is highly concentrated.

Thus, absent advice from antitrust counsel, providers and other sellers and purchasers in the health-care sector should avoid participation in surveys concerning projected or future charges or payments for services. Indeed, they should avoid even discussing these subjects with competitors. Avoidance is particularly important if the survey or discussion relates to the current or future prices of specific, identified competitors. Such surveys may facilitate a per se unlawful price-fixing agreement among competing providers.[80] Even if no actual price-fixing agreement results, exchanges of competitively sensitive information among competitors still can be unlawful under rule-of-reason analysis if their effect is to raise or stabilize prices (or lower or stabilize wages or the price of some other input).[81]

Key factors in assessing whether the exchange of price information among competitors will survive challenge under the rule of reason include (1) the susceptibility of the relevant market to tacit collusion or oligopolistic, inter-

---

78. *See* Am. Soc'y of Internal Med., 105 F.T.C. 505 (1985) (FTC Advisory Opinion discussing Society establishment and dissemination of relative-value guides).

79. *See* United States v. Utah Soc'y for Healthcare Human Res. Admin., 1994-2 Trade Cas. (CCH) ¶ 70,795 (D. Utah 1994) (consent decree) (challenge to hospital exchange of wage information).

80. *See* Todd v. Exxon Corp., 275 F.3d 191, 198 (2d Cir. 2001) (explaining that exchange of wage information among competing employers may facilitate a per se unlawful wage-fixing agreement); Morton Salt Co. v. United States, 235 F.2d 573, 576-77 (10th Cir. 1953) (noting that a price exchange may lead to further action resulting in a price-fixing agreement).

81. *See* United States v. U.S. Gypsum Co., 438 U.S. 422 (1978); United States v. Container Corp., 393 U.S. 333 (1969); Mitcheal v. Intracorp, Inc., 179 F.3d 847, 859 (10th Cir. 1999) ("Mere exchanges of information, even regarding price, are not necessarily illegal.").

dependent competitive behavior, particularly the level of market concentration, the fungibility of the products or services whose prices are exchanged, and the price-elasticity of demand of the products or services; (2) the nature of the information exchanged, particularly whether the prices subject to the exchange or survey are current or future prices or historical prices, whether the information is aggregated, and whether the information identifies the prices of specific parties or transactions or is masked; (3) whether the information is otherwise publicly available, particularly whether, if the exchange is among sellers, the information is available to purchasers; (4) whether participants in the exchange or survey meet to discuss the information and whether the information contains any instructions about how it should be used; (5) whether the information is gathered and disseminated by the parties themselves or by an independent third party; and (6) the purpose for the exchange.[82]

Statement 6 of the federal antitrust enforcement agencies' *Health Care Enforcement Statements* discusses "provider participation in exchanges of price and cost information." It provides an antitrust safety zone if (1) the survey or exchange is implemented by a third party; (2) the statistics disseminated are based on data that is at least three months old; and (3) the statistics disseminated are based on data from at least five providers, no single provider's data accounts for more than 25 percent of the statistics, and the information is sufficiently aggregated or masked so that recipients cannot identify the prices or costs of particular providers participating in the survey.[83]

The Antitrust Division has brought enforcement actions against obstetricians for exchanging information on the prices they charged for deliveries[84] and against hospitals for exchanging information about the wages paid nurses.[85] In a private class-action suit filed by current and former medical-school residents, the plaintiffs allege that the resident-stipend surveys conducted by the American Medical Association and the Council of Teaching Hospitals, which they post on the Internet, are facilitating practices in a nationwide conspiracy

---

82. *See generally Todd*, 275 F.3d at 207-13.
83. *Health Care Enforcement Statements, supra* p. 12 n.41, Statement 6.
84. United States v. Burgstiner, 1991-1 Trade Cas. (CCH) ¶ 69,422 (S.D. Ga. 1991) (consent decree).
85. United States v. Utah Soc'y for Healthcare Human Res. Admin., 1994-2 Trade Cas. (CCH) ¶ 70,795 (D. Utah 1994) (consent decree).

among graduate medical education programs to reduce the stipends paid to medical residents and fellows.[86]

The federal enforcement agencies have issued numerous advisory opinions discussing the exchange or dissemination of provider prices. Relatively recent opinion letters from both the Antitrust Division and FTC discuss and approve physician-sponsored surveys of reimbursement by health plans with which the physicians contract.[87]

---

86. Resident Physicians Antitrust Litig., No. 02-0873 (D.D.C., filed May 7, 2002) (complaint), *at* http://www.residentcase.com/select_pleadings/complaint.pdf.

87. *See, e.g.,* FTC Staff Advisory Opinion to Medical Group Management Association (Nov. 3, 2003) (fee survey by association of medical groups), *at* http://www.ftc.gov/bc/adops/mgma031104.pdf; FTC Staff Advisory Opinion to PriMed Physicians (Feb. 6, 2003) (survey of prices paid physicians by payers), *at* http://www.ftc.gov/bc/adops/030206dayton.htm; Antitrust Division Business Review Letter to Washington State Medical Association (Sept. 23, 2002) (physician fee and reimbursement survey), *at* http://www.usdoj.gov/atr/public/busreview/200260.pdf.

Other agency advice letters discussing the exchange or dissemination of pricing information include FTC Staff Advisory Opinion to Business Health Cos., Inc. (Oct. 18, 1996) (survey of hospital prices), *at* http://www.ftc.gov/bc/adops/waco_fin.htm; Antitrust Division Business Review Letter to Seeskin, Pass, Blackburn & Co. (June 29, 1994) (compilation and dissemination of dentists' fee information), *at* http://www.usdoj.gov/atr/public/busreview/cafdfs.htm; Antitrust Division Business Review Letter to Birmingham Cooperative Clinical Benchmarking Demonstration Project (June 20, 1994) (collection and reporting of hospital performance and pricing information), *at* http://www.usdoj.gov/ atr/public/busreview/bccbdp.htm; Antitrust Division Business Review Letter to New Jersey Hospital Association (Feb. 18, 1994) (hospital salary and wage survey), *at* http://www.usdoj.gov/ atr/public/busreview/njha.htm; Antitrust Division Business Review Letter to Hyatt, Imler, Ott & Blount, P.C. (June 12, 1992) (hospital price survey), *reprinted in* 3 *HCAL, supra* p. 14 n.47, App. C28; FTC Staff Advisory Opinion to American Dental Association (Feb. 15, 1990) (survey of payer fees for dental services), *reprinted in id.,* App. D28; Antitrust Division Business Review Letter to St. Louis Area Business Health Coalition (Mar. 24, 1988) (survey of prices for most frequently purchased hospital services), *reprinted in id.,* App. C25; Antitrust Division Business Review Letter to Lexecon Health Services (June 20, 1986) (compilation and publication of provider-specific price information), *reprinted in id.,* App. C17; FTC Staff Advisory Opinion to North Texas Chapter, American College of Surgeons (Dec. 12, 1985) (survey of fees charged by surgeons), *reprinted in id.,* App. D18; Antitrust Divi-

3. Unilateral Pricing Conduct by Firms with Market Power

In general, no antitrust violation results simply because one provider can and does offer lower prices than its competitors, even if that provider enjoys a competitive advantage over its rivals, such as greater economies of scale and thus lower costs. There are situations, however, where unilateral pricing conduct by a seller or purchaser with market power potentially can raise antitrust concern.

a.   Monopoly and Monopsony Pricing

As noted before, firms with monopoly power or monopsony power do not violate the antitrust laws by charging above-competitive prices for their output or paying below-competitive prices for their inputs if they obtained their market power lawfully and are not maintaining or increasing their power by predatory means.[88] Indeed, in the case of providers complaining about low reimbursement from health plans, the courts have uniformly held that even if the health plan has monopsony power, it still violates no antitrust law if it pays only what it must to obtain the quantity of services it wants.[89] Of course, the answer may be different if the higher or lower price results from an agreement among competing sellers or purchasers.

b.   Predatory Pricing

Predatory pricing occurs where (1) a firm with substantial market power prices its products or services below some measure of its costs until its competitors are

---

sion Business Review Letter to Stark County Health Care Coalition (Aug. 30, 1985) (gathering and dissemination of various types of health-care information), *reprinted in id.*, App. C16; FTC Staff Advisory Opinion to Utah Society of Oral & Maxillofacial Surgeons (Feb. 8, 1985) (physician fee survey), *reprinted in id.*, App. D14.

88. *See supra* pp. 34 (monopolization), 39 (monopsonization).

89. *See, e.g.*, Griffiths v. Blue Cross & Blue Shield, 147 F. Supp. 2d 1203, 1210, 1216 (N.D. Ala. 2001) ("It is well established that an insurer such as Blue Cross, who in effect purchases health care services on behalf of its subscribers, does not violate Section 1 by using its market power to negotiate discounted fees that healthcare providers agree to accept as full payment for services"; "Blue Cross's alleged use of market power to obtain discounts for its customers from health care providers does not constitute willful acquisition or maintenance of monopoly power for purposes of a Section 2 claim").

driven from the market or are so competitively crippled that they cannot constrain the seller's market power, and (2) entry and expansion barriers are sufficient so that, after the period of the seller's below-cost pricing, the seller can recoup the losses it suffered and then reap supracompetitive profits by raising its price above the competitive level for a sustained period of time.[90] The strategy, which probably occurs infrequently, is risky because losses during the below-cost pricing period are certain but subsequent recoupment of those losses and then monopoly profits are not. Importantly, short-term below-cost pricing, by itself, is not unlawful; indeed, it benefits consumers.

Allegations of predatory pricing are rare in health-care antitrust cases. In one case, a payer argued unsuccessfully that its competitor replaced it as an employer's health plan by offering the employer predatory prices.[91]

c.   Price Discrimination

In general, it is not unlawful for a seller to charge different purchasers different prices as a means of competition. Agreements between sellers and buyers embodying discriminatory prices, for example, are subject to rule-of-reason analysis under Section 1 of the Sherman Act, and none has been found unlawful.[92] Price discrimination in the sale of commodities (but not services), however, can violate Section 2(a) of the Robinson-Patman Act.[93] When the claimant is a competitor of the seller (so-called "primary-line" price discrimination), it must prove that the seller's price discrimination meets the test

---

90. *See generally* Brooke Group, Ltd. v. Brown & Williamson Tobacco Co., 509 U.S. 209 (1993); Matsushita Elec. Indus. Co. v. Zenith Radio Corp., 475 U.S. 574 (1986) (allegation of a conspiracy among competitors to engage in predatory pricing).

91. Coventry Health Care v. Via Christi Health Sys., Inc., 176 F. Supp. 2d 1207 (D. Kan. 2001).

92. *See, e.g.*, Callahan v. A.E.V., Inc., 182 F.3d 237, 248-49 (3d Cir. 1999); *cf.* Brand Name Prescription Drugs Antitrust Litig., 288 F.3d 1028, 1030-32 (7th Cir. 2002) ("Price discrimination is . . . quite common in competitive industries."; "price discrimination is not (in general) unlawful"). On the other hand, a seller's ability to price discriminate can suggest that it has market power. Brand Name Prescription Drugs Antitrust Litig., 186 F.3d 781, 786 (7th Cir. 1999).

93. For a helpful pamphlet providing a brief overview of the Robinson-Patman Act, *see* AMERICAN BAR ASSOCIATION SECTION OF ANTITRUST LAW, A PRIMER ON THE FEDERAL PRICE DISCRIMINATION LAWS (2000).

for predatory pricing violative of Section 2 of the Sherman Act—that is, the seller's prices must be below some measure of its costs and it must be able to recoup its losses through future supracompetitive prices.[94] There is no health-care antitrust case in which a plaintiff has met this burden. On the other hand, where the plaintiff is the seller's customer, alleging that the seller charged it a higher price than its competitor (so-called "secondary-line" price discrimination), the plaintiff has an easier burden. All it must show is that the price differential was significant and sustained, and then the necessary injury to competition can be inferred.[95] Thus, a supplier of commodities such as medical supplies or pharmaceuticals should exercise some care in charging different prices to its customers who compete against one another.

In health care, price discrimination issues arise most frequently where a hospital vendor has granted a nonprofit hospital a discriminatory price (that is, a price lower than that granted the hospital's for-profit competitors). In this situation, the question is usually whether the Nonprofit Institutions Act (NPIA)[96] exempts that price discrimination from Section 2(f) of the Robinson-Patman Act, which prohibits purchasers from knowingly inducing or receiving an unlawful discriminatory price (and from Section 2(a), which prohibits the seller from granting unlawful price discriminations).[97] The NPIA provides that the Robinson-Patman Act does not apply to "purchases of their supplies for their own use by . . . hospitals and charitable institutions not operated for profit." Thus, a seller's sales to nonprofit hospitals and other charitable institutions are exempt from both the seller and buyer provisions of the Robinson-Patman Act if the nonprofit purchaser consumes the commodity (pharmaceuticals, for example) in a manner that constitutes its "own use." In general, this means, for hospital purchasers, that the commodity is used in the treatment of its own patients or by those closely connected to the hospital.[98]

---

94. *See supra* pp. 87-90; *see also Brooke Group,* 509 U.S. at 222-24; United States v. AMR Corp., 335 F.3d 1109, 115 (10th Cir. 2003).

95. FTC v. Morton Salt Co., 334 U.S. 37, 46-48 (1948); *see also* Falls City Indus. v. Vanco Beverage, Inc., 460 U.S. 428, 436 (1983).

96. 15 U.S.C. § 13c.

97. The NPIA is discussed *supra*, at p. 60.

98. *See* Abbott Labs. v. Portland Retail Druggists' Ass'n, 425 U.S. 1 (1976) (holding, in general, that resale of pharmaceuticals by the hospital to its inpatients, outpatients, employees, and medical staff constitute the hospital's "own use," while prescription renewals for former patients and sales to walk-in customers do not).

As hospitals have evolved into "health systems" providing services far beyond inpatient acute-care hospital services and entering into different types of arrangements with other entities, the definition of "own use" has expanded as well. Although there are few decisions, numerous FTC advisory opinions discuss the meaning of "own use" in a plethora of specific factual situations. In the case of hospital systems, the nonprofit hospital may, in general, transfer the commodity for the use of its nonprofit subsidiaries (or other nonprofit entities) for their "own use" without destroying the exemption.[99] But the Supreme Court has specifically held that purchases of commodities by state-owned facilities that compete with private-sector firms, such as the purchase

---

99. *E.g.,* FTC Staff Advisory Opinion to Dunlap Memorial Hospital (Jan. 6, 2004) (sales of pharmaceuticals by nonprofit hospital to non-affiliated nonprofit clinic at cost), *at* http://www.ftc.gov/ os/2004/01/040106dunlaplet.pdf; FTC Staff Advisory Opinion to Arkansas Children's Hospital (Mar. 13, 2003) (sales of pharmaceuticals to affiliated clinics), *at* http://www.ftc.gov/os/2003/03/ 030313ach.htm; FTC Staff Advisory Opinion to Valley Medical Center (Mar. 13, 2003) (resales of pharmaceuticals to nonprofit hospital's contract workers), *at* http://www.ftc.gov/os/2003/03/030313vbmc.htm; FTC Staff Advisory Opinion to Viquest and Pitt County Memorial Hospital (Mar. 8, 2003) (resale of vaccines by nonprofit hospital to affiliated wellness center), *at* http://www.ftc.gov/bc/adops/viquestet.htm; FTC Staff Advisory Opinion to Connecticut Hospital Association (Dec. 20, 2001) (exemption applies to re-sales to retired hospital employees), *at* http://www.ftc.gov/opa/2001/12/ chaadvisopinionletter.htm; FTC Staff Advisory Opinion to Harvard Vanguard Medical Associates, Inc. (Dec. 18, 2001) (exemption applies to resales by nonprofit clinic to patients), *at* http://www.ftc.gov/bc/adops/harvardvma.htm; FTC Staff Advisory Opinion to BJC Health System (Nov. 9, 1999) (exemption applies to transfers from hospital to related clinics for resale to health-system employees), *at* http://www.ftc.gov/bc/adops/bjclet.htm; FTC Staff Advisory Opinion to Wesley Health Center (Apr. 29, 1999) (exemption applies to resales by nonprofit residential health-care facility to volunteer workers), *at* http://www.ftc.gov/bc/adops/wesleyhealthcare.htm; FTC Staff Advisory Opinion to North Mississippi Health Services (Jan. 7, 1998) (exemption applies to resales of pharmaceuticals by nonprofit hospital's cancer fund to indigent patients who were not hospital's patients), *at* http:// www.ftc.gov/bc/adops/normiss2.fin.htm; FTC Staff Advisory Opinion to Henry County Memorial Hospital (Apr. 10, 1997) (exemption would not apply to resales by nonprofit hospital to hospital PHO subscribers), *at* http:/ /www.ftc.gov/bc/adops/henry.htm.

of pharmaceuticals by a state hospital that competes with independent, for-profit pharmacies, are not exempt from the Robinson-Patman Act.[100]

d. Selective Discounting and Bundled Pricing

In general, it is not unlawful for providers, regardless of their market power, to offer the same services to different purchasers at different prices. Hospitals, for example, frequently engage in selective discounting of this type based on the volume of patients a payer will steer to them, granting larger discounts to larger payers. A question can arise, however, when a large provider with market power offers a discount on all its services (a "bundled discount") to a payer when competing with a competitor that offers fewer such services and thus cannot realistically match the aggregate dollar amount of the discount offered by its more diversified competitor. For example, a hospital with substantial market power in the market for outpatient surgical services might offer a payer a significant discount off both its inpatient and outpatient services in return for the payer's steering all its subscribers to the hospital's outpatient surgical services.

Because a freestanding outpatient surgery center does not offer the full panoply of hospital services, it cannot match the amount of that discount even if it offers the same or even a larger percentage discount off the price of its outpatient services. The arrangement, thus, can have the effect of an exclusive contract for outpatient surgical services between the hospital and payer. The freestanding center may be foreclosed from the subscriber's patients, and, depending on other facts relating to the market (particularly the percentage of all referrals the payer controls), the hospital may be able to maintain its dominance over the market for outpatient surgical services.[101]

---

100. Jefferson County Pharm. Ass'n, Inc. v. Abbott Labs., 460 U.S. 150 (1983).
101. For a discussion of a situation similar to this, *see* Rebecca Simmons, *The Enhancement of Anticompetitive Activity Through Group Purchasing Organizations: A Case Study*, ABA ANTITRUST HEALTH CARE CHRONICLE, Spring 2003, at 2 [hereinafter Simmons]. For helpful discussions of this issue, although not focusing specifically on health care, *see* Willard K. Tom, Deputy Director, Bureau of Competition, Federal Trade Commission, "Anticompetitive Aspects of Exclusive Dealing and Related Practices," Prepared Remarks Before the ABA Section of Antitrust Law Spring Meeting (Apr. 15, 1999), *reprinted in* 4 *HCAL*, p. 14 n.46, App. E88; A. Douglas Melamed, Principal Deputy Assistant Attorney General, Antitrust Division, "Exclusionary Vertical Agree-

The legal status of bundled discounting is not clear. Some cases indicate that such discounts constitute predatory conduct, which may result in a violation of Section 2 of the Sherman Act if the hospital has substantial market power in the relevant market for outpatient services, and the discount forecloses a substantial percentage of the market to its smaller competitors unable to offer a similar discount.[102] Other cases, however, would seem to require that the hospital's discount amount to predatory pricing—that the hospital's price, at a minimum, be below an appropriate measure of its cost of providing the discounted services.[103]

One case found this type of discount unlawful where a pharmaceutical manufacturer bundled discounts on its patented and non-patented drugs.[104] Another found that a similar discount on different blood tests would be unlawful only if it "threatens equally or more efficient firms."[105] In another, a jury returned a verdict of $521 million where a vendor of regular and specialty hospital beds bundled its discount on both in sales to group-purchasing organizations, foreclosing another vendor who sold only the specialty beds.[106] A more recent case involving a hospital and freestanding outpatient surgery center upheld such a contract without discussing the specific issue.[107]

Related to bundled discounts, an antitrust issue can arise when a hospital with substantial market power conditions a discount (or a deeper discount) on

---

ments," Prepared Remarks Before the ABA Section of Antitrust Law Spring Meeting (Apr. 2, 1998), *at* http://www.usdoj.gov.atr/public/speeches/1623.htm.

102. *See* LePage's, Inc. v. 3M, 324 F.3d 141 (3d Cir. 2003) (en banc), *petition for cert. filed*, 72 U.S.L.W. 3007 (U.S. June 20, 2003) (No. 01-1865); Avery Dennison Corp. v. ACCO Brands, Inc., 2000-1 Trade Cas. (CCH) ¶ 72,882 (C.D. Cal. 2000); Minn. Mining & Mfg. Co. v. Appleton Papers, Inc., 35 F. Supp. 2d 1138 (D. Minn. 1999).

103. *See* Concord Boat Corp. v. Brunswick Corp., 207 F.3d 1039 (8th Cir. 2000); *see also LePage's*, 324 F.3d at 177-78 (Greenberg, J., dissenting).

104. SmithKline Corp. v. Eli Lilly & Co., 575 F.2d 1056 (3d Cir. 1978).

105. Ortho Diagnostic Sys. v. Abbott Labs., 920 F. Supp. 455, 469 (S.D.N.Y. 1996).

106. Kenetic Concepts, Inc. v. Hillenbrand Indus., Inc., No. 95-CV-0755 (W.D. Tex., Sept. 27, 2002) (jury verdict). For discussions of this case, *see* Simmons, *supra* p. 99 n.101; Ellen L. Goldman, *Firm Wins $174 Million Antitrust Verdict*, N.Y. LAWYER, Oct. 7, 2002.

107. Surgical Care Ctr. v. Hosp. Dist. No. 1, 2001-1 Trade Cas. (CCH) ¶ 73,215, at 89,933 (E.D. La. 2001), *aff'd*, 309 F.3d 836 (5th Cir. 2002).

a payer's agreement not to contract with the hospital's smaller competitor. In the *PeaceHealth* case, for example, a jury found that a hospital's threat to increase its prices to a managed-care plan if the plan included a competing hospital in its network constituted one part of a scheme to attempt to monopolize primary and secondary hospital services.[108]

4. *Most-Favored-Nation Provisions*

A "most-favored-nations" (MFN) provision in a provider agreement obligates the provider not to charge, or accept from, other payers a lower price than that received from the payer. Although courts, for the most part, have rejected antitrust challenges to MFN provisions, viewing them as a typical and legitimate device for a purchaser to ensure low prices,[109] the enforcement agencies have obtained consent decrees in numerous challenges to them.[110] The Antitrust Division has indicated a continuing enforcement interest in MFN provisions.[111]

---

108. McKenzie-Willamette Hosp. v. PeaceHealth, No. 02-6032-HA (D. Ore. Oct. 31, 2003) (jury verdict awarding plaintiff $5.4 million in single damages for attempted monopolization). For discussions of the decision, *see* Mark Taylor, *Casualty of Court: Oregon Verdict Sends Message: 'Watch Out for Juries,'* Mod. Healthcare, Nov. 10, 2003, at 12; Tim Christie, *PeaceHealth Liable in Antitrust Lawsuit,* Eugene Register Guard, Nov. 1, 2003, *available at* http://www.registerguard.com/news/2003/11/01/ al.hospitalsuit. 1101.html.

109. *E.g.*, Blue Cross & Blue Shield United v. Marshfield Clinic, 65 F.3d 1406, 1415 (7th Cir. 1995); Ocean State Physicians Health Plan v. Blue Cross & Blue Shield, 883 F.2d 1101, 1109-10 (1st Cir. 1989). *But cf.* Reazin v. Blue Cross & Blue Shield, 899 F.2d 951, 971 & n.30 (10th Cir. 1990) (noting that MFN contributed to defendant's market power but finding it unnecessary to "reach the question . . . whether use of the [MFN] clause could itself violate section 2").

110. *See, e.g.*, United States v. Med. Mut., 1999-1 Trade Cas. (CCH) ¶ 72,465 (N.D. Ohio 1999) (consent decree and competitive impact statement); United States v. Delta Dental Plan, 943 F. Supp. 172 (D.R.I. 1996) (denying defendant's 12(b)(6) motion), and 1997-2 Trade Cas. (CCH) ¶ 71,860 (D.R.I. 1997) (consent decree and competitive impact statement); United States v. Vision Serv. Plan, 1996-1 Trade Cas. (CCH) ¶ 71,404 (D.D.C. 1996) (consent decree).

111. *See* Deborah P. Majoras, Deputy Assistant Attorney General, Antitrust Division, Prepared Remarks Before the Federal Trade Commission Health Care

The agencies claim that use of MFN provisions by a dominant payer in a market suppresses selective discounting by providers that may facilitate entry by new managed care plans into the area.[112] The provision can chill provider discounting because a provider subject to an MFN provision, when considering whether to accept lower prices from other payers, may refrain from offering discounts to those payers because its offering discounts to them might trigger the MFN provision, potentially resulting in lower aggregate revenues. The provider considering whether to offer other payers a discount must attempt to compare the effect on its profits based on the additional revenues it will receive by contracting with another plan at a deeply discounted price and the loss of revenues it will suffer by lowering its price to the payer with the MFN requirement. If business from the latter constitutes a significant portion of the provider's business, its losses from lowering its price to that payer may significantly exceed any gain from contracting with other plans at a lower price. In this way, MFN provisions can operate as an entry barrier to new plans seeking to enter the market or a barrier to expansion by existing payers, and this can enhance the payer's market power as both a seller of health-care financing products and a purchaser of health-care services from providers.

The agencies also claim that MFN provisions may facilitate coordinated pricing among providers, particularly where the providers are closely affiliated with or control a dominant payer using an MFN provision. In this circumstance, the agencies believe that providers use MFN provisions to give one another mutual assurance that prices will not be lowered below those agreed to with the affiliated payer. On the other hand, MFN provisions can have

---

and Competition Law and Policy Workshop (Sept. 9, 2002) ("we continue to receive and evaluate complaints about managed care plans' use of [MFN] clauses to determine if they merit more complete investigation and, ultimately, any enforcement action. These types of clauses generally operate to protect insurers against other plans getting better reimbursement rates from providers and generally create disincentives for providers to lower reimbursement rates."), *at* http://www.usdoj.gov/atr/public/speeches/200195.htm.

112. *See* Gail Kursh, Chief, Professions and Intellectual Property Section, Antitrust Division, "Report from the Antitrust Division on Recent Enforcement Initiatives in the Health Care Field," Prepared Remarks Before the National Health Lawyers Association Antitrust in the Healthcare Field Seminar (Feb. 16, 1995) (on file with editor).

procompetitive effects and thus should not be condemned too quickly without a thorough analysis of their procompetitive and anticompetitive effects.[113]

5. Peer Review of Fees

Fee peer review is a procedure by which insurance carriers, health maintenance organizations, preferred provider organizations, and other third-party payers (or consumers themselves) receive advice from health-care providers (the peer-review panel) as to whether particular health-care provider charges were reasonable in the circumstances.[114] Today, fee peer-review programs are somewhat of an anachronism because of the growth of managed-care organizations during the 1980s and 1990s, which exercise substantial control over the level of physician fees themselves. Typically, medical societies sponsored and operated such programs. Today, many health plans contract with an outside firm to provide this service.

Nevertheless, if a fee peer-review panel includes competing physicians, there is a risk that the review activities could result in a price-fixing agreement or an unlawful agreement among competitors to exchange fee information leading to price stabilization.[115] Moreover, while the Health Care Quality Improvement Act provides health-care providers with immunity from antitrust damages for their professional review actions, the Act defines professional review actions as those based on the competence or professional conduct of a physician and expressly excludes actions based primarily on a physician's fees.[116] In addition, conducting fee peer review, even for an insurer, does not constitute the "business of insurance," and thus the McCarran-Ferguson Act's limited exemption for the business of insurance does not provide any protection.[117]

---

113. For a helpful discussion of the economics of MFNs, *see* William J. Lynk, *Some Basics About Most Favored Nations Contracts in Health Care Markets*, 45 Antitrust Bull. 491 (2000).

114. Some peer-review programs also assess whether the services rendered were medically necessary within the terms of the health-insurance policy between the insurer and its subscriber.

115. *See* Ratino v. Med. Serv., 718 F.2d 1260, 1270 (4th Cir. 1983).

116. 42 U.S.C. § 11,151(a); *see generally supra* pp. 59-60, discussing the Health Care Quality Improvement Act.

117. Union Life Ins. Co. v. Pireno, 458 U.S. 119 (1982) (holding the McCarran Act exemption inapplicable to a chiropractic fee peer-review program); *see generally supra* pp. 55-56, discussing the McCarran Act.

For those participating in the peer review of fees, the risk of antitrust liability can be minimized by following rather simple guidelines:

1. *No anticompetitive purpose or intent.* The legitimate reasons for the peer-review process should be spelled out.
2. *Voluntary participation.* Physicians should not be threatened with sanctions for electing not to participate in the program or not to follow the peer-review panel's decision.
3. *Nonbinding decisions.* There should be no attempt to pressure or discriminate against physicians or payers who refuse to adhere to the review panel's decision with respect to fees.
4. *Nondissemination of decisions to other competing providers.* The panel's decisions or recommendations should be disclosed only to the parties involved in the proceeding. The concern is that if the fees the panel finds reasonable become known to area physicians generally, the physicians will then effectively adopt those amounts as their charges.[118]

Little antitrust concern arises where a payer contracts with an independent third-party firm to review its participating providers' charges and advise it

---

118. The most in-depth discussion of relevant factors in evaluating the lawfulness of fee peer-review programs is the FTC's advisory opinion to the Iowa Dental Association. Iowa Dental Ass'n, 99 F.T.C. 648 (1982). The federal enforcement agencies have issued a number of advisory opinions about such programs. *See* FTC Advisory Opinion to the American Medical Association (Feb. 14, 1994) (full-Commission advisory opinion approving peer-review program but disapproving sanctions for "fee gouging"), *at* http://www.ftc.gov/bc/adops/009.htm; FTC Staff Advisory Opinion to National Society of Plastic and Reconstructive Surgeons (Apr. 23, 1991), *reprinted in* 3 *HCAL*, supra p. 14 n.46, App. D30; FTC Staff Advisory Opinion to American Dental Association (Feb. 15, 1990), *reprinted in id.*, App. D28; FTC Staff Advisory Opinion to Passaic County Medical Society (Jan. 3, 1986) (refusing to approve medical society fee peer-review program because society members would be required to participate and be bound by panel's decision on fees), *reprinted in id.*, App. D19; FTC Staff Advisory Opinion to Tarrant County Medical Society (Jul. 12, 1984), *reprinted in id.*, App. D12; FTC Staff Advisory Opinion to American Podiatry Association (Aug. 18, 1983), *reprinted in id.*, App. D4; Antitrust Division Business Review Letter to International Chiropractors Association (Mar. 2, 1977), *reprinted in id.*, App. C3.

whether they are reasonable. These agreements raise no significant antitrust risk because there is no agreement among, or participation by, competitors in making this determination.[119] Concern could arise, however, where payers who contract with some of the same providers use (and especially if they agree to use) the same third-party firm to advise them about the reasonableness of their providers' fees because those prices could become fixed or stabilized.

6. Hospital Control of Hospital-Based Physician Pricing

Hospitals have sometimes attempted to control or affect the prices that their hospital-based physicians charge for their services by mandating those prices themselves or reserving the right to approve the physicians' fees or changes in their fees, or including provisions in hospital-based physician contracts with maximum prices or that require the physicians to charge prices that are "competitive" in the area. The purpose for these types of provisions is usually to prevent the physicians from exercising any market power that they might have. In several cases, physicians under such obligations have alleged that these types of restraints constitute unlawful vertical price-fixing agreements. The arrangements, however, are not vertical price-fixing agreements because the hospital is not selling the physicians any product or service and mandating that the physicians resell that product or service at a price established by the hospital.[120] Because hospital services and physician services are economic complements (that is, quantity demanded of one decreases as the price of the other increases), the hospital has an interest in ensuring that the physicians cannot exercise any market power they might have because their doing so could adversely affect the quantity of hospital services demanded.[121]

Some hospitals have contracts with hospital-based physician groups that obligate the physicians to participate in and accept fee levels provided in payer contracts agreed to by the hospital. Because these physician services are an integral part of the hospital's services to patients and other physicians, the

---

119. *See, e.g.*, Mitchael v. Intracorp, Inc., 179 F.3d 847 (10th Cir. 1999); Zinzer v. Rose, 868 F.2d 938 (7th Cir. 1989).
120. For a discussion of vertical price-fixing agreements, *see supra* p. 47.
121. *See, e.g.*, Konik v. Champlain Valley Physicians Hosp. Med. Ctr., 733 F.2d 1007, 1019 (2d Cir. 1984); Rockland Physician Assocs. v. Grodin, 616 F. Supp. 945 (S.D.N.Y. 1985); *see also* Arizona v. Maricopa County Med. Soc'y, 457 U.S. 332, 346-48 (1982).

arrangements may facilitate competition among hospitals. Courts have addressed such arrangements only infrequently and have applied the rule of reason because the hospital and physicians typically are not competitors in providing the physician services in question.[122] If a hospital uses two or more competing practice groups for such services, however, horizontal price-fixing concerns could arise if the hospital sets or coordinates their prices.

7. *Payer Control of Participating Provider Prices*

In a series of relatively old cases, where the payer, in its provider agreements with participating providers, prohibited the providers from balance billing or set the co-payment amounts the providers could charge their patients, providers challenged these restraints as unlawful vertical price-fixing agreements. Courts uniformly rejected these challenges, holding that the agreements were no more than contracts for the purchase of services between the payer and provider and that the restraints did not result in vertical price-fixing agreements because the providers did not purchase and resell a product or service from the payer.[123] The analysis and result may be different, however, where the payer is provider-controlled, and thus the agreement relating to prices may be horizontal rather than vertical.[124] In this situation, the analysis follows that explained before.[125]

C. Non-Price Joint Activities Among Competitors

Downward pressures on reimbursement from both governmental and com-

---

122. *See* Westchester Radiological Assocs. v. Empire Blue Cross & Blue Shield, 707 F. Supp. 708 (S.D.N.Y.) (rejecting a claim of unlawful use of monopsony power by Blue Cross plan to force hospitals to include radiology services in price for hospital services and accept reimbursement for both, thus lowering reimbursement for radiologists), *aff'd per curiam*, 884 F.2d 707 (2d Cir. 1989).

123. *See, e.g.*, Med. Arts Pharmacy, Inc. v. Blue Cross & Blue Shield, 675 F.2d 502 (2d Cir. 1982) (per curiam); Sausalito Pharmacy, Inc. v. Blue Shield, 1981-1 Trade Cas. (CCH) ¶ 63,885 (N.D. Cal. 1981), *aff'd per curiam*, 677 F.2d 47 (9th Cir. 1982); *see also* Kartell v. Blue Shield, 749 F.2d 922 (1st Cir. 1984) (upholding Blue Shield's prohibition of its participating physicians' balance-billing subscribers).

124. *See, e.g.*, Hahn v. Oregon Physicians' Serv., 868 F.2d 1022 (9th Cir. 1989).

125. *See supra* pp. 75-81.

mercial payers have forced health-care providers to seek ways to increase revenues and decrease costs. As a result, providers have faced tremendous competitive pressures, which in turn have led many individual and institutional health-care providers to integrate through consolidations, joint ventures, and other collaborative activities. These collaborative efforts may increase the providers' efficiencies and therefore be procompetitive. On the other hand, they may also give rise to antitrust liability when they foster price-fixing, group boycotts, market divisions, or market power. The antitrust enforcement agencies have encouraged the formation of procompetitive collaborative ventures[126] but have aggressively enforced the antitrust laws where health-care providers have collectively resisted efforts to reduce health-care costs through unlawful means. If properly structured and operated, legitimate joint activities among competitors can flourish in health-care markets.

1. Mergers[127]

The early and mid-1990s witnessed a wave of mergers among competing hospitals, a phenomenon that seemed to dissipate around 1998 or 1999.[128]

---

126. *See* Antitrust Division Business Review Letter to Marin General Hospital and Ross Hospital (Feb. 11, 1997) (opining that Antitrust Division would not challenge hospital joint venture to provide behavioral services), *at* http://www.usdoj.gov/atr/public/busreview/1044.htm; FTC Staff Advisory Opinion to Erlanger Medical Center and Memorial Hospital (May 31, 1995) (opining that FTC would not challenge hospital joint venture to provide obstetrical and gynecological services), *at* http://www.ftc.gov/ bc/adops/ erlang.htm. Both letters contain extensive analyses of the proposed joint ventures.

127. For a more in-depth discussion of mergers in the health-care sector, *see* ABA SECTION OF ANTITRUST LAW, HEALTH CARE MERGERS AND ACQUISITIONS HANDBOOK (2003).

128. *See generally* Alison E. Cuellar & Paul J. Gertler, *Trends in Hospital Consolidation: The Formation of Local Systems*, HEALTH AFFAIRS, Nov.–Dec. 2003, at 77, 78 [hereafter *Hospital Consolidation*] (noting that hospital mergers and acquisitions peaked at 310 in 1997 and fell to 132 in 2000); *see also By the Numbers*, MOD. HEALTHCARE, Dec. 22, 2003, at 4 (reporting that hospital merger and acquisition transactions fell from 110 in 1999 to 58 in 2002, and physician-practice transactions fell from 135 in 1999 to 36 in 2002).

During the 1990s, the Antitrust Division, FTC, and state attorneys general lost a series of litigated hospital-merger cases.[129] Since then, some concern has arisen that hospital mergers resulted in a number of hospital systems obtaining market power.[130] On the other hand, providers claim that the numerous mergers in the managed-care industry have resulted in managed-care plans obtaining market power as purchasers of the providers' services.[131]

---

129. FTC v. Tenet Health Care Corp., 186 F.3d 1045 (8th Cir. 1999); FTC v. Butterworth Health Corp., 121 F.3d 708 (6th Cir. 1997) (per curiam unpublished opinion reprinted at 1997-2 Trade Cas. (CCH) ¶ 71,683), *aff'g* 946 F. Supp. 1285 (W.D. Mich. 1996); United States v. Mercy Health Servs., 107 F.3d 632 (8th Cir. 1997), *vacating as moot and remanding with instructions to dismiss,* 902 F. Supp. 968 (N.D. Iowa 1995); FTC v. Freeman Hosp., 69 F.3d 260 (8th Cir. 1995); FTC v. Hosp. Bd., 38 F.3d 1184 (11th Cir. 1994); California v. Sutter Health Sys., 130 F. Supp. 2d 1109 (N.D. Cal. 2001) (amended opinion); United States v. Long Island Jewish Med. Ctr., 893 F. Supp. 121 (E.D.N.Y. 1997); Adventist Health Sys./West, 117 F.T.C. 224 (1994).

   Government losses in these cases were one catalyst for the FTC's establishing a merger litigation task force in August 2002 to, among other things, review the effects of consummated mergers. *See* Press Release, FTC, Federal Trade Commission Announces Formation of Merger Litigation Task Force (Aug. 28, 2002), *at* http://www.ftc.gov/opa/2002/08/mergerlitigation. htm; Mark Taylor, *Competitive Edge? FTC Task Force to Look into Mergers,* Competition, Mod. Healthcare, Sept. 2, 2002, at 10.

130. A number of studies issued together by the Blue Cross and Blue Shield Association in October 2002 concluded that hospital consolidations are a significant cause of higher hospital prices. *See, e.g.,* Joe Hay, et al., *Executive Summary: Hospital Cost in the U.S.* (Oct. 2002) (on file with editor). Popular business publications have made the same claim. *See, e.g.,* Joseph Weber, *The New Power Play in Health Care,* Bus. Week, Jan. 28, 2002, at 90; David Wessel, *After a Respite, the Health-Care Cost Spiral Resumes,* Wall St. J, May 9, 2002, at A2. A more recent study appears to reach the same conclusion. *Hospital Consolidation, supra* p. 107 n.128, at 78. In response to the Blue Cross reports, the American Hospital Association commissioned a report rebutting this conclusion. Margaret E. Guerin-Calvert, et al., *Economic Analysis of Healthcare Cost Studies Commissioned by Blue Cross Blue Shield Association* (2003) (on file with editor).

131. *See* American Medical Association, Competition in Health Insurance: A Comprehensive Study of U.S. Markets (2001) (on file with editor) (finding that markets for managed-care plans in many areas of the U.S. are highly concentrated); Donald Palmisano, President-Elect, American Medical Association, "Taking the Payer Side Seriously: Why the Federal Trade Commission Should Redi-

Relatively few mergers actually present competitive concerns. Nevertheless, both federal and state enforcement authorities have challenged hospital and other mergers in the health-care sector as violations of Section 7 of the Clayton Act (or Sections 1 or 2 of the Sherman Act).[132] The FTC, for example, has brought a number of actions challenging mergers among pharmaceutical manufacturers,[133] pharmaceutical wholesalers,[134] commercial laboratories,[135] and other providers of health-care products and services.[136] In several older actions, the Antitrust Division challenged several mergers of nursing-home chains.[137] While neither agency thus far has challenged any merger of physician practices, state attorneys general have challenged several,[138] and the Antitrust Division has issued business review letters threatening to challenge two such mergers.[139] In other business review letters discussing

---

rect Its Efforts in Health Care Antitrust Enforcement," Prepared Remarks Before the Federal Trade Commission Workshop on Health Care Competition Law and Policy (Sept. 9, 2002) (arguing that enforcement agencies should redirect antitrust efforts from providers to combat payer market power), *at* http://www.ftc.gov/ogc/healthcare/palmisano.pdf.

132. Most modern courts hold that the standards of analysis for mergers under Section 7 of the Clayton Act and Section 1 of the Sherman Act have become identical. *See, e.g.*, United States v. Rockford Mem'l Corp., 898 F.2d 1278, 1281 (7th Cir. 1990). For the requirements of a Section 2 violation, *see supra* pp. 34-41.

133. *E.g.*, Glaxo Wellcome PLC, Dkt. No. C-3990 (FTC Jan. 30, 2001) (consent order), *at* http://www.ftc.gov/os/2001/01/glaxosmithklinedo.pdf.

134. FTC v. Cardinal Health, Inc., 12 F. Supp. 2d 34 (D.D.C. 1998).

135. Quest Diagnostic, Inc., Dkt. No. C-4074 (FTC Apr. 8, 2003) (consent order), *at* http://www/ftc.gov/os/2003/04/questdo.pdf.

136. In addition, the FTC has urged at least one state attorney general to disapprove a hospital merger over which he had authority. FTC Staff Letter to the Attorney General of Louisiana (Apr. 1, 2003) (involving the proposed acquisition of Slidell Memorial Hospital by Tenet Healthcare Corp.), *at* http://www.ftc.gov/be/v030008.htm.

137. *E.g.*, United States v. Beverly Enters., 1984-1 Trade Cas. (CCH) ¶ 66,052 (M.D. Ga. 1984) (consent decree).

138. *E.g.*, Wisconsin v. Marshfield Clinic, 1997-1 Trade Cas. (CCH) ¶ 71,855 (W.D. Wis. 1997) (consent decree); Maine v. Me. Heart Surgical Assocs., P.A., 1996-2 Trade Cas. (CCH) ¶ 71,653 (Me. Sup. Ct. 1996) (consent decree).

139. Antitrust Division Business Review Letter to Gastroenterology Associates, Ltd., GI Associates, P.C., and Valley Gastroenterologists (Jul. 7, 1997), *at* http://www.usdoj.gov/atr/public/busreview/1178.htm; Antitrust Division

physician-practice mergers, however, the Antitrust Division has opined that it would not file a challenge.[140] To date, the Antitrust Division has also challenged one merger of managed-care organizations.[141]

The general antitrust analytical framework for analyzing mergers does not vary from industry to industry. Mergers are categorized as horizontal, vertical, or conglomerate depending upon the relationship, if any, of the merging parties. Vertical mergers raise antitrust issues only infrequently, where, for example, one of the merging firms sells a resource necessary for competitors of the other to compete effectively and the resource is difficult or impossible to obtain from other sources.[142] Horizontal mergers, the primary focus of Section 7, raise antitrust concern where (1) the merged entity will be able to exercise market power by itself, or (2) the merger results in a highly concentrated relevant market in which market participants likely will engage in tacit collusion with regard to competitively sensitive variables such as price. In either situation, it is reasonably probable that the transaction will lessen competition substantially.[143]

Business Review Letter to Danbury Surgical Associates (Aug. 28, 1987), *reprinted in* 3 *HCAL, supra* p. 14 n.47, App. C24.

140. Antitrust Division Business Review Letter to Orthopaedic Associates of Mobile, P.A., and Bone & Joint Center of Mobile (Apr. 16, 1997), *at* http://www.usdoj.gov/atr/public/busreview/1098.htm; Antitrust Division Business Review Letter to CVT Surgical Center and Surgery Associates of Baton Rouge (Apr. 16, 1997), *at* http://www.usdoj.gov/atr/public/busreview/1099.htm; Antitrust Division Business Review Letter to Terence L. Smith (Oct. 17, 1996) (merger of anesthesiology groups), *at* http://www.usdoj.gov/atr/ public/ busreview/0954.htm; Antitrust Division Business Review Letter to Pulmonary Associates, Ltd., and Albuquerque Pulmonary Consultants, P.A. (Oct. 31, 1994), *at* http://www.usdoj.gov/atr/public/busreview/pulmon.htm.

141. United States v. Aetna, Inc., 1999-2 Trade Cas. (CCH) ¶ 72,730 (N.D. Tex. 1999) (consent decree and competitive impact statement).

142. *See generally* U.S. Dep't of Justice, Merger Guidelines § 4.2 (1984), *reprinted in* 4 Trade Reg. Rep. (CCH) ¶ 13,103. These merger guidelines, the predecessor to the *1992 Merger Guidelines* that discuss only horizontal mergers, provide helpful guidance for the analysis of non-horizontal mergers.

143. *See 1992 Merger Guidelines, supra* p. 12 n.39, §§ 0.1, 2.1, 2.2; *see also* United States v. E.I. du Pont de Nemours & Co., 353 U.S. 586, 607 (1957) ("the test of a violation of § 7 is whether at the time of suit there is a reasonable probability that the acquisition is likely to result in the condemned restraints").

Although there are abundant merger opinions providing guidance,[144] the most important starting point in analyzing horizontal mergers is the *1992 Merger Guidelines*, last revised in 1997, which apply to mergers between both competing sellers and competing buyers.[145] The *1992 Merger Guidelines* provide for a five-step analysis, which generally follows the decisional law, to assess a horizontal merger's likely effect on competition. Briefly, that analysis involves a determination of (1) the definition and measurement of concentration of the relevant market in which the merging firms operate;[146] (2) the potential adverse competitive effects flowing from the merger;[147] (3) whether entry into the relevant market by new firms would be "timely, likely, and sufficient" to counteract any adverse effects of the merger on competition;[148] (4) whether the merger would result in "significant net efficiencies" not likely to be achieved absent the merger;[149] and (5) whether either merging party qualifies as a "failing firm."[150]

---

144. *See generally ALD V, supra* p. 9 n.23, at 315-68.

145. *1992 Merger Guidelines, supra* p. 12 n.39, § 0.1 (explaining that "[i]n order to assess potential monopsony concerns, the [enforcement agencies] will apply an analytical framework analogous to the framework of these Guidelines").

146. *Id.*, §§ 1.1-.5. The level of market concentration (that is, the number and relative sizes of firms in the market) is measured by the Herfindahl-Hirschman Index (HHI). *Id.* § 1.5. A relevant market's post-merger HHI is calculated by adding the market shares of the merging firms, squaring the market share of each firm in the relevant market, and adding the squares. The calculation can result in a number between almost zero (a perfectly competitive market) and 10,000 (a single-firm monopoly). The HHI increase resulting from the merger is calculated by multiplying the market shares of the merging firms by each other and then multiplying that product by two. According to the *1992 Merger Guidelines*, a merger resulting in a post-merger HHI of less than 1,000 presents no competitive concern because the market remains unconcentrated. The market is moderately concentrated if the post-merger HHI is between 1,000 and 1,800; in this situation, the merger warrants no further analysis if the increase in the HHI is 100 or less. If the merger results in a post-merger HHI above 1,800, the market is highly concentrated; further analysis is warranted if the merger increases the HHI by 50 points or more, and the agencies will presume the merger is anticompetitive if the increase is more than 100 points. *Id.* § 1.15.

147. *Id.* §§ 2.1-.2.

148. *Id.* §§ 3.2-.4.

149. *Id.* § 4.

150. *Id.* § 5.

More explicitly, the analysis of a hospital merger (or any merger) might require a 10-step analysis:

1. Definition of the relevant product market. In hospital-merger cases, courts have almost universally found (or the parties have stipulated) that the relevant product market is the cluster of acute-care inpatient services offered by general acute-care hospitals.[151] The relevant product market may be narrower in the case of a merger between competing specialty hospitals (for example, psychiatric hospitals) or where the competitive concern with a general acute-care hospital merger is limited to particular services the merging hospitals offer (for example, obstetrics).
2. Definition of the relevant geographic market. Thus far, courts have defined relatively broad relevant geographic markets in hospital-merger cases.[152]
3. Identification of competitors in the relevant market. Because the relevant product market for hospital-merger analysis usually includes only inpatient services, outpatient facilities are not normally deemed competitors.[153] They would be included if the effect on outpatient services from the merger were a competitive concern.
4. Calculation of the merged firm's post-merger market share based on licensed beds, staffed beds, patient days, admissions, and revenues.
5. Calculation of the post-merger level of market concentration and the increase in concentration resulting from the merger.
6. Comparison of the results in (4) and (5) to the benchmarks of the *1992 Merger Guidelines*. In general, agency challenges to hospital mergers

---

151. *E.g.*, FTC v. Tenet Health Care Corp., 186 F.3d 1045, 1051 (8th Cir. 1999) (parties stipulated that relevant product market was "delivery of primary and secondary inpatient hospital care services").
152. *E.g.*, United States v. Mercy Health Servs., 902 F. Supp. 968, 976-87 (N.D. Iowa 1995) (finding that market included hospitals from 70 to 100 miles from merging hospitals), *vacated as moot and remanded with instructions to dismiss*, 107 F.3d 632 (8th Cir. 1997).
153. *E.g.*, Am. Med. Int'l, 104 F.T.C. 1, 194 (1984). *But see* United States v. Carilion Health Sys., 707 F. Supp. 840, 844-45, 847 (W.D. Va.) (including outpatient providers in relevant market), *aff'd*, 892 F.2d 1042 (4th Cir. 1989) (per curiam unpublished opinion reprinted at 1989-2 Trade Cas. (CCH) ¶ 68,859).

have involved mergers resulting in post-merger market concentration and market shares substantially above the minimum levels that trigger concern under the *1992 Merger Guidelines.*

7. Assessment of entry and expansion barriers in the market. Especially in states with certificate-of-need regulation, entry barriers into hospital markets are usually considered high.[154]

8. Assessment of qualitative market-specific factors that would facilitate or inhibit interdependent, oligopolistic economic behavior or, in the language of the *1992 Merger Guidelines,* "coordinated interaction."[155]

9. Assessment of efficiency effects, if any, from the merger. Efficiency justifications have played a major role in hospital-merger litigation, but the courts have indicated that the benefits from the efficiencies must be passed on to consumers.[156] Moreover, the *1992 Merger Guidelines* set relatively stringent requirements for the claimed efficiencies to count in favor of the transaction.

10. Assessment of whether either merging firm is a "failing firm"[157] or "weakened competitor." A merging hospital's status as a "failing firm" is an absolute defense,[158] while its mere weakness as a competitor is simply one factor the court considers in determining the merger's likely effect on competition.[159]

Importantly, while sufficient quantitative evidence—high post-merger concentration and market share statistics—results in a rebuttable presumption

---

154. FTC v. Univ. Health, Inc., 938 F.2d 1206, 1219 (11th Cir. 1991) (explaining that "Georgia's [CON] law . . . is a substantial barrier to entry by new competitors and to expansion by existing ones").

155. *1992 Merger Guidelines, supra* p. 12 n.39, § 2.1.

156. *See Univ. Health,* 938 F.2d at 1223. For a helpful discussion of the role of efficiencies in hospital-merger analysis, *see* Debra A. Valentine, General Counsel, Federal Trade Commission, "Health Care Mergers: Will We Get the Efficiencies Claims Right?," Prepared Remarks Before the St. Louis University School of Law (Nov. 14, 1997), *at* http://www.ftc.gov/speeches/other/healthc2.htm.

157. For a discussion of the stringent requirements for "failing firm" status, *see 1992 Merger Guidelines, supra* p. 12 n.39, § 5.

158. *See* California v. Sutter Health Sys., 130 F. Supp. 2d 1109, 1133 (N.D. Cal. 2001) (sustaining the defense).

159. *See Univ. Health,* 938 F.2d at 1221.

of unlawfulness, or a prima facie case,[160] courts also place substantial emphasis on qualitative factors suggesting that the concentration and market-share statistics present an inaccurate prediction of the merger's future effect on competition.[161] In a sense, the quantitative evidence is used as a screen to determine if more in-depth analysis is warranted. Plaintiffs, in addition, need to tell a competitive story explaining how and why the merger is likely to lead to anticompetitive effects instead of merely relying on market share and concentration figures.

Statement 1 of the *Health Care Enforcement Statements* provides an antitrust safety zone for small hospital mergers. Under it, the federal enforcement agencies will not challenge, except in extraordinary circumstances, a hospital merger between two acute-care hospitals where, over the previous three years, one had fewer than 100 beds and an average daily inpatient census of fewer than 40 patients. According to Statement 1, the *1992 Horizontal Merger Guidelines* apply to all other hospital mergers.

Thus far, hospital-merger decisions have focused in large part on three issues: (1) definition of the relevant geographic market,[162] (2) the claimed efficiencies from the transaction,[163] and (3) the role that the nonprofit status of the merging hospitals should play in assessing the likely competitive effects of the transaction.[164] As to the first, courts have defined relevant geo-

---

160. *See, e.g.*, United States v. Long Island Jewish Med. Ctr., 983 F. Supp. 121, 136 (E.D.N.Y. 1997).

161. *See generally* United States v. General Dynamics Corp., 415 U.S. 486 (1974) (upholding merger resulting in high concentration because acquired firm lacked resources to remain a strong competitor and thus its current market share overstated its future competitive strength).

162. *See, e.g.*, FTC v. Tenet Health Care Corp., 186 F.3d 1045, 1052-54 (8th Cir. 1999); FTC v. Freeman Hosp., 69 F.3d 260, 264 (8th Cir. 1995); *Sutter Health Sys.*, 130 F. Supp. 2d at 1120-24; United States v. Mercy Health Servs., 902 F. Supp. 968, 980-81 (N.D. Iowa 1995), *vacated as moot with instructions to dismiss*, 107 F.3d 632 (8th Cir. 1997).

163. *See, e.g., Long Island Jewish Med. Ctr.*, 983 F. Supp. at 149; FTC v. Butterworth Health Corp., 946 F. Supp. 1285, 1300 (W.D. Mich. 1996), *aff'd per curiam*, 121 F.3d 708 (6th Cir. 1997) (unpublished opinion reprinted at 1997-2 Trade Cas. (CCH) ¶ 71,863).

164. *Compare* United States v. Carilion Health Sys., 707 F. Supp. 840, 846, 849 (W.D. Va. 1989) (emphasizing hospital's nonprofit status); *Butterworth Health Corp.*, 946 F. Supp. at 1297 (noting nonprofit status might deter hospital with market power from exercising it), *with* FTC v. Univ. Health, Inc., 938 F.2d 1206, 1224 (11th Cir. 1991) (explaining that Supreme Court has re-

graphic markets broadly, insisting that plaintiffs include not only hospitals that area patients currently use, but also those to which patients (or health plans) likely would turn if the merging hospitals, by themselves or with others in their service areas, attempted to raise their prices by a significant amount.[165] As to likely efficiencies from the transaction, courts, in general, have paid them more heed in hospital-merger cases than in other merger cases. Courts, however, have required that the benefits of the efficiencies be passed on to consumers for the efficiencies to count in favor of the transaction.[166] As to the hospitals' nonprofit status, courts, in general, have held that this factor is a relevant, but not determinative, factor in determining whether the hospitals would exercise market power after the merger.[167]

Although the federal enforcement agencies will always seek to block a merger they believe unlawful, state attorneys general may permit the merger to proceed if the merging parties (1) enter a consent decree requiring them to achieve the efficiencies from the merger they claim and (2) agree to relief constraining their competitive behavior.[168] The federal agencies reject these types of "conduct remedies," insisting instead on a "structural remedy" preventing the transaction or requiring divestiture. Private parties also have challenged hospital mergers.[169]

---

jected argument that nonprofit entities enjoy any implicit exemption from the antitrust laws); Hosp. Corp. of Am. v. FTC, 807 F.2d 1381, 1390 (7th Cir. 1986) ("no one has shown that [nonprofit status] makes the enterprise unwilling to cooperate to reduce competition").

165. *E.g.*, *Tenet Health Care Corp.*, 186 F.3d at 1052 (explaining that "the FTC must present evidence on the critical question of where consumers of hospital services could practicably turn for alternative services . . . . This evidence must address where consumers could practicably go, not on where they actually go.").

166. *E.g.*, United States v. Long Island Jewish Med. Ctr., 983 F. Supp. 121, 149 (E.D. N.Y. 1997).

167. *E.g., Butterworth Health Corp.*, 946 F. Supp. at 1297.

168. *See, e.g.*, Wisconsin v. Kenosha Hosp. & Med. Ctr., 1997-1 Trade Cas. (CCH) ¶ 71,669 (E.D. Wis. 1997). For an interesting "point-counterpoint" discussion about the appropriateness of this type of remedy, *see* Robert Langer, *State Attorneys General and Hospital Mergers*, ABA ANTITRUST HEALTH CARE CHRONICLE, Fall 1997; Carl S. Hisiro & Kevin J. O'Connor, *State Attorneys General and Hospital Mergers*, ABA ANTITRUST HEALTH CARE CHRONICLE, Winter 1997.

169. *E.g.*, Santa Cruz Med. Clinic v. Dominican Santa Cruz Hosp., 1995-2 Trade Cas. (CCH) ¶ 71,254 (N.D. Cal. 1995).

While the enforcement authorities thus far have focused primarily on hospital mergers, the agencies have investigated and challenged mergers in other health-care sector industries as well. For example, the Antitrust Division has challenged one merger of managed-care firms, alleging that the merger of the Aetna and Prudential health plans in two Texas metropolitan areas would generate anticompetitive effects in the markets for certain types of health plans and in the purchase of physician services.[170] Mergers of physician practices also may warrant scrutiny where the relevant market is concentrated and entry barriers are significant, although neither federal agency has challenged a physician-practice merger thus far. As noted before, the Antitrust Division has issued business review letters both approving and threatening to challenge such mergers.[171]

Acquisitions of physician practices by hospitals (or managed-care plans) are analyzed as vertical mergers, or as horizontal mergers if the hospital already employs physicians in the same medical specialties as the acquired physicians.[172] When analyzed as a vertical merger, the competitive effect of potential concern occurs in the relevant product market for hospital services rather than in the relevant market for the physicians' services; the primary question is whether the acquisition forecloses such a large percentage of all patients in the relevant market to other hospitals that they are unable to constrain the competitive behavior of the hospital acquiring the physician practices.[173] For this to occur, the acquired practices must control a significant percentage of all patient referrals for hospital services in the relevant market, and the acquisition must provide the hospital with significant market power in the market for hospital services because of its foreclosure effect on other hospitals in the market.

When hospitals or physician practices purport to merge, it is important that they implement a form of transaction that will result in the creation of a single entity rather than merely a joint venture (as discussed in the next section) or mere cartel—that is, they must totally integrate rather than partially integrate. A number of hospitals, for example, have implemented so-called

---

170. United States v. Aetna, Inc., 1999-2 Trade Cas. (CCH) ¶ 72,730 (N.D. Tex. 1999) (consent decree and competitive impact statement).
171. *See supra* p. 109-10 and nn.139, 140.
172. *See generally* HTI Health Servs., Inc. v. Quorum Health Group, Inc., 960 F. Supp. 1104, 1112 n.4 (S.D. Miss. 1997).
173. *Id.* at 1112 n.4, 1114.

"virtual mergers," in which the hospitals do not merge their assets and each retains certain "reserved powers" over its facilities.[174] Depending on the degree of actual integration and other factors, these transactions may or may not result in a single entity for antitrust purposes. If the transaction does not result in a single entity, then Section 1 of the Sherman Act applies to the hospitals' activities through the new organization. For example, in *New York v. St. Francis Hospital*,[175] the New York attorney general successfully challenged the joint-negotiation and market-allocation activities of a purported virtual merger of two hospitals as per se violations of Section 1. There, although the hospitals had intended to integrate their operations through the new organization, it appears they never actually did so. In the *Susquehanna Health System* decision, on the other hand, where the hospitals participating in an alliance integrated their operations almost completely, the court held that they constituted a single entity.[176]

The same issue can arise when physicians purportedly "merge" their practices, but the transaction results in little actual practice integration and is more of an office-sharing arrangement than a merger. This can occur, for

---

174. For discussions of the antitrust ramifications of virtual mergers, *see* Mark J. Botti, Assistant Chief, Litigation II Section, Antitrust Division, "Virtual Mergers of Hospitals: When Does the *Per Se* Rule Apply?," Prepared Remarks Before the American Health Lawyers Association Antitrust in the Health Care Field Seminar (Feb. 14, 2000), *reprinted in* 3 *HCAL, supra* p. 14 n.47, App. E83; John J. Miles, "A Conceptual and Practical Approach to the Antitrust Analysis of Virtual Mergers," Prepared Remarks Before the American Health Lawyers Association Antitrust in the Health Care Field Seminar (Feb. 14, 2000) (on file with editor); Roxane C. Busey, "Antitrust Aspects of 'Virtual Mergers' and Affiliations," Prepared Remarks Before the Northwestern University Health Care Antitrust Forum (Oct. 21, 1999) (on file with editor).
175. 94 F. Supp. 2d 399 (S.D.N.Y. 1999).
176. HealthAm. Pa., Inc. v. Susquehanna Health Sys., 278 F. Supp. 2d 423 (M.D. Pa. 2003). For a helpful analysis of the *Susquehanna* decision, *see* Robert W. McCann, *I Think (I Am Integrated), Therefore I Am: Joint Operating Agreements and the* Susquehanna *Decision,* Health L. Rep. (BNA), Sept. 18, 2003, at 1449. For particularly helpful discussions, outside the health-care context, of the variables that courts consider in making the single-entity determination, *see* Freeman v. San Diego Ass'n of Realtors, 322 F.3d 1133, 1147-50 (9th Cir.), *cert. denied,* 124 S.Ct. 355 (2003); Fraser v. Major League Soccer, L.L.C., 284 F.3d 47, 55-60 (1st Cir. 2002) (holding that league was not a single entity).

example, where separate physician practice groups, while retaining their independent organizations, form a larger organization with the separate practice organizations as members (often a limited-liability company with relatively little authority over the operations of the individual practice organizations).[177] Where the larger organization then negotiates payer contracts on behalf of the members, a per se violation of Section 1 can result.[178]

Finally, Section 7A of the Clayton Act,[179] the Hart-Scott-Rodino premerger notification provisions, requires parties to certain large acquisition transactions to notify the FTC and Department of Justice of the transaction and to wait 30 days for the agencies to review it before the transaction may be consummated. In general, the parties must report the merger if (1) the acquiring party will hold, in the aggregate, more than $200 million of the acquired firm's voting securities and assets, or (2) the acquiring firm would hold more than $50 million but not more than $200 million of such securities and assets, and one party to the transaction has annual net sales or total assets of $100 million or more and the other party has sales or assets of $10 million or more.[180]

---

177. *See* Surgical Specialists, Dkt. No. C-4101 (FTC Nov. 14, 2003) (consent order) (enforcement action against Yakima, Washington, physician limited liability company alleging unlawful concerted negotiations of price with payer by three medical groups that, according to the complaint, "did not . . . want to combine or integrate their practices"), *at* http://www.ftc.gov/05/ 2003/09/surgicalemp.pdf.
178. *See supra* pp. 67-75, (discussing joint negotiations by provider networks). The joint negotiations in *Surgical Specialists* led not only to an FTC enforcement action, but also to suits by the state attorney general, a class of purchasers, and a former member of the group. *See* Press Release, Washington State Office of Attorney General, Yakima Physicians Barred from Jointly Negotiating Reimbursement Rates (Sept. 9, 2003), *at* http:// www.atg.wa.gov/releases/rel_ssy_09240.html.
179. 15 U.S.C. § 18a.
180. Civil penalties for violations of the premerger notification requirements can be substantial. *See, e.g.,* United States v. Gemstar-TV Guide Int'l, Inc., 2003-2 Trade Cas. (CCH) ¶ 74,082 (D.D.C. 2003) (consent decree) (assessing $5.7 million civil penalty for violation of § 7A). To prevent a violation of Section 7A and possibly Section 1 of the Sherman Act for "gun jumping," parties to a proposed merger should take care not to coordinate their competitive activities prior to the expiration of Section 7A's waiting period and consummation of the transaction. *See* United States v. Computer Assocs. Int'l, Inc., 2002-2 Trade Cas. (CCH) ¶ 73,883 (D.D.C. 2002)

2. Joint Ventures

Hospitals or other health-care providers may enter into joint-venture arrangements to operate specific facilities or equipment, to provide certain services together, and for many other purposes. Common hospital joint ventures include those for group purchasing, shared services, ambulatory care facilities, ancillary services, long-term care facilities, imaging centers, breast cancer screening clinics, durable medical equipment, and home-health services. In addition, physicians have formed joint ventures to provide services or goods complementary or functionally related to their own professional services. Physicians also have established joint ventures to provide ancillary products and services to their patients.[181]

Joint ventures are "combinations" of the participants and thus meet the concerted-action requirement of Section 1 of the Sherman Act. Joint ventures among competitors often raise the question of whether the arrangement is a legitimate joint venture whose purpose and effect is likely to be procompetitive by generating efficiencies in the delivery of its products or services, creating a new product, or facilitating entry into a new market, or whether the combination is little more than a cartel whose purpose and likely effect is anticompetitive. The answer to this question depends primarily on the purpose for the venture, the extent of integration in and efficiencies from the venture (for example, production of a new or better product or service, or production of products or services the parties already produce at a lower average cost), whether the parties continue to compete against one another, and the venture's market power. In a true joint venture, the venturers typically pool their capital, integrate particular operations, and share the economic risk of profit or loss.[182]

Joint ventures can take many forms, serve many purposes, and involve parties in different economic relationships. They can engage in research and development, production, marketing, and distribution. They can focus on producing or obtaining an input used by the venturers (a group-purchasing pro-

---

(consent decree and competitive impact statement) ($638,000 civil penalty for "gun jumping" in violation of both § 7A and § 1).

For helpful advice on premerger notification filings, *see* ABA SECTION OF ANTITRUST LAW, PREMERGER NOTIFICATION MANUAL (3d ed. 2003).

181. *See, e.g.*, Home Oxygen & Med. Equip. Co., 122 F.T.C. 278 (1994) (consent order) (joint ventures among pulmonologists to provide home oxygen).

182. *E.g.*, Arizona v. Maricopa County Med. Soc'y, 457 U.S. 332, 356 (1982).

gram, for example) or on producing an output (a joint venture to provide magnetic resonance imaging services, for example). Joint ventures can consist of competitors, parties in a vertical relationship, or parties in a conglomerate relationship. They may produce and sell products or services the joint venturers already produce and sell individually, or they might provide a new product or service (or the same product or service in a new geographic market) that none of the venturers currently provide or could provide individually. Although, given all these variables, generalizations are both difficult and dangerous, joint ventures likely to raise the most serious antitrust concerns are those among competitors to market products or services that they already sell individually. This is not to suggest, however, that other joint ventures do not warrant careful antitrust scrutiny, depending on the circumstances.

Every joint venture should be analyzed from two perspectives: (1) its formation and (2) its operation or conduct. The formation of a joint venture is usually evaluated under Section 7 of the Clayton Act, which prohibits anticompetitive acquisitions, to determine whether it likely will substantially lessen competition.[183] As in the case of mergers, the questions are whether the joint venture will be able to exercise market power by itself or whether the relevant market in which the venture operates will be sufficiently concentrated that the venture and its competitors likely will engage in tacit collusion. The Department of Justice and FTC *1992 Horizontal Merger Guidelines* are helpful in the assessment of joint-venture formation. Another essential resource is the *Collaboration Guidelines*,[184] which integrate the antitrust analysis of a joint venture's formation and its subsequent operation.

Even where there is no current horizontal or vertical relationship among the venturers, antitrust concern about the venture's formation may arise when one of the venturers currently produces the product or service the venture will produce, the market for that product or service is highly concentrated, and, but for participating in the venture, other venturers would have entered that market individually and reduced the level of market concentration.[185]

---

183. *See* United States v. Penn-Olin Chem. Co., 378 U.S. 158 (1964) (applying § 7 to joint venture). The formation of joint ventures, like mergers and acquisitions, can be subject to the premerger reporting requirements of Section 7A of the Clayton Act if the parties and the transaction are sufficiently large to meet the Act's reporting thresholds.

184. *Collaboration Guidelines, supra* p. 12 n.40.

185. For a discussion of this "potential competition" theory, *see ALD V, supra* p. 9 n.23, at 354-61.

Because the joint venture is a combination among its venturers who are separate entities for purposes of antitrust analysis,[186] its operations must be evaluated under Section 1 of the Sherman Act. Although rule-of-reason analysis typically is applied to all aspects of the joint venture, courts will not hesitate to treat as per se unlawful any operational aspect of the joint venture's conduct that falls within the parameters of the per se rule, such as horizontal price-fixing[187] or market-allocation agreements,[188] unless they are ancillary restrictions reasonably necessary for the venture's efficient operation and carefully limited in their implementation, scope, and effect.[189]

Physician joint ventures formed to provide medical services different from, but related to, the physicians' own medical services (sometimes referred to as "physician ancillary joint ventures")[190] also can pose antitrust risks. For example, such a joint venture might be formed by a group of physicians to provide clinical laboratory, physical therapy, outpatient diagnostic imaging, or specialty hospital services to which the investing physicians refer their patients and provide services through the venture. The FTC has closely examined these types of "self-referral" joint ventures where they allegedly resulted in the ventures' obtaining market power because the physicians controlled a large percentage of referrals for the type of service the venture provides.[191] In addition, physicians in separate practices participating

---

186. *See, e.g.,* NCAA v. Bd. of Regents, 468 U.S. 85, 99 (1984).

187. *E.g., Maricopa,* 457 U.S. at 344-48.

188. Gen. Leaseways, Inc. v. Nat'l Truck Leasing Ass'n, 744 F.2d 588 (7th Cir. 1984).

189. *See Collaboration Guidelines, supra* p. 12 n.40, §§ 3.2, 3.36(b); Augusta News Co. v. Hudson News Co., 269 F.3d 41, 48 (1st Cir. 2001); Addamax Corp. v. Open Software Found., Inc., 152 F.3d 48, 51-52 (1st Cir. 1998) (explaining that ancillary restraints in joint ventures are those that are "legitimately related" to the joint venture's efforts and are judged under the rule of reason); Rozema v. Marshfield Clinic, 977 F. Supp. 1362, 1374 (W.D. Wis. 1997) (where the agreement "contributes to productivity through integrated efforts, the Rule of Reason is the norm").

190. *See generally* Kevin J. Arquitt, Director, Bureau of Competition, Federal Trade Commission, "A New Concern in Health Care Antitrust Enforcement: Acquisition and Exercise of Market Power by Physician Ancillary Joint Ventures," Prepared Remarks Before the National Health Lawyers Association Antitrust in the Healthcare Field Seminar (Jan. 30, 1992) (on file with editor).

191. *See, e.g.,* Homecare Oxygen & Med. Equip. Co., 118 F.T.C. 706 (1994) (consent order).

in such joint ventures must ensure that their venture does not become a vehicle through which they fix the prices for their professional services.[192]

The Department of Justice and FTC 1996 *Health Care Enforcement Statements* discuss several types of health-care provider joint ventures: (1) hospital joint ventures for high-technology and other expensive equipment (Statement 2); (2) hospital joint ventures for specialized clinical or other expensive health-care services (Statement 3); (3) joint-purchasing arrangements (Statement 7); (4) physician network joint ventures (Statement 8); and (5) multiprovider networks (Statement 9).[193]

For hospital joint ventures involving high-technology and other expensive equipment, Statement 2 provides an antitrust safety zone for those that include only the number of hospitals whose participation is needed to support the equipment.[194] For example, if two hospitals cannot each recover the cost of individually purchasing MRI equipment over its useful life, they may join together with a third hospital that likewise could not have supported the MRI over its life. However, if the third hospital could have independently purchased, operated, and marketed the MRI equipment services, its participation would negate safety-zone protection. A hospital is considered able to "support" high-technology or other expensive equipment if it could recover the costs of owning, operating, and marketing the equipment and its services over its useful life.[195]

If the joint venture for this type of equipment falls outside the safety zone, then traditional rule-of-reason analysis applies if "the joint venture arrangement is not one that uses the joint venture label but is likely merely to restrict competition and decrease output."[196] This requires (1) definition of the relevant market; (2) assessment of competitive effects by, for example, examining the market structure for the venture's product or service; (3) evaluation of the venture's efficiencies; and (4) examination of any collateral or

---

192. *See* Urological Stone Surgeons, Inc., 125 F.T.C. 513 (1998) (challenging a price-fixing agreement for their professional services among urologists participating in a lithotripsy joint venture).
193. For discussion of the Statement 8 and 9 joint ventures, *see supra* pp. 85-91.
194. Statement 2 carefully notes, however, that the antitrust safety zone applies only to agreements among the venturers that are "reasonably necessary to the venture." *Health Care Enforcement Statements, supra* p. 12 n.41, Statement 2 n.4.
195. *Id.* Statement 2 n.2.
196. *Id.* at n.5.

purportedly ancillary agreements that may restrain competition but are unnecessary to the venture's efficient operation.[197]

Statement 3 of the *Health Care Enforcement Statements*, discussing hospital joint ventures to provide specialized clinical or other expensive health-care services (such as a center of excellence for cancer treatment), contains no antitrust safety zone. It does provide for evaluation under the rule of reason as long as the venture is not a sham hiding a horizontal market-allocation agreement with little or no integration.[198] The steps in the analysis are the same as in rule-of-reason examination under Statement 2.

3. Agreements Allocating Services

Agreements among actual or potential competitors to divide or allocate among themselves the products or services they offer or the geographic areas or customers they serve, absent integration, are per se unlawful under Section 1 of the Sherman Act.[199] That principle applies in health-care antitrust cases as in others.[200] Indeed, market-allocation agreements arguably have greater anticompetitive effect than price-fixing agreements because they prevent competition with respect to all competitive variables, not just price.

Statement 3 of the *Health Care Enforcement Statements* addresses situations in which hospitals provide highly specialized clinical services jointly. To the extent that they agree to do so and not to provide the services individually, a type of horizontal market-allocation agreement results. This type of joint venture, however, is not usually per se unlawful because of the substantial efficiencies that the joint venture may generate. Statement 3 warns, however, that if the hospitals enter into such an arrangement without the requisite economic integration (sometimes referred to as a "sham" joint venture), a per se unlawful market-allocation agreement might result.

---

197. For a more detailed discussion of the analysis the agencies would undertake under the rule of reason, *see Collaboration Guidelines, supra* p. 12 n.40, §§ 3.3-3.37.
198. *Health Care Enforcement Statements, supra* p. 12 n.41, Statement 3 n.9.
199. *See supra* p. 44; *see generally* Palmer v. BRG of Ga., 498 U.S. 46 (1990).
200. *See* Blue Cross & Blue Shield United v. Marshfield Clinic, 65 F.3d 1406, 1415-16 (7th Cir. 1995) (finding that clinic engaged in per se unlawful market allocation through agreements with an HMO and its affiliated physicians).

Market-allocation agreements among competing hospitals as to the services they will and will not offer used to be a common phenomenon, particularly prior to repeal in 1986 of the National Health Planning and Resources Development Act of 1974—the federal health-planning act. Now, hospitals should avoid such agreements unless they are ancillary to a bona fide joint venture that generates substantial efficiencies in the delivery of the affected services.[201]

4. Joint Purchasing

Joint purchasing of materials or services by health-care entities, particularly by group-purchasing organizations, is a common activity that can generate substantial efficiencies by lowering the purchasers' costs of inputs. Thus, they are usually judged under the rule of reason.[202] Group-purchasing organizations can be an efficient form of joint venture providing a procompetitive response to marketplace forces demanding more effective cost containment.[203] If not properly structured and operated, however, joint-purchasing arrangements may be challenged by actual or potential suppliers of the group as price-fixing arrangements, group boycotts, attempts to monopolize (or to monopsonize), or unlawful exclusive dealing arrangements.[204]

---

201. *See, e.g.*, FTC Staff Advisory Opinion to Wichita, Kansas, Chamber of Commerce (May 22, 1991) (advising that agreement among area hospitals to collectively allocate services, equipment, or facilities among themselves would constitute a per se violation of § 1), *reprinted in* 3 *HCAL*, p. 14 n.47, App. D29; Antitrust Division Business Review Letter to Westlake Health Campus Association (Aug. 27, 1980), *reprinted in id.*, App. C10.

202. *See, e.g.*, Addamax Corp. v. Open Software Found., Inc., 888 F. Supp. 274, 282 (D. Mass. 1995) (explaining that "[b]ecause joint purchasing agreements often produce legitimate economies of scale, courts have generally refused to find these agreements illegal under the *per se* standard"), *aff'd*, 152 F.3d 48 (1st Cir. 1998).

203. Northwest Wholesale Stationers, Inc. v. Pac. Stationery & Printing Co., 472 U.S. 284, 295 (1985); *see also* White & White, Inc. v. Am. Hosp. Supply Corp., 540 F. Supp. 951 (W.D. Mich. 1982), *rev'd on other grounds*, 723 F.2d 495 (6th Cir. 1983); *see generally* Kathryn M. Fenton, *Antitrust Implications of Joint Efforts by Third Party Payors to Reduce Costs and Improve the Quality of Health Care*, 61 Antitrust L.J. 17, 35-37 (1992).

204. *See, e.g.*, *Northwest Wholesale Stationers*, 472 U.S. at 288 (group boycott); *White & White*, 540 F. Supp. at 1027-29 (unlawful exclusive dealing agree-

Perhaps the five most common antitrust questions about group-purchasing programs are (1) whether the program results in an unlawful price-fixing agreement among participating purchasers; (2) whether the program provides the participants with monopsony power as purchasers of the products or services purchased through the program; (3) whether the program may facilitate the stabilization of prices at which the participants sell their own products or services; (4) whether an agreement among participants to exclude their competitors in the output market from participation in the program constitutes an unlawful group boycott; and (5) whether the exclusive dealing or "sole source" supply contracts entered into by some group-purchasing programs with their vendors are unlawful.[205]

1. *Buyer price-fixing.* Frequently, group-purchasing programs result in a form of horizontal price-fixing agreement because the program acts as the participants' agent in negotiating purchase prices with vendors. The Supreme Court and other courts have held that naked price-fixing agreements among competing purchasers, just like those among competing sellers, are per se unlawful.[206] Most group-purchasing programs, however, probably involve sufficient integration of the purchasing and distribution functions so that their price-fixing activities with regard to purchase prices are analyzed under the

---

ment); Langston Corp. v. Standard Register Co., 553 F. Supp. 632 (N.D. Ga. 1982) (same); Antitrust Division Business Review Letter to Ohio Hospital Purchasing Consortium (June 9, 1982), *reprinted in* 3 *HCAL, supra* p. 14 n.47, App. C13; FTC Staff Advisory Opinion to Louisiana Health Care Association (Apr. 23, 1982) (price-fixing and monopsonization), *reprinted in id.,* App. D2.

205. The antitrust theories applicable to group-purchasing organizations or programs can depend on the organization's structure and organization, particularly whether its activities are controlled by its purchaser-members. If so, its activities result from agreements subject to Section 1 of the Sherman Act, just as the activities of provider-controlled contracting networks, discussed *supra* at pp. 85-91, do.

206. *See, e.g.,* Mandeville Island Farms, Inc. v. Am. Crystal Sugar Co., 334 U.S. 219 (1948); *see also* Todd v. Exxon Corp., 275 F.3d 191, 201 (2d Cir. 2001) (dicta).

rule of reason and thus are unlawful only if the group has significant monopsony power in the affected relevant markets.[207]

2. *Monopsony power.* In determining whether a group-purchasing program may have monopsony power, the first step is to define the relevant market. In the case of many group-purchasing programs for many supplies, the relevant geographic markets for the products they purchase might be regional or national because many vendors operate on a regional or national basis and can turn to more distant areas over a wide geographic area to make sales. Although a number of variables require examination, the most important is the purchasers' aggregate market share of purchases in the relevant market. A significant market share, probably at least 30 percent, is a necessary, but not sufficient, condition for monopsony power to exist. The possible monopsony power of group-purchasing programs is one of the concerns addressed by Statement 7 of the *Health Care Enforcement Statements,* entitled "Joint Purchasing Arrangements Among Health Care Providers."

3. *Output market price stabilization.* Price stabilization in the output market can be a concern if the participants in the group-purchasing program are competitors in the market for their outputs (hospital services, for example), and the price of the input purchased through the program constitutes a significant percentage of the cost of their output. In this situation, it becomes easier for the participants to collude tacitly with respect to their output prices. This concern is another addressed by Statement 7.

4. *Exclusion of competitors.* Exclusion of their competitors from the program by program purchaser-members is an issue the Supreme Court addressed explicitly in *Northwest Wholesale Stationers,* holding that while the agreement to exclude a competitor from a group-purchasing program might constitute a group boycott, the boycott is not per se unlawful unless, at a minimum, the boycotting parties together have a substantial degree of market power or their excluded competitor needs access to the program to compete against them effectively.[208]

---

207. *Cf. Northwest Wholesale Stationers,* 472 U.S. at 295 (discussing efficiencies from group-purchasing programs in the context of a group-boycott claim).

208. *Id.* at 296-97.

5. *Exclusive dealing.* Exclusive dealing and sole-source contracts between the group-purchasing organization and selected vendors, which foreclose competing vendors from the program members' purchases, are analyzed under the traditional exclusive-dealing antitrust framework.[209] Many group-purchasing programs are "preferred-provider"-type programs that do not require their participants to purchase through the program, and this characteristic significantly decreases the probability of any significant anticompetitive effect. Nevertheless, based on complaints from vendors who claim to have been excluded from such programs, Congress, in April 2002, asked the Antitrust Division and FTC to reexamine their health-care antitrust guidelines, discussed next, regarding group-purchasing programs.[210]

The Antitrust Division and FTC explain, in Statement 7 of their *Health Care Enforcement Statements*, that most joint-purchasing arrangements among hospitals or other health-care providers do not raise antitrust concerns. Through joint purchasing, the participants frequently can obtain volume discounts, reduce transaction costs, and obtain consulting advice that may not be available to each participant individually.

Statement 7 establishes an antitrust safety zone for group-purchasing arrangements where (1) the participants' purchases account for less than 35 percent of the total sales of the purchased product or service in the relevant market, and (2) the cost of the products and services purchased jointly ac-

---

209. *See, e.g., White & White*, 723 F.2d at 500; *see generally* Simmons, *supra* p. 99 n.101, at 2.

210. Letter from Senate Judiciary Subcommittee on Antitrust, Business Rights, and Competition to Charles A. James, Assistant Attorney General, Antitrust Division, and Timothy J. Muris, Chairman, Federal Trade Commission (Apr. 30, 2002), *reprinted in* 4 HCAL, *supra* p. 14 n.47, App. E107; *see also Kohl Seeks Tighter GPO Controls,* MOD. HEALTHCARE, Oct. 27, 2003, at 3 (noting Senate Judiciary request to FTC and Antitrust Division to reexamine policy guidelines on group purchasing).

Situations also arise when the group produces the input rather than merely purchasing it. The basic analysis of the two situations is the same. For an example of the analysis of this type of input-production joint venture, *see* Sewell Plastics, Inc. v. Coca-Cola Co., 720 F. Supp. 1196 (W.D.N.C. 1989), *aff'd without published op.*, 912 F.2d 463 (4th Cir. 1990) (opinion reprinted at 1990-2 Trade Cas. (CCH) ¶ 69,165).

counts for less than 20 percent of the total revenues from all products or services sold by each participant. The first requirement relates to the question of the group's monopsony power, the second to the question of whether the purchasers' output prices might be adversely affected through tacit collusion.

A group-purchasing arrangement need not fall within the safety zone to be lawful. Statement 7 explains that in addition to the above, the following factors are relevant in determining whether the program raises antitrust concerns:

1. Whether the participants are required to use the group-purchasing arrangement for all their purchases. If so, the antitrust risk is greater than in programs that do not require exclusivity. Members can be asked to commit to purchase a specified amount through the arrangement so that a volume discount or other favorable contract can be negotiated.
2. Whether an independent employee or agent conducts negotiations on behalf of the participants. Use of an outside, independent party lowers the antitrust risk that participants will use the group as a vehicle for discussing and coordinating prices of the health-care services they offer.
3. Whether communications between the purchasing group and individual participants are kept confidential and not discussed with other participants. This also lessens the likelihood of anticompetitive communications among the participants.
4. Whether other group-purchasing arrangements exist in the market. If so, the risk of group monopsony power is lower than otherwise, as is the risk from excluding a competitor from the arrangement, because the excluded party has other alternatives and entry by new purchasing groups may be easy.

5. *Professional Associations*

Professional associations, such as medical societies, are normally treated as combinations of their members for purposes of the antitrust laws, and thus their actions are subject to Section 1 of the Sherman Act.[211] Moreover, many

---

211. *E.g.*, DM Research, Inc. v. Coll. of Am. Pathologists, 170 F.3d 53, 57 (1st Cir. 1999) ("Such organizations may . . . operate essentially as a means of

of their activities have the potential to restrain competition, including activities directly affecting the fees of their members, ethical restraints on advertising and solicitation, membership requirements, quality standards, and other ethical rules.

In general, the courts have treated the activities of professional associations—particularly those that might affect the quality of care rendered by members—leniently, applying rule-of-reason analysis to professional activities other than those with clear anticompetitive effects and no plausible procompetitive justification. One reason for this may be the Supreme Court's suggestion in *Goldfarb v. Virginia State Bar* that the public-service aspect of some professions might "require that a particular practice, which could properly be viewed as a violation of the Sherman Act in another context, be treated differently."[212] Moreover, some activities of professionals or their associations may not constitute commercial conduct and thus not be subject to the antitrust laws. There is, however, no "learned professions" exemption

---

coordinating the actions of their independent members; and in some cases have been viewed as the joint actions of the members."); Cal. Dental Ass'n v. FTC, 128 F.3d 720, 728 (9th Cir. 1997) ("Professional associations are 'routinely treated as continuing conspiracies of their members'"), *remanded on other grounds*, 526 U.S. 756 (1999). *But cf.* Viazis v. Am. Ass'n of Orthodontists, 314 F.3d 758, 764 (5th Cir. 2002) ("Despite the fact that '[a] trade association by its nature involves collective action by competitors[,] . . . [it] is not by its nature a walking conspiracy, its every denial of some benefit amounting to an unreasonable restraint of trade.'").

That an association is a combination of its members does not mean, however, that all its members are liable if the association commits an antitrust violation. *See, e.g.*, AD/SAT v. Associated Press, 181 F.3d 216, 234 (2d Cir. 1999) ("There must . . . be some evidence of actual knowledge of, *and participation in*, the illegal scheme in order to establish a violation of the antitrust laws by a particular association member"); Nat'l Camp Ass'n, Inc. v. Am. Camping Ass'n, Inc., 2001-1 Trade Cas. (CCH) ¶ 73,130, at 89,385 (S.D.N.Y. 2000) (explaining that plaintiff must adduce evidence that association members, in their individual capacities, consciously committed themselves to the conspiracy).

212. 421 U.S. 773, 788 n.17 (1975); *see also* United States v. Ore. State Med. Soc'y, 343 U.S. 326, 336 (1951) (explaining that the "historic direct relationship between patient and physician" may be quite different from "the usual considerations prevailing in ordinary commercial matters" and that "forms of competition usual in the business world may be demoralizing to the ethical standards of a profession").

from the antitrust laws,[213] and courts have not hesitated to apply the per se rule or an abbreviated version of the rule of reason where appropriate.[214] Even if the association is a nonprofit entity, the FTC has jurisdiction over it under Section 5 of the FTC Act if it confers economic benefits on its members, as most professional associations do.[215]

Naked price-fixing agreements among competing professionals, whether resulting from association activities[216] or outside the association,[217] clearly are per se unlawful[218] and may be prosecuted criminally. The same is true of naked product, geographic, or customer market-allocation agreements.[219]

On the other hand, the rule of reason applies to most other professional association activity that might restrain competition, at least where there is a plausible procompetitive or quality-of-care justification for it. In *California Dental Association v. Federal Trade Commission*,[220] for example, the Supreme Court rejected application of the per se rule to both the association's price-related and nonprice constraints on its members' advertising. It even went further and held that the quick-look standard applied by the FTC and then the circuit court of appeals was too quick, remanding the case for a more in-depth analysis of the association's procompetitive justifications for the restraints. On remand, after a more thorough examination of the association's proffered justifications, the court held that the FTC had failed to prove that, on balance, the restrictions were unreasonably anticompetitive.[221]

Challenges to restrictions on advertising by professionals have long been a major enforcement focus of the FTC.[222] Another subject of enforcement interest has been ethical restraints limiting the form in which professionals

---

213. *E.g.*, Wilk v. Am. Med. Ass'n, 719 F.2d 207, 221 (7th Cir. 1983).
214. *E.g.*, FTC v. Ind. Fed'n of Dentists, 476 U.S. 447 (1986).
215. *See supra* p. 49-50.
216. *See* United States v. Lake Country Optometric Soc'y, No. W95CR114 (W.D. Tex., Jul. 9, 1996) (guilty plea for fixing price of eye exams; $75,000 fine and five-year probation), *summarized at* [1988-1996 Transfer Binder] Trade Reg. Rep. (CCH) ¶ 45,095, at 44,781.
217. *See* United States v. A. Lanoy Alston, D.M.D., P.C., 974 F.2d 1206 (9th Cir. 1992) (agreement among dentists about acceptable co-payment amounts).
218. *See, e.g.*, Arizona v. Maricopa County Med. Soc'y, 457 U.S. 332 (1982).
219. *Cf.* Blackburn v. Sweeney, 53 F.3d 825 (7th Cir. 1995) (applying per se rule to customer-allocation agreement between law firms).
220. 526 U.S. 756 (1999).
221. Cal. Dental Ass'n v. FTC, 224 F.3d 942 (9th Cir. 2000).
222. *E.g.*, Am. Psychological Ass'n, 115 F.T.C. 993 (1992) (consent order).

practice. Years ago, for example, in *American Medical Association v. United States*, the Supreme Court condemned an association's attempts to prevent its members from accepting employment by HMOs,[223] and during the 1970s and 1980s, the FTC brought a number of cases challenging restraints on modes of practice that associations opined were unethical.[224]

Every organization has requirements that applicants must meet for membership. Where the requirement is not masking conduct that would constitute a per se violation (such as exclusion because the applicant would refuse to join the association's price-fixing conspiracy), courts consistently apply the rule of reason to the association's decision.[225] On the other hand, some courts have indicated that where the purpose of the requirement is to serve the members' own economic interests, rather than the public interest, the requirement may be unlawful.[226]

Many professional associations or similar bodies have established accreditation or quality standards members must meet to retain their membership or obtain certification. Again, the courts almost universally apply the rule of reason to quality-related standards, and most have been upheld.[227] And

---

223. 317 U.S. 519 (1943).
224. *E.g.*, Am. Acad. of Optometry, 108 F.T.C. 25 (1986) (consent order) (challenge to ethical restraint that, inter alia, prohibited optometrists from practicing in commercial settings such as retail stores).
225. *E.g.,* Marrese v. Am. Acad. of Orthopaedic Surgeons, 706 F.2d 1448 (7th Cir. 1983); *see also* Nat'l Ass'n of Review Appraisers & Mortgage Underwriters, Inc. v. Appraisers Found., 64 F.3d 113 (8th Cir. 1995).
226. *E.g.*, Kreuzer v. Am. Acad. of Periodontology, 735 F.2d 1479, 1494 (D.C. Cir. 1984).
227. *See, e.g.*, Found. for Interior Design Edu. Research v. Savannah Coll. of Art & Design, 244 F.3d 521, 530 (6th Cir. 2001) ("accreditation serves an important public purpose and can enhance competition"); Blue Dane Simmental Corp. v. Am. Simmental Ass'n, 178 F.3d 1035, 1041 (8th Cir. 1999) ("Generally, the decision of the classifying organization 'will be conclusive and the courts will not intervene.'"); DM Research, Inc. v. Coll. of Am. Pathologists, 170 F.3d 53, 57 (1st Cir. 1999) (noting that association standards are "commonplace, and often very useful"); Poindexter v. Am. Bd. of Surgery, 911 F. Supp. 1510, 1519 (N.D. Ga. 1994) ("Courts have long recognized that establishing and monitoring product and service standards is a legitimate and beneficial function of trade and professional associations. Restrictions on access by imposition of educational and training requirements and a degree of self-regulation are definitional aspects of the term 'profession.'"); Koefoot v. Am. Coll. of Surgeons, 652 F. Supp. 882 (N.D. Ill. 1987).

a number of courts have held that associations do not violate the antitrust laws when they provide information and make recommendations to their members about matters of professional interest but do not force members to follow the recommendation or act in any particular way.[228]

D. Vertical Integration and Exclusionary Conduct

"Predatory" or "unreasonably exclusionary" conduct is conduct, usually undertaken by firms with market power, that excludes competitors from the market, impedes existing competitors from growing, or weakens competitors to the extent that they no longer can constrain the competitive behavior of other market participants, and that lacks offsetting procompetitive benefits.[229] The conduct may result from unilateral action or from horizontal or vertical agreements. Vertical agreements (such as those between a hospital and physicians creating and implementing a physician-hospital organization) often are procompetitive because they combine complementary products for better and more cost-efficient health-care delivery. However, they can also adversely affect competition when they deny (or raise the cost of) a needed or valuable input to a rival.

1. Selective and Exclusive Managed-Care Contracting

One method by which managed-care plans obtain higher discounts or lower prices from providers than they otherwise could obtain is by contracting with fewer than all providers wishing to participate in their health plan. In this way, they can "steer" greater volume to their participating providers, which induces those providers to offer lower prices than they otherwise would.[230] The extreme form of selective contracting is exclusive contracting, in which

---

228. *E.g.*, Schachar v. Am. Acad. of Ophthalmology, 870 F.2d 397, 399 (7th Cir. 1989); *see also* Am. Council of Certified Podiatric Physicians & Surgeons v. Am. Bd. of Podiatric Surgery, Inc., 323 F.3d 366, 373 (6th Cir. 2003) (finding no violation in part because defendant had no "enforcement devices" to enforce its allegedly anticompetitive views).

229. *See, e.g.*, United States v. Microsoft Corp., 253 F.3d 34, 58 (D.C. Cir. 2001) (en banc) (per curiam).

230. *See* Stop & Shop Supermarket Co. v. Blue Cross & Blue Shield, 239 F. Supp. 2d 180, 188 (D.R.I. 2003).

the managed-care plan contracts with only one provider group for specific services for its patients, such as anesthesia. The arrangement thus forecloses other providers from providing care to the plan's members. Exclusivity may run the other way as well—that is, a provider group may agree to provide its services only to a single managed-care plan. These arrangements are vertical agreements and thus are subject to rule-of-reason analysis.[231] A health plan's unilateral decision about with whom to contract rarely raises an antitrust issue;[232] however, its agreement with providers about which to include or exclude in its plan may, in limited circumstances.

If analyzed from the standpoint of its effect on competition rather than its effect on competitors with whom the plan refuses to contract, selective and exclusive contracting should raise significant antitrust issues infrequently. Obviously, the arrangement injures excluded providers, but the exclusion results in an unreasonable restraint on competition only if it is likely to result in higher prices or lower quality for consumers.[233] This result is unlikely unless the arrangement permits the provider with the exclusive arrangement to obtain, maintain, or increase its market power, an unlikely result unless that provider's competitors are forced from the market or considerably weakened. Competition, therefore, would be adversely affected only if the arrangement excluded (or significantly weakened) a substantial percentage of providers from a significant percentage of the market for a significant period

---

231. All Care Nursing Serv., Inc. v. High Tech Staffing Servs., Inc., 135 F.3d 740, 748-49 (11th Cir. 1998) (applying rule of reason to preferred provider arrangement for purchase of temporary nursing services; noting there was no group boycott of sellers by purchasers because all sellers could bid on the preferred provider contract); *Stop & Shop*, 239 F. Supp. 2d at 189-91; Drug Emporium, Inc. v. Blue Cross, 104 F. Supp. 2d 184, 188 (W.D.N.Y. 2000); Cont'l Orthopedic Appliances, Inc. v. Health Ins. Plan, 40 F. Supp. 2d 109, 117 (E.D.N.Y. 1999).

232. *E.g.*, Cont'l Orthopedic Appliances, Inc. v. Health Ins. Plan, 956 F. Supp. 367, 373 (E.D.N.Y. 1997).

233. Capital Imaging Assocs., P.C. v. Mohawk Valley Med. Assocs., Inc., 996 F.2d 537, 546 (2d Cir. 1996) (dismissing provider's claim that HMO unlawfully refused to contract with it, in part because plaintiff failed to prove "an increase in prices for and a deterioration of the quality of" the relevant medical service); *Stop & Shop*, 239 F. Supp. 2d at 193 (denying defendant's motion for summary judgment because plaintiffs adduced evidence that selective contracting arrangement had increased prices).

of time.[234] This, in turn, would require the plaintiff to define the relevant market[235] and prove that that the health plan participating in the exclusive arrangement controls a large percentage of referrals for the medical services affected by the agreement.[236] Especially because the managed-care plan, as a purchaser of the providers' services, has no incentive to enter an arrangement that would provide its suppliers with market power,[237] the antitrust claims of providers excluded from health plans because of a policy of selective or exclusive contracting must be viewed with some caution.[238]

Where the health plan or network refusing to contract with a provider is controlled by providers or providers otherwise have substantial input into the plan's selection of providers, the analysis is somewhat different, because the requisite agreement for Section 1 purposes is horizontal and the exclusion results in a group boycott.[239] Even here, however, courts have applied the rule of reason and upheld the exclusion, especially where participation in the plan was not necessary for the excluded providers to remain viable competitors and the network offered a procompetitive justification for its action.[240]

---

234. *E.g.*, Orthopedic Studio, Inc. v. Health Ins. Plan., 1996-1 Trade Cas. (CCH) ¶ 71,319, at 76,500 (E.D.N.Y. 1996)

235. *See, e.g.*, Surgical Care Ctr. v. Hosp. Serv. Dist. No. 1, 309 F.3d 836 (5th Cir. 2002) (affirming district court's dismissal, in part, because plaintiff failed to define relevant geographic market).

236. *Stop & Shop*, 239 F. Supp. 2d at 193 (denying defendant's motion for summary judgment, in part, because plaintiff adduced evidence that it would be foreclosed from 60 percent of market).

237. *Id.* at 188 ("[n]or is it rational to infer that Blue Cross [excluded plaintiffs] to lessen competition among pharmacies selling prescription pharmaceuticals").

238. It also is important to distinguish between a health plan's mere agreement to contract with a provider for services and its agreement with that provider not to contract with other providers. The former should raise no antitrust issues, although the latter can be proved by circumstantial evidence of the parties' conduct.

239. *See, e.g.*, Am. Chiropractic Ass'n v. Trigon Healthcare, Inc., 151 F. Supp. 2d 723 (W.D. Va. 2001).

240. *See* Doctor's Hosp. v. Southeast Med. Alliance, Inc., 123 F.3d 301 (5th Cir. 1997); Levine v. Cent. Fla. Med. Affiliates, 72 F.3d 1538 (11th Cir. 1996); J. Allen Ramey, M.D., P.C., Inc. v. Pac. Found. for Med. Care, 999 F. Supp. 1355 (S.D. Cal. 1998); *see generally Health Care Enforcement Statements, supra* p. 12 n.41, Statement 9.B.2.c. (explaining that "[a] rule of reason analysis is

Selective contracting can take many forms. For example, the managed-care plan may simply contract with less than all providers wishing to partici-pate; the plan may contract with all providers but denominate some as "preferred providers," the use of which requires less out-of-pocket expense to the plan's subscribers; a provider may offer plans a deeper discount if they exclude one or more providers from their plan panel. In all cases, the basic antitrust concern is the same: whether providers are foreclosed from patients to the extent that participating providers may obtain the ability to increase prices or decrease quality and whether, if so, the arrangement generates procompetitive benefits, such as lowering the providers' average cost so they can offer lower prices and thus compete more effectively.

The analysis is similar where the arrangement between a plan and its providers is exclusive in the sense that participating providers agree not to participate in competing plans. This type of arrangement can also generate procompetitive benefits.[241] The antitrust concern is whether competing plans are sufficiently foreclosed from obtaining the providers they need so that the plan using this type of exclusive arrangement is able to obtain market power and thus able to raise its prices.[242]

2. *"All-Products" Provisions*

Some health insurers and managed-care plans regularly include, in their pro-vider agreements with physicians, a requirement that, to participate in one of the insurer's plans, the physicians must participate in other or all of the insurer's plans. For example, a managed-care organization offering an indemnity plan, an HMO, a PPO, and a senior plan may require its participating physicians to participate in the HMO and senior plans in order to participate in the indem-nity or PPO plans. Physicians may not wish to participate in all plans, either

---

usually applied in judging the legality of a . . . network's exclusion of providers or classes of providers from the network, or its policies on refer-ring enrollees to network providers").

241. *See generally* FTC Bureau of Competition, Bureau of Consumer Protec-tion, and Bureau of Economics Letter to Nevada Commissioner of Insur-ance (Nov. 5, 1986) (arguing against department of insurance policy that would prohibit such arrangements), *reprinted in* 3 *HCAL, supra* p. 14 n.47, App. D24.

242. *See generally* U.S. Healthcare, Inc. v. Healthsource, Inc., 986 F.2d 589 (1st Cir. 1993), *aff'g* 1992-1 Trade Cas. (CCH) ¶ 69,697 (D.N.H. 1992).

because the rates of reimbursement are different or because the plans differ in other respects, such as the degree of "hassle factors."

It seems unlikely that, as a general matter, all-products provisions raise significant antitrust concern except in narrow circumstances. Although they may resemble tying arrangements, they are not tying arrangements as a technical matter because the managed-care plan is not selling the participating providers any good or service conditioned on the providers' purchasing a second good or service.[243] Moreover, all-products provisions typically will not exhibit the anticompetitive effect that raises concern about tying agreements—market foreclosure in the market for the tied product. In addition, such provisions arguably generate procompetitive benefits, such as ensuring that subscribers are not forced to change physicians if they switch from one of the insurer's plans to another.

On the other hand, as the Antitrust Division explained in its competitive impact statement accompanying the consent decree in the Aetna-Prudential merger challenge, all-products provisions may facilitate the exercise of monopsony power by payers by making it more difficult for physicians to reject the payer's contract offer with respect to a particular type of plan.[244] For example, with an all-products requirement in a provider agreement, a physician rejecting participation in a payer's HMO will lose the patients from all the payer's plans, not just its HMO members; and the more patients a physician has to replace, the more difficult it is for the physician to reject the payer's offer.[245] Whether the provision would constitute an unreasonable restraint on competition by itself in this situation is unclear.

3. *Provider Diversification Through Vertical Integration*

In the face of declining inpatient census and increasingly restrictive third-party reimbursement practices, hospitals have turned to ownership of other types of health-care businesses, such as those providing long-term care, durable medical equipment (DME), home health, rehabilitation services, and

---

243. *Cf.* Brokerage Concepts, Inc. v. U.S. Healthcare, Inc., 140 F.3d 494, 511 (3d Cir. 1998) (holding that no tying arrangement resulted where insurer conditioned pharmacy's inclusion in its network on the pharmacy's purchasing third-party-administration services from insurer).
244. United States v. Aetna, Inc., 1999-2 Trade Cas. (CCH) ¶ 72,730, at 86,380 (N.D. Tex. 1999) (competitive impact statement).

hospice care to supplement decreased inpatient revenues. Typically, the hospital or health system will establish such a business through a newly created wholly-owned subsidiary, a joint venture with an existing supplier, or by merger. Such arrangements can raise significant antitrust concerns, particularly if the hospital "steers" or "channels" all its patients requiring the affected product or service to its affiliated provider and those patients constitute a significant percentage of all customers in the relevant geographic market for those products or services. The analysis normally focuses on the degree to which other providers of the services are foreclosed from potential patients and customers because of the arrangement and the type of conduct the hospital uses to steer patients to its affiliated provider. In some situations, the degree of foreclosure may be sufficient that competing providers cannot continue as a competitive constraint on the hospital-affiliated provider, and the latter may obtain substantial market power.

Actual challenges based on this situation have come primarily from DME and home-health suppliers harmed by a hospital system's entry into their markets. Relevant legal theories vary depending on the method by which the hospital entered that market and its conduct after entry. If the hospital acquires the affiliated provider through merger or through the creation of a joint venture, the transaction is a vertical merger subject to Section 7 of the Clayton Act. If the hospital entered by a joint venture and the parties agree that the hospital will refer all its patients requiring the affected product or service to its joint venture, the agreement is an exclusive dealing agreement subject to Section 1 of the Sherman Act.[246] If the hospital enters the market by creating its own wholly-owned subsidiary to provide the products or services[247] (or by merger), a single entity would result, and thus no conspiracy

---

245. *See, e.g.*, Marius Schwartz, Economic Director of Enforcement, Antitrust Division, "Buyer Power Concerns and the *Aetna/Prudential* Merger," Prepared Remarks Before the 5th Annual Health Care Antitrust Forum, Northwestern University School of Law (Oct. 20, 1999) (explaining that impediments to physicians replacing patients lost through rejecting payer offers exacerbates payer market power as a purchaser), *at* http://www.usdoj.gov/atr/public/speeches/3924.pdf.
246. *See, e.g.*, Advanced Health-Care Servs., Inc. v. Radford Cmty. Hosp., 910 F.2d 139 (4th Cir. 1990).
247. If the arrangement involves commodities rather than services, the plaintiff may also challenge it under Section 3 of the Clayton Act, 15 U.S.C. § 14.

between those organizations would be possible thereafter.[248] In that situation, however, a plaintiff might claim that the hospital tied its services and those of its affiliated provider by requiring its patients to use the affiliated provider. Similarly, a plaintiff might allege monopolization or attempted monopolization in violation of Section 2 of the Sherman Act, claiming that the hospital "leveraged" its market power in the market for hospital services or that it denied the plaintiff access to an "essential facility" (here, hospital referrals) in monopolizing or attempting to monopolize the market for the "downstream" product or service.[249]

Hospitals can decrease or eliminate the antitrust risk from these arrangements by not steering their patients to their affiliated provider. Rather, for example, than automatically referring hospital patients needing DME at discharge to the hospital's affiliated DME company, the hospital's discharge planner might provide the patient (or a patient representative) with a list of area providers, permit the patient to select the provider of his or her choice, and have the patient sign a form indicating that he or she chose among the providers.

4. Opposition to Certificate-of-Need Applications

In states with certificate-of-need (CON) laws, it is common for hospitals, either individually or concertedly, to oppose the certificate-of-need applica-

---

248. *E.g.*, Heritage Home Health Care, Inc. v. Capital Region Health Care Corp., 1996-2 Trade Cas. (CCH) ¶ 71,584 (D.N.H. 1996).

249. *See, e.g.*, M & M Med. Supplies & Serv., Inc. v. Pleasant Valley Hosp., 981 F.2d 160 (4th Cir. 1992); *see also* Key Enters. v. Venice Hosp., 919 F.2d 1550 (11th Cir. 1990), *vacated with instructions to dismiss*, 9 F.3d 893 (11th Cir. 1993); Del. Health Care, Inc. v. MCD Holding Co., 957 F. Supp. 535 (D. Del. 1997). Although the *Venice Hospital* decision was vacated, it provides a relatively in-depth analysis of the vertical integration/diversification issue. The *Delaware Health* decision provides an in-depth discussion of relevant geographic market definition in diversification cases.

Significantly, the Supreme Court has never recognized the essential facilities doctrine in the context of a Section 2 claim and has stated that leveraging does not violate Section 2 unless the defendant actually monopolizes the downstream market or a dangerous probability exists that it will do so. Verizon Communications, Inc. v. Law Offices of Curtis V. Trinko, LLP, No. 02-682, slip op. at 11, 15 n.4, 2004 WL 51011 at 6, 7 n.4 (U.S. Jan. 13, 2004).

tions of their competitors. Because, however, this activity constitutes "petitioning the government" in an effort to induce governmental action, it is exempt from successful antitrust challenge in most circumstances under the *Noerr-Pennington* doctrine.[250] That exemption applies whether the opposition is unilateral or results from concerted action, and it applies even if the objectors' intent in seeking government action is anticompetitive.

The exemption, however, does not apply to petitioning activity when the parties exert coercive force on the governmental agency[251] or the petitioning is a "sham"—that is, where parties "use the governmental *process*—as opposed to the outcome of that process—as an anticompetitive weapon."[252] The sham exception to the exemption would apply, for example, where the objectors' arguments against the CON are so objectively baseless that no reasonable person could expect them to succeed, and the objectors' subjective intent is not to persuade the state to reject the CON application but, rather, simply to delay the applicant's project.[253]

Whether knowing misrepresentations made to the government in the context of seeking governmental action constitute "sham" petitioning is somewhat unclear. Older cases indicated they are.[254] Recent decisions appear to suggest they are not unless the misrepresentations are material[255] and affect the "legitimacy"[256] of the government's decision.

Behind-the-scenes market-allocation agreements between CON applicants to settle CON disputes also may raise antitrust concern.[257]

---

250. *See supra* pp. 49-55, discussing the antitrust exemption for solicitation of governmental action.
251. *See* Superior Court Trial Lawyers Ass'n v. FTC, 493 U.S. 411, 424-25 (1990).
252. *See, e.g.*, City of Columbia v. Omni Outdoor Adver., Inc., 499 U.S. 365, 380 (1991) ("A classic example is the filing of frivolous objections to the license application of a competitor, with no expectation of achieving denial of the license but simply in order to impose expense and delay."); Armstrong Surgical Ctr., Inc. v. Armstrong County Mem'l Hosp., 185 F.3d 154, 158 (3d Cir. 1999); Boulware v. Nevada, 960 F.2d 793, 798 (9th Cir. 1992).
253. *See generally* Prof'l Real Estate Investors, Inc. v. Columbia Pictures Indus., Inc., 508 U.S. 49, 60-61 (1993) (explaining test for "sham" litigation).
254. St. Joseph's Hosp. v. Hosp. Corp. of Am., 795 F.2d 948, 955 (11th Cir. 1986).
255. *Armstrong Surgical Ctr.*, 185 F.3d at 163.
256. Kottle v. Northwest Kidney Ctr., 146 F.3d 1056, 1063 (9th Cir. 1998).
257. *See, e.g.*, Florida v. HCA, Inc., 2003-1 Trade Cas. (CCH) ¶ 74,027 (M.D. Fla. 2003) (consent decree).

5. Hospital Efforts to Impede Medical-Staff Competition

In recent years, hospitals have expressed increasing concern about efforts by their medical-staff members to compete against the hospital.[258] A particular area of concern is the establishment of independent specialty hospitals, such as heart hospitals, orthopedic surgery hospitals, and outpatient surgery centers, by members of the hospital's medical staff.

The physicians establishing the facilities claim that they are merely attempting to increase competition by offering higher-quality services at lower prices than the hospital. The hospitals counter that the physicians are "cream skimmers," taking high-margin business to their facilities and leaving the hospital with money-losing but important services such as emergency services. Moreover, the hospitals argue that the physicians take only low-acuity patients with high-reimbursement commercial insurance, while leaving the hospital with the more seriously ill, uninsured, and Medicaid patients. The hospitals also argue that the physicians have an unfair competitive advantage because of their financial incentive and ability to refer their patients to a facility in which they have an economic interest, regardless of whether that facility is the best choice for the patient.[259]

Competing facilities owned by a hospital's medical-staff members have alleged that hospitals have engaged in a number of different types of exclusionary conduct to impede their efforts to establish viable competing facilities.

---

258. *See generally* Lawrence P. Casalino et al., *Focused Factories? Physician-Owned Specialty Hospitals,* HEALTH AFFAIRS, Nov.–Dec. 2003, at 56; *see also* Julie Piotrowski, *Niche Facilities Hit: Moratorium Raises New Self-Referral Issues for Docs,* MOD. HEALTHCARE, Dec. 22/29, 2003, at 28; Patrick Reilly, *Lobbying Offensive: Congress Asked to Limit Physician Investments,* MOD. HEALTHCARE, Sept. 29, 2003, at 8; Markian Hawryluk, *GAO: Boutique Hospitals Treat Healthier Patients,* AM. MED. NEWS, June 16, 2003, at 10.

259. *See* Williamson v. Sacred Heart Hosp., 41 F.3d 667 (11th Cir. 1995) (per curiam unpublished opinion reprinted at 1995-1 Trade Cas. (CCH) ¶ 70,905) (upholding hospital decision rejecting plaintiff's application for staff privileges where plaintiff competed with defendant hospital, in part because the antitrust laws do not require a firm to support or assist its competitors); *cf.* Mahan v. Avera St. Luke's, 621 N.W.2d 150 (S.D. 2001) (non-antitrust case upholding hospital's decision rejecting privilege applications of physicians working with group that opened surgery center competing with hospital); *see generally* Mark Taylor, *Doc Investors in For-Profit Hospitals Denied Staff Privileges,* MOD. HEALTHCARE, Jul. 15, 2002, at 12.

These efforts have included hospital policies to exclude such physicians from their medical staffs, attempts to persuade other physicians not to refer to the physicians' facility, exclusive contracts with payers for the services in question,[260] the use of bundled discounts with payers,[261] refusals to enter into transfer agreements with such facilities,[262] and similar types of conduct.

If a hospital has substantial market power in the market for the services provided by the physicians' facility, these types of conduct can raise monopolization or attempted monopolization concerns under Section 2 of the Sherman Act. If the conduct results from agreements between the hospital and others (such as payers or other members of the hospital's medical staff) and if the agreements appear to restrain competition unreasonably in the market for the affected services, issues under Section 1 of the Sherman Act may arise as well. Or, if the hospital has market power in the market for inpatient hospital services and conditions its sales of those services on a payer's also purchasing the services in question from it, a tying arrangement might result. The analysis generally focuses on the extent to which competitors of the hospital are foreclosed from patients by the conduct and the effect of that foreclosure on the hospital's market power.

At present, there are few decisions discussing this factual situation in detail, although several cases are pending.[263] In the *Surgical Care Center of Hammond* case,[264] the court rejected a claim of this type under Section 2 of the Sherman Act by a physician-established ambulatory surgery center, primarily because it found that the plaintiff failed to prove the hospital's market power in the market for outpatient surgery. In addition, it found that the hospital's exclusive contract with a payer was not predatory based in part on the testimony of the plaintiff's own expert.[265] More litigation focusing on this issue is likely in the near future.[266]

---

260. *See, e.g.*, Rome Ambulatory Surgery Ctr., LLC v. Rome Mem'l Hosp., No. 01-CV-0023 (DNH-GJB) (N.D.N.Y., filed Aug. 22, 2002) (first amended complaint).

261. *See* Surgical Care Ctr. v. Hosp. Serv. Dist. No. 1, 2001-1 Trade Cas. (CCH) ¶ 73,215 (E.D. La. 2001), *aff'd*, 309 F.3d 836 (5th Cir. 2002).

262. *Id.*

263. *E.g., Rome Ambulatory Surgery Ctr.*

264. *Surgical Care Ctr.*, 2001-1 Trade Cas. (CCH) ¶ 73,215.

265. *Id.* at ¶ 89,943.

266. Hospital efforts to prevent this type of competition from its medical staff can raise other antitrust issues as well. For example, when staff members an-

6. *Hospital and Hospital System Full-Line Forcing*

Situations arise in which a hospital refuses to contract with a payer for one service unless the payer agrees to contract with the hospital for all its services, or a multi-hospital system refuses to contract with a payer for the services of one of its hospitals unless the payer contracts with all the system's hospitals. These are examples of "full-line forcing"—that is, arrangements under which a seller requires a buyer to purchase its full service line. In general, full-line forcing arrangements are analyzed using tying and leverage arrangement analysis,[267] but there can be some unusual twists.

In the first situation, the arrangement will usually involve the sale of separate products, a requirement for an unlawful tying arrangement,[268] but because the payer remains free to purchase the tied services from other hospitals as well, it can be difficult to determine the extent to which (if any) the hospital's competitors are foreclosed from the tied market and thus the effect the arrangement has on the market power of the hospital insisting on the arrangement (and thus the effect on consumers). No decisions yet discuss the appropriate analysis in the factual context here.[269]

---

nounce their intent to build a competitive facility, the hospital might offer to form a joint venture with the physicians to offer the service. If, because of the hospital's interest in the venture, the hospital and venture coordinate their competitive behavior rather than compete, the market loses what would have been a new independent competitor, which raises an antitrust problem if the market for the service is highly concentrated and the independent venture would have significantly deconcentrated it. Potential-competition merger theory applies to this situation. *See generally* United States v. Penn-Olin Chem. Co., 378 U.S. 158 (1964); *see also* United States v. Marine Bancorp., 418 U.S. 602 (1974). In addition, the parties' coordinated behavior may, itself, raise an antitrust issue. For example, since the new joint venture is not a single entity for antitrust purposes and assuming the hospital offers the affected services itself, an agreement between the hospital and venture about the price either or both will charge, or joint negotiations on behalf of both with payers, may constitute horizontal price-fixing agreements. At present, there are no decisions directly addressing either situation.

267. *See generally ALD V, supra* p. 9 n.23, at 212-14.
268. *See* Jefferson Parish Hosp. Dist. No. 2 v. Hyde, 466 U.S. 2, 20 (1984).
269. In *Lancaster Community Hospital v. Antelope Valley Hospital District,* 940 F.2d 397 (9th Cir. 1991), the plaintiff hospital alleged that the defendant

In the second situation, that where the hospital system insists that the payer contract with all its hospitals as a condition to contracting with any, it is not clear whether the system is selling separate products in the sense necessary for an unlawful tying arrangement, particularly if all its hospitals offer the same services. Moreover, the degree of foreclosure again is unclear because the payer remains free to contract with the system's competitors and, to the extent it wants a broad panel of providers, probably will do so. Indeed, in that situation, the payer would probably have contracted with all the system's hospitals without being forced to do so, in which case there is no tying arrangement at all.[270]

In the second situation and particularly where the system's hospitals are in separate relevant geographic markets, a question can arise whether the hospital is using the market power of one of its hospitals (a flagship hospital, for example, with substantial market power in certain tertiary services) to increase the market power of its other hospitals. Suppose, for example, the system's flagship hospital refuses to participate in the payer's plan unless the plan agrees to increase its reimbursement to the system's non-flagship hospitals. Older Supreme Court decisions, in another industry, suggest that this conduct is problematic where competitors of the non-flagship hospital are foreclosed because of the policy,[271] but no decisions discuss whether this arguable "transfer" of market power from one of the system's hospitals to others creates significant antitrust concern. Theory would suggest that the system as a whole cannot increase its aggregate market power through this

---

hospital required that payers purchase all its medical/surgical services as a condition to purchasing its perinatal services, but the decision focuses on the applicability of the state-action exemption given the defendant's status as a special-district hospital, and there is no discussion of the merits.

270. *See Jefferson Parish Hosp. Dist.*, 466 U.S. at 13 (explaining that the concern with tying arrangements is that the purchaser must purchase a product it either does not want or would prefer to purchase from someone else); Will v. Comprehensive Accounting Corp., 776 F.2d 665 (7th Cir. 1985) ("The joint sale of two products is a 'tie' only if the seller exploits its control of the tying product 'to force the buyer into the purchase of a tied product that the buyer either did not want at all, or might have preferred to purchase elsewhere on different terms.'").

271. *See* Schine Chain Theatres, Inc. v. United States, 334 U.S. 110 (1948); United States v. Griffith, 334 U.S. 100 (1948) (defendant film exhibitors used their market power in one geographical area to prevent their competitors in other areas from obtaining desired first-run films).

arrangement[272] and, therefore, whether the policy raises antitrust concern is questionable. A payer might argue, however, that the policy is anticompetitive because absent its having to contract with the unwanted hospital, that hospital's competitors would offer the payer a lower price for greater patient volume, and the policy may hinder the ability of payers to steer subscribers to lower-cost hospitals.[273] Competing hospitals also might object to the extent that the policy induces payers not to contract with them or forecloses them from patients who otherwise might have used their facilities. The policy is common and may become a fertile ground for future health-care antitrust litigation.

Finally, a problem could arise if the hospital system ties its hospital services and the services of its employed physicians by refusing to contract with payers for the former unless payers also contract for the latter. This clearly is a tying arrangement and thus may raise substantial antitrust concern where the health system has significant market power in the market for hospital services.

7. Pharmaceutical Industry Collusive and Exclusionary Conduct

The FTC has been quite active in challenging different types of antitrust problems arising in the pharmaceutical industry.[274] Its enforcement actions have included challenges to pharmaceutical company horizontal and vertical

---

272. *See* RICHARD A. POSNER, ANTITRUST LAW 198-207 (2d ed. 2001).
273. *See* Thomas R. McCarthy, *Contracting Practices by Hospitals*, Antitrust Insights (NERA Economic Consulting), Mar./Apr. 2003, at 1, *available at* http://www.nera.com/wwt/newsletter_issues/5954/pdf.
274. For overviews of the FTC's activities in the pharmaceutical industry, *see* Federal Trade Commission, Bureau of Competition, "FTC Actions in Pharmaceutical Services and Products" (Oct. 2003), at http://www.ftc.gov/bc/031\rxupdate.pdf; Timothy J. Muris, Chairman, Federal Trade Commission, "Everything Old Is New Again: Health Care and Competition in the 21st Century," Prepared Remarks Before the 7th Annual Competition in Health Care Forum, Northwestern University School of Law (Nov. 7, 2002), *at* http://www.ftc.gov/speeches/02speech.htm; Timothy J. Muris, Chairman, Federal Trade Commission, Prepared Statement of the Federal Trade Commission Before the Committee on Energy and Commerce, Subcommittee on Health, U.S. House of Representatives (Oct. 9, 2002), *reprinted in* 4 HCAL, *supra* p. 14 n.47, App. E112.

mergers[275] and a challenge to an exclusive contract between a pharmaceutical manufacturer and a supplier of an essential input for one of its drugs that allegedly permitted the manufacturer to raise the price of the drug dramatically.[276]

In addition, the FTC has challenged agreements between branded-drug manufacturers and generic manufacturers settling patent-infringement litigation by the former against the latter in which the branded manufacturer allegedly paid the generic manufacturer to delay its entry into the market.[277] The Commission has obtained consent decrees in several of these cases.[278] In the single litigated FTC case, the commissioners reversed an administrative law judge's initial decision in favor of the respondents and held that the agreements there, by which a branded-drug manufacturer, in the context of settling patent-infringement litigation, paid generic manufacturers to delay their entry into the market, unreasonably restrained competition.[279] The FTC also has challenged unilateral conduct by branded-drug manufacturers in which they

---

275. *E.g.*, Glaxo Wellcome, PLC, Dkt. No. C-3990 (FTC Jan. 26, 2001) (consent order) (horizontal merger), *at* http://www.ftc.gov/os/2001/01/ glaxosmithklinedo.pdf; Merck/Medco, Dkt. No. C-3853 (FTC Feb. 24, 1999) (vertical merger), *at* http://www.ftc.gov.os/1999/02/9510097merck.do.htm.

276. FTC v. Mylan Labs., 62 F. Supp. 2d 25 (D.D.C. 1999).

277. For helpful discussions of this issue, *see* M. Howard Morse, *Settlement of Intellectual Property Disputes in the Pharmaceutical and Medical Device Industries: Antitrust Rules*, 10 Geo. Mason L. Rev. 359 (2002); Kevin D. McDonald, *Patent Settlements and Payments that Flow the "Wrong" Way*, ABA Antitrust Health Care Chronicle, Winter 2002, at 2; Thomas B. Leary, Commissioner, Federal Trade Commissioner, "Antitrust Issues in Settlement of Pharmaceutical Patent Disputes, Part II," Prepared Remarks Before the American Bar Association and American Health Lawyers Association Antitrust in the Healthcare Field Seminar (May 17, 2001), *at* http:// www.ftc.gov/ speeches/leary/learypharmaceuticalsettlement.htm; Thomas B. Leary, Commissioner, Federal Trade Commission, "Antitrust Issues in Settlement of Pharmaceutical Patent Disputes," Prepared Remarks Before the 6th Annual Health Care Antitrust Forum, Northwestern University School of Law (Nov. 3, 2000), *at* http://www.ftc.gov/speeches/leary/ learypharma.htm.

278. *E.g.*, Abbott Labs., Dkt. No. C-3945 (FTC May 22, 2000) (consent order), *at* http://www.ftc.gov/os/2000/05/c3945.do.htm.

279. Schering Plough Corp., Dkt. No. D-9297 (FTC Dec. 8, 2003) (Commission Opinion), *at* http://www.ftc.gov/os/adjpro/d9297/031218commission opinion.pdf.

allegedly attempted to extend drug patents by abusing Food and Drug Administration patent registration procedures.[280]

State attorneys general and private parties also have been active in the pharmaceutical industry, filing several treble-damage actions for damages on their own behalf and as parens patriae on behalf of their states' citizens to recover damages suffered by them.[281] For the most part, these cases have sought damages for the same types of practices challenged by the FTC.[282]

---

280. For several articles discussing these issues in detail, *see Symposium: Antitrust Issues in the Pharmaceutical Industry*, 71 Antitrust L.J. (2003).

281. *See, e.g.*, Cardizem CD Antitrust Litig., 332 F.3d 896 (6th Cir. 2003) (market-allocation patent-infringement settlement agreement; holding the agreement per se unlawful); Valley Drug Co. v. Geneva Pharms., Inc., 344 F.3d 1294 (11th Cir. 2003) (same; but holding rule of reason applicable); In re Ciprofloxacin Hydrochloride Antitrust Litig., 261 F. Supp. 2d 188 (E.D.N.Y. 2003) (same; holding rule of reason applicable); Buspirone Patent Litig., 185 F. Supp. 2d 363 (S.D.N.Y. 2002) (denying defendants' Rule 12(b)(6) motion where defendants allegedly abused FDA patent-listing procedure).

282. *E.g.*, Bristol-Myers-Squibb, Dkt. No. C-4076 (FTC April 18, 2003) (consent order), *at* http://www.ftc.gov/os/2003/04/bristolmyerssquibbdo.pdf; Biovail Corp., Dkt. No. C-4060 (FTC Oct. 2, 2002) (consent order), *at* http://www.ftc.gov/os/2002/10/biovaildo.pdf.

CHAPTER 4

PREVENTING AND MINIMIZING ANTITRUST PROBLEMS

A. Antitrust Compliance Programs

1. Goals of a Compliance Program

Many organizations have formal antitrust compliance policies and programs to minimize and properly manage antitrust risk. The form and content of these programs vary, and they should be specifically tailored to an organization based on its structure and activities in health care and the types of antitrust issues it might experience, in consultation with an experienced antitrust counsel.[1]

Antitrust compliance programs can achieve a number of important goals, but their overriding objective is to prevent conduct by the organization that clearly violates antitrust law. The compliance program should include (1) establishing a formal written organizational policy to comply with antitrust law; (2) establishing an affirmative antitrust-compliance obligation for the organization's personnel and agents; (3) educating the organization's personnel and agents about antitrust law, particularly about conduct that clearly is prohibited; (4) establishing an affirmative obligation for the organization's personnel to report questionable conduct within the organization; (5) establishing and implementing procedures for responding promptly and effectively to reports of possible violations and for monitoring the organization's compliance with the policy and with antitrust law; and (6) periodic antitrust audits of certain aspects of the organization's operations that are prone to antitrust concerns by counsel to help ensure compliance with the antitrust laws and to identify and correct any problematic conduct.

Antitrust compliance is important because the antitrust laws are an integral part of our free-enterprise system, and a compliance program is a cost-effective means of minimizing and managing the risk of antitrust liability. The time, expense, and resources necessary to establish and administer an

---

1. *See generally* ABA SECTION OF ANTITRUST LAW, ANTITRUST COMPLIANCE MANUALS: A COMPENDIUM OF STATE-OF-THE-ART MANUALS FOR TODAY'S CORPORATIONS (1995).

antitrust compliance program are minuscule compared to those normally required to defend against antitrust investigations or claims, or to pay the substantial treble damages, attorneys fees, or fines that may result from a violation.

An antitrust compliance program also may enable an organization to avoid and deal more effectively with price-fixing and other serious violations of antitrust law that may be the subject of criminal prosecution. The Antitrust Division has formal leniency policies for both corporations and individuals reporting their antitrust violations, and early detection and self-reporting of a serious antitrust violation is essential to take advantage of these policies.[2] Under these policies, only a single corporation (or individual) involved in an antitrust conspiracy can obtain leniency, and an organization's early detection of unlawful conduct by its employees or agents may enable the organization to approach the government for leniency before other conspirators do so. The U.S. Sentencing Commission also recognizes an "effective program to prevent and detect violations of law" as a possible mitigating factor that may permit a downward adjustment to criminal penalties against an organization convicted of an antitrust violation.[3]

2. *See* U.S. Dep't of Justice, Corporate Leniency Policy (1993), *reprinted in* 4 Trade Reg. Rep. (CCH) ¶ 13,113; U.S. Dep't of Justice, Leniency Policy for Individuals (1994), *reprinted in* 4 Trade Reg. Rep. (CCH) ¶ 13,114. *See also* Scott D. Hammond, Director of Criminal Enforcement, Antitrust Division, "When Calculating the Costs and Benefits of Applying for Corporate Amnesty, How Do You Put a Price on an Individual's Freedom?", Prepared Remarks (Mar. 8, 2001), *at* http://www.usdoj.gov/atr/public/speeches/7647.pdf; Scott D. Hammond, Director of Criminal Enforcement, Antitrust Division, "Detecting and Deterring Cartel Activity Through an Effective Leniency Program," Prepared Remarks Before the International Workshop on Cartels (Nov. 21-22, 2000), *at* http://www.usdoj.gov/atr/public/speeches/9928.pdf; Gary R. Spratling, Deputy Assistant Attorney General, Antitrust Division, "Making Companies an Offer They Shouldn't Refuse: The Antitrust Division's Corporate Leniency Policy – An Update," Prepared Remarks Before the Bar Association of the District of Columbia's 35th Annual Symposium on Associations and Antitrust (Feb. 16, 1999), *at* http://www.usdoj.gov/atr/public/speeches/2247.pdf.
3. *See* U.S. SENTENCING COMMISSION, FEDERAL SENTENCING GUIDELINE MANUAL, § 8A1.2 n.3(k) (2002) [hereinafter *Sentencing Guidelines*] (defining effective compliance program), and § 8C.2.5(f) (authorizing downward adjustment to corporate fine). A compliance program cannot be used to reduce an organization's criminal fine if certain high-level personnel participate in, condone, or will-

2. *Essential Features of a Compliance Program*

Federal antitrust law does not require that organizations establish and administer a formal antitrust compliance program and does not prescribe the essential features of such programs. The U.S. Sentencing Commission, however, has described the criteria it uses to evaluate whether a program has been reasonably designed, implemented, and enforced, so that it is deemed "effective" and therefore qualifies the organization for a reduced criminal fine. These criteria provide useful guidance for health-care organizations seeking to implement a compliance program, even though criminal antitrust enforcement and penalties have not been common against health-care providers or payers. In summary, these criteria require that the organization:

1. establish compliance standards and procedures for employees and agents that are reasonably capable of reducing the prospect of criminal conduct;
2. assign the overall responsibility to oversee compliance with the standards and procedures to specific high-level personnel;
3. use due care not to delegate such authority to individuals with a propensity to engage in illegal activities;
4. conduct training programs or take other steps to communicate the compliance standards and procedures to employees and agents effectively;
5. take reasonable steps to achieve compliance by creating systems reasonably designed to detect criminal conduct and implementing and publicizing a system for reporting suspected criminal conduct that personnel can use without fear of retribution;

---

fully ignore the illegal conduct, or if the organization unreasonably delays reporting the violation to appropriate governmental authorities once it becomes aware of illegal conduct. *Sentencing Guidelines,* § 8C.2.5(f). *See also* Gary R. Spratling, Deputy Assistant Attorney General, Antitrust Division, "Corporate Crime in America: Strengthening the Good Citizen Corporation – The Experience and View of the Antitrust Division," Prepared Remarks Before a National Symposium Sponsored by the U.S. Sentencing Commission (Sept. 8, 1995) (describing Sentencing Commission criteria and information requirements the Antitrust Division may consider before agreeing that an organization's compliance program warrants sentence mitigation), *at* http://www.usdoj.gov/atr/public/speeches/0456.htm.

6. enforce the standards consistently through appropriate disciplinary mechanisms; and
7. take all reasonable steps to respond appropriately to any offenses that are detected to prevent further similar offenses, including necessary modifications to the compliance program.

As the Sentencing Commission criteria underscore, an effective compliance program entails much more than a formal written policy of compliance with the antitrust laws, or written standards and procedures that are reasonably capable of ensuring compliance. The organization also must educate its personnel about the program and must take affirmative steps to monitor and ensure compliance with the program's standards and procedures on an ongoing basis.

Health-care organizations have confronted government antitrust investigations and enforcement most frequently with respect to mergers, joint ventures, provider conduct in jointly negotiating and contracting for services with payers, and other types of agreements or collective action among competitors on prices and other terms of services. Private actions have focused significantly on medical-staff decisions (resulting from both peer review and exclusive contracts) by hospitals. Accordingly, a compliance program should focus particular attention on personnel and conduct pertinent to these potentially competitively significant matters.

B. Managing Business Records

Health-care organizations create, communicate, and store a tremendous volume of information in the course of providing patient care and processing claims for payment and reimbursement. Although these business records are of substantial importance in ensuring quality patient care and compliance with the billing requirements of governmental and private payers, they generally are not of substantial importance to an organization's possible exposure to antitrust risks. Rather, antitrust concerns arise primarily from business records about matters that are competitively significant, such as contracts between payers and providers, prices and fees, networks and joint ventures, consolidation and integration strategies and transactions, and peer-review and credentialing activities.

A health-care organization should have an effective program for managing business records, particularly electronic records such as e-mail, pertaining to these subjects to ensure prompt detection of conduct exposing it to potential antitrust liability. This also will help to ensure that important actions, goals, and decisions of the organization with competitive significance are not described inaccurately or inappropriately.

Many health-care organizations have general programs for the storage and regular periodic destruction of business records, including electronic storage media. Health-care organizations have affirmative legal obligations to maintain certain records for prescribed time periods. Although there are no such requirements under federal antitrust law, existing programs for the retention and periodic destruction of records still should be reviewed with experienced antitrust counsel and coordinated with the organization's antitrust compliance program.

From the perspective of antitrust law, an organization's program for managing business records also should focus on the initial preparation of records pertinent to matters of competitive significance. This is important because business records (including e-mail and other electronic records) describing an organization's conduct, intentions, goals, and perceived market position may be used either for or against it in future antitrust investigations and litigation. Accordingly, personnel responsible for matters of competitive significance should be familiar with and sensitive to antitrust principles and concerns, not only in recommending, approving, or carrying on such activities, but also in the preparation of communications and business records about these matters. In addition, the organization should consider establishing procedures requiring that all such records be prepared or approved by designated management personnel and stored in a centralized manner to facilitate internal review, monitoring, and retrieval.

Management of business records has become increasingly challenging in health care because of the increased use of e-mail and electronic storage media. The resulting decentralization of archived records pertinent to an organization's competitively significant business activities may result in increased antitrust risk. Health-care organizations should specifically address these concerns in their programs for managing the creation, review, storage, and periodic destruction of documents and other business records. In particular, organizations should create and implement a formal and effective document-retention program that will retain the organization's documents for appropriate and required periods and then destroy them.

C. Responding to an Agency Investigation

Health-care organizations have been the focus of numerous antitrust investigations and enforcement actions in recent years. Accordingly, they should be prepared to deal effectively with formal or informal inquiries by federal and state antitrust enforcement officials about their competitive conduct and the markets in which they operate.[4] It is important that they understand how to respond when an antitrust enforcement agency contacts them, whether the contact is by compulsory process, a written request for information, or a telephone call.[5] An investigation may occur in the course of an agency's review of a proposed transaction reported under the pre-merger notification requirements of Section 7A of the Clayton Act;[6] in response to complaints by providers, payers, competitors, consumers, or other governmental agencies about allegedly anticompetitive conduct; from articles on newspapers or trade magazines; or at the initiative of a federal or state enforcement official. Federal and state antitrust officials frequently conduct investigations jointly and have developed published policies reflecting their interaction.[7]

A health-care organization may be contacted as a target or subject of an investigation and possible enforcement action, or as a witness (for example, as a possible victim of anticompetitive conduct or a general source of mar-

---

4. *See generally* Mark J. Botti, Attorney, Antitrust Division, "Comments on the Nuts and Bolts of a Civil Investigation by the Department of Justice Involving the Health Care Industry," Prepared Remarks Before the American Bar Association Section of Antitrust Law Healthcare Antitrust Seminar (Oct. 25, 1996), *reprinted in* 4 *HCAL, supra* p. 14 n.47, App. E66.

5. For a helpful discussion, *see* Charles A. James, "Defense Techniques in Government Antitrust Investigations," Prepared Remarks Before the American Bar Association Section of Antitrust Law Antitrust in Health Care Seminar (Oct. 15, 1998) (on file with editor).

6. *See supra,* pp. 107-09.

7. The state attorneys general and federal enforcement agencies have issued a written protocol for joint investigations of mergers that, as a practical matter, applies to other types of investigations as well. U.S. Dep't of Justice & Federal Trade Comm'n, Protocol for Coordination in Merger Investigations Between the Federal Enforcement Agencies and State Attorneys General (1998), *reprinted in* 4 Trade Reg. Rep. (CCH) ¶ 13,420.

ket information).[8] An organization also may seek to encourage or actively assist in an investigation directed at conduct that threatens competition in the areas it serves. The agencies also frequently contact health-care providers, payers, and others informally in connection with their analyses of proposed conduct or transactions submitted for review under the FTC advisory opinion and Antitrust Division business review procedures.

The agencies have broad authority to investigate possible violations of antitrust law prior to asserting actual claims in court or in an FTC adjudicatory proceeding. The agencies are authorized to issue civil investigative demands (CIDs),[9] and the FTC is authorized to issue civil subpoenas and access orders.[10] The Department of Justice also is authorized to issue grand jury subpoenas as part of a criminal investigation.[11] Most state attorneys general also have broad pre-complaint investigatory powers, and they frequently use them in health-care antitrust investigations. Information initially obtained by an agency during a civil investigation may be used for criminal prosecution by the Antitrust Division where evidence of price-fixing or other serious antitrust violations is discovered. Thus, care must be exercised in disclosing information in a civil investigation that would be privileged under the Fifth Amendment in a criminal investigation.[12]

Once an organization is aware that an agency is investigating its conduct or other matters of interest or concern, it should promptly consult legal counsel and designate one or more key individuals to work under the direction of

---

8. See U.S. Dep't of Justice, U.S. Attorneys' Manual, tit. 9-11.151 (2002) [hereinafter *USAM*] (describing Department of Justice policy to advise a grand jury witness who is a "target" or "subject" of his or her status and rights; defining "target" as someone as to whom the prosecutor or grand jury has substantial evidence linking the person to the commission of a crime; defining "subject" as a person whose conduct is within the scope of an investigation).

9. 15 U.S.C. § 57b-1 (FTC); 15 U.S.C. § 1312 (Antitrust Division).

10. 15 U.S.C. § 49.

11. Fed. R. Crim. P. 17.

12. See United States v. Price Bros. Co., 721 F. Supp. 869 (E.D. Mich. 1989) (defendant's cooperation in FTC investigation did not prevent transfer of investigation to Antitrust Division and subsequent criminal prosecution); 15 U.S.C. § 56(b) (authorizing FTC to disclose investigative materials to Department of Justice for criminal enforcement purposes); *USAM, supra* n.8, tit. 7, ch. III.E (describing policies and procedures of the Antitrust Division for the issuance and enforcement of CIDs).

counsel in dealing with the matter. If the organization knows or has reason to believe that its own conduct is the focus of an investigation, it should take appropriate steps to maintain applicable privileges with respect to communications within the organization and with counsel. The organization also should promptly determine whether any of its personnel or agents have been contacted by the agency and should instruct its personnel about how to respond to such contacts. Finally, the organization should ensure that its employees retain all potentially relevant documents to guard against a subsequent government obstruction-of-justice claim.

1. Early Stages of an Investigation

An agency's initial contact with an organization or its personnel may be formal (for example, service of a CID or subpoena or a personal visit by an agent of the Federal Bureau of Investigation) or informal (for example, a letter or telephone call from agency personnel asking that the organization provide information voluntarily). Formal inquiries should be handled promptly by legal counsel to ensure that the organization fully complies with its legal obligations without inadvertently waiving any available privilege.[13]

An organization that is contacted informally should direct the inquiry to its counsel. The organization's representative or counsel should obtain the identity of the contacting person and the agency he or she represents, the nature of the inquiry, the organization's connection to the inquiry, the precise questions the agent seeks to have answered, and the time within which the agency needs or would like a response. Counsel should promptly determine from the investigating agency whether the organization, its personnel, or its agents are a subject or target of the investigation or merely sources of information. The organization also should promptly suspend any normal document-destruction program and notify appropriate personnel to retain all pertinent business records in their

---

13. *See generally ALD V, supra* p. 9 n.23, at 674-80, 732-47 (in-depth discussion of the agencies' investigative authority and procedures). CID recipients are subject to serious penalties for failure to comply fully with a validly issued CID. *See* 15 U.S.C. § 50 (willful neglect or refusal to comply with court-ordered compulsory process issued by FTC punishable by fine or imprisonment of up to one year or both); 18 U.S.C. § 1505 (willful withholding, misrepresentation, concealment, destruction, or falsifying of documentary material or oral testimony demanded by a CID punishable by fine or imprisonment for up to five years or both).

possession. The organization then should work carefully with its counsel to gather and evaluate information about the subject matter of the investigation, with appropriate sensitivity to considerations of privilege.

2. *Responding to an Agency Civil Investigative Demand or Subpoena*

An organization served with an agency CID or subpoena must promptly determine whether it will comply, negotiate with the agency to reduce the scope of information requested, file an action in court to set aside or modify the subpoena, or refuse to comply and wait for the agency to seek a court order enforcing the CID.[14] Most CID recipients seek to narrow the scope of information sought in some respects, and the agency staff frequently accommodates these requests. Recipients of CIDs or subpoenas only infrequently challenge them formally, given the agencies' broad authority to conduct investigations and the willingness of agency staff to negotiate the actual terms.[15] A petition to modify or set aside a CID from the Antitrust Division must be filed in federal court within 20 days after the CID is served on the recipient, and it is rarely granted.[16]

Subpoenas and CIDs also may require oral testimony under oath by an organization's personnel or agents. Individuals who testify may be represented by counsel during their testimony, but other parties (including the organization) are not entitled to be present directly or through counsel.[17] Any witness's counsel may make objections but may not cross-examine, and the

---

14. 15 U.S.C. § 1314(a).
15. *See, e.g.,* Blue Cross & Blue Shield v. Klein, 1996-2 Trade Cas. (CCH) ¶ 71,600 (N.D. Ohio 1996), *aff'd mem.,* 117 F.3d 1420 (6th Cir. 1997) (affirming denial of petition to quash CID seeking information on recipient's use of most-favored-nations clauses in provider agreements; remanding to determine whether CID was reasonable in scope); Finnell v. United States, 535 F. Supp. 410, 413 (D. Kan. 1982) (rejecting challenge to CID based on lack of relevance to an investigation, citing "presumption of validity"). *But see* Major League Baseball v. Crist, 331 F.3d 1177 (11th Cir. 2003) (quashing state attorney general's CID where the conduct under investigation was clearly exempt from antitrust law).
16. 15 U.S.C. § 1314(b). A comparable motion relating to a grand jury subpoena must be made "promptly" in the federal district court in which the grand jury proceeding takes place. *See* FED. R. CRIM. P. 17(c).
17. 15 U.S.C. § 1312(i) (2), (7).

witness may refuse to answer only on the basis of a legal privilege, including self-incrimination.[18] Testimony still may be compelled under a grant of immunity, which prohibits use of that testimony and information derived from it against the witness.[19] Given these limitations, a testifying individual should be fully prepared by counsel prior to testifying.

3. Dealing With the Agency

Given the agencies' broad prosecutorial discretion and investigative powers, health-care organizations typically seek to cooperate in agency antitrust investigations. Establishing and maintaining effective communications and credibility with agency staff is very important, whether the organization is a target or subject of the investigation, only a witness, or is seeking to encourage enforcement against others.

Most civil enforcement actions brought by the agencies are settled by a consent decree or final judgment with the Antitrust Division or a consent order to cease and desist with the FTC. Certain procedural steps must be completed before the proposed decree or order can be entered as a final order.[20] The agencies have entered into numerous settlements with health-care organizations resolving antitrust claims involving a plethora of subjects. Their published explanations of settlement terms and the underlying antitrust claims are important sources of guidance about potential enforcement concerns and the likely terms of future settlements resolving similar conduct.[21]

---

18. *Id.* § 1312(i)(7). In a grand jury proceeding, a witness is not entitled to be represented by counsel. *See* FED. R. CRIM. P. 6(d); United States v. Mondujano, 425 U.S. 564, 605 (1976).

19. *See* 18 U.S.C. § 6002; *see also ALD V, supra* p. 9 n.23, at 747-49 (discussing legal principles and procedures pertinent to grants of immunity); *USAM, supra* p. 124 n.8, tit. 7, ch. III.F (describing policies and procedures of the Antitrust Division for conducting a grand jury investigation, including requests for and grants of immunity).

20. *See* 15 U.S.C. §§ 1311-1314.

21. The FTC staff issues an Analysis to Aid Public Comment and the Department of Justice issues a Competitive Impact Statement to aid those wishing to submit comments before a settlement is considered for final approval by the FTC or a federal district court. These analyses and the terms of proposed relief are published in the *Federal Register* and are available on the agencies' Web sites. In addition, they are published in services, such as Commerce Clearing House's Trade Regulation Reporter.

Importantly, a settlement may prohibit conduct that would not itself violate the law, to "fence in" the defendants or respondents, both to cure the effects of a violation and to help ensure the violation does not recur.

Responding effectively to an antitrust investigation in health care is frequently a complex and delicate matter, requiring knowledge of both antitrust law and health care, as well as experience in dealing with the enforcement staff of the responsible agency.[22] Accordingly, experienced legal counsel should be consulted as soon as a health-care organization learns of an investigation in which it is or may be a target, subject, or witness, or in which it wishes to provide assistance or encouragement.

---

22. *See generally USAM, supra* p. 124 n.8, tit. 7, ch. III (describing policies and procedures of the Antitrust Division for investigations and case development).

ANTITRUST WEB SITES

ABA Section of Antitrust Law – www.abanet.org/antitrust/. (For more anti-trust links, see www.abanet.org/antitrust/sites.html.)

ABA Section of Antitrust Law Health Care Committee – www.abanet.org/antitrust/committees/health/home.html.

ABA Section of Health Law – www.abanet.org/health/home/html.

American Antitrust Institute – www.antitrustinstitute.org.

American Health Lawyers Association Antitrust Practice Group – www.healthlawyers.org/pg/antitrust.

Antitrust and Trade Regulation Statutes – www.usdoj.gov/atr/foia/divisionmanual/ch2.htm; www.ftc.gov/ogc/stat2.htm.

Federal Trade Commission – www.ftc.gov.

Federal Trade Commission/Health Care Staff Advisory Opinions – www.ftc.gov/bc/advisory.htm.

Federal Trade Commission/Speeches – www.ftc.gov/speeches/speech1.htm.

Federal Trade Commission & U.S. Department of Justice Guidelines for Collaborations Among Competitors – www.ftc.gov/os/2000/04/ftcdojguidelines.pdf.

Federal Trade Commission & U.S. Department of Justice Health Care and Competition Law and Policy Hearings/Transcripts and Materials – www.ftc.gov/ogc/healthcarehearings/index.htm.

National Association of Attorneys General/Antitrust – www.naag.org/issues/issue-antitrust.php

U.S. Department of Justice, Antitrust Division – www.usdoj.gov/atr/index.html.

U.S. Department of Justice, Antitrust Division/Business Review Letters – www.usdoj.gov/atr/public/busreview/letters.htm.

U.S. Department of Justice, Antitrust Division/Speeches – www.usdoj.gov/atr/public/speeches/speeches/htm.

U.S. Department of Justice & Federal Trade Commission Merger Guidelines – www.ftc.gov/bc/docs/horizmer.htm.

U.S. Department of Justice & Federal Trade Commission Statements of Antitrust Enforcement Policy in Health Care – www.usdoj.gov/atr/public/guidelines/1791.pdf.

TABLE OF CASES

Blue Cross & Blue Shield United v. Marshfield Clinic, 65 F.3d 1406, 1411 (7th Cir. 1995)   18 n.13, 35 n.75

Blue Cross & Blue Shield United v. Marshfield Clinic, 65 F.3d 1406, 1415 (7th Cir. 1995)   44 n.126, 101 n.109

Blue Cross & Blue Shield United v. Marshfield Clinic, 65 F.3d at 1413-14   36 n.81

Blue Cross & Blue Shield v. Klein, 1996-2 Trade Cas. (CCH) ¶ 71,600 (N.D. Ohio 1996), *aff'd mem.,* 117 F.3d 1420 (6th Cir. 1997)   155 n.15

Blue Dane Simmental Corp. v. Am. Simmental Ass'n, 178 F.3d 1035, 1041 (8th Cir. 1999)   131 n.227

Boczar v. Manatee Hosp. & Health Sys., 993 F.2d 1514, 1517-19 (11th Cir. 1993)   72 n.12

Bogan v. Hodgkins, 166 F.3d 509, 515 (2d Cir. 1999)   45 n.129

Bolt v. Halifax Hosp. Med. Ctr., 891 F.2d 810, 818-19 (11th Cir. 1990)   26 n.39, 72 n.11

Boulware v. Nevada, 960 F.2d 793, 796, 798 (9th Cir. 1992)   2 n.6, 139 n.252

Brader v. Allegheny Gen. Hosp., 167 F.3d 832, 839 (3d Cir. 1999)   59 n.203

Brader v. Allegheny Gen. Hosp., 64 F.3d 869, 873-74 (3d Cir. 1995)   16 n.4

Brader v. Allegheny Gen. Hosp., 64 F.3d 869, 876 (3d Cir. 1995)   64 n.229

Brand Name Prescription Drugs Antitrust Litig., 123 F.3d 599, 603 (7th Cir. 1997)   21 n.22

Brand Name Prescription Drugs Antitrust Litig., 186 F.3d 781, 786 (7th Cir. 1999)   96 n.92

Brand Name Prescription Drugs Antitrust Litig., 288 F.3d 1028, 1030-32 (7th Cir. 2002)   96 n.92

Bristol Hotel Mgmt. Corp. v. Aetna Cas. & Sur. Co., 20 F. Supp. 2d 1345 (S.D. Fla. 1998)   56 n.185

Broad. Music, Inc. v. Columbia Broad. Sys., 441 U.S. 1, 19 (1979)   33 n.68, 43 n.121

Brokerage Concepts, Inc. v. U.S. Healthcare, Inc., 140 F.3d 494, 511, 513-14 (3d Cir. 1998)   17 n.9, 136 n.243

Bronx Legal Servs v. Legal Servs. for N.Y. City, 2003-1 Trade Cas. (CCH) ¶ 73,954, at 95,720 (S.D.N.Y. 2003)   49 n.153

In re Monosodium Glutamate Antitrust Litig., 2003-1 Trade Cas. (CCH) ¶ 73,963 (D. Minn. 2003)   67 n.242

Ind. Fed'n of Dentists v. FTC, 476 U.S. 447, 458-59 (1986)   30 nn.58 & 59

Int'l Bhd. of Teamsters v. Philip Morris, Inc., 196 F.3d 818 (7th Cir. 1999)   63 n.223

Int'l Healthcare Mgmt. v. Hawaii Coalition for Health, 332 F.3d 600 (9th Cir. 2003)   87 n.68

Intergraph Corp. v. Intel Corp., 195 F.3d 1346 (Fed. Cir. 1999)   37 n.89

InterVest, Inc. v. Bloomberg, L.P., 340 F.3d 144, 165-66 (3d Cir. 2003)   27 n.44

J. Allen Ramey, M.D., P.C., Inc. v. Pac. Found. for Med. Care, 999 F. Supp. 1355, 1361 (S.D. Cal. 1998)   66 n.234, 134 n.240

Jackson v. Radcliffe, 1992-1 Trade Cas. (CCH) ¶ 69,808, at 67,755 (S.D. Tex. 1992)   74 n.19

Jefferson County Pharm. Ass'n, Inc. v. Abbott Labs., 460 U.S. 150 (1983)   99 n.100

Jefferson Parish Hosp. Dist. No. 2 v. Hyde, 466 U.S. 2 (1984)   2 n.5, 70 n.4

Jefferson Parish Hosp. Dist. No. 2 v. Hyde, 466 U.S. 2, 14 (1984)   47 n.139

Jefferson Parish Hosp. Dist. No. 2 v. Hyde, 466 U.S. 2, 20 (1984)   142 n.268

Jefferson Parish Hosp. Dist. No. 2 v. Hyde, 466 U.S. 2, 29 (1984)   48 n.144

Jefferson Parish Hosp. Dist. No. 2 v. Hyde, 466 U.S. 2, 29-30 (1984)   78 n.36

Jefferson Parish Hosp. Dist. No. 2 v. Hyde, 466 U.S. 2, 43-44 (1984)   76 n.26

Jefferson Parish Hosp. Dist. No. 2 v. Hyde, 466 U.S. 2, 31 & n.52 (1984)   79 n.43

Jefferson Parish Hosp. Dist. No. 2 v. Hyde, 466 U.S. at 16-17, 18-25 (1984)   76 n.27, 77 n.28

Johnson v. Univ. Health Servs., Inc., 161 F.3d 1334 (11th Cir. 1998)   66 n.236

Kansas v. Utilicorp United, Inc., 497 U.S. 199 (1990)   62 n.219

Kartell v. Blue Shield, 749 F.2d 922 (1st Cir. 1984)   106 n.123

Kenetic Concepts, Inc. v. Hillenbrand Indus., Inc., No. 95-CV-0755 (W.D. Tex., Sept. 27, 2002)   100 n.106

Key Enters. v. Venice Hosp., 919 F.2d 1550 (11th Cir. 1990), *vacated with instructions to dismiss*, 9 F.3d 893 (11th Cir. 1993)   138 n.249

Sewell Plastics, Inc. v. Coca-Cola Co., 720 F. Supp. 1196 (W.D.N.C. 1989), *aff'd without published op.*, 912 F.2d 463 (4th Cir. 1990) (opinion reprinted at 1990-2 Trade Cas. (CCH) ¶ 69,165)   127 n.210

Sheet Metal Div. of Capital Dist. Sheet Metal, Roofing & Air Conditioning Contractors Ass'n v. Local 38, Sheet Metal Workers Int'l Ass'n, 208 F.3d 18, 26 (2d Cir. 2000)   57 n.191

Simon v. Value Behavioral Health, Inc., 208 F.3d 1073 (9th Cir. 2000)   63 n.223

Singh v. Blue Cross/Blue Shield, 308 F.3d 25, 32 (1st Cir. 2003)   59 n.202

Smith v. N. Mich. Hosps., 703 F.2d 942, 955 (6th Cir. 1983); *Nilavar*, 142 F. Supp. 2d at 876-77   79 n.41

Smith v. NCAA, 139 F.3d 180, 185 (3d Cir. 1998)   49 nn.149 & 150

Smith v. Ricks, 31 F.3d 1478, 1485 (9th Cir. 1994)   59 n.204

SmithKline Corp. v. Eli Lilly & Co., 575 F.2d 1056 (3d Cir. 1978)   100 n.104

Spectrum Sports, Inc. v. McQuillan, 506 U.S. 447, 456, 458 (1993)   4 n.10, 37 n.91

Spectrum Sports, Inc. v. McQuillan, 506 U.S at 459   37 n.92

Spence v. Southeastern Alaska Pilots Ass'n, 1991-1 Trade Cas. (CCH) ¶ 69,453 (D. Alaska 1990)   57 n.194

St. Joseph's Hosp. v. Hosp. Corp. of Am., 795 F.2d 948, 955, 956 (11th Cir. 1986)   54 n.179, 139 n.254, 25 n.36

St. Paul Fire & Marine Ins. Co. v. Barry, 438 U.S. 531 (1978)   2 n.5, 55 n.182

Standard Oil Co. v. United States, 221 U.S. 1, 60-70 (1911)   28 n.45

State Oil Co. v. Kahn, 522 U.S. 3, 10, 18-19 (1997)   28 n.45, 30 n.58, 47 n.137

Steamfitters Local Union No. 420 Welfare Fund v. Philip Morris, Inc., 171 F.3d 912 (3d Cir. 1999)   63 n.223

Stop & Shop Supermarket Co. v. Blue Cross & Blue Shield, 239 F. Supp. 2d 180, 186, 187, 188, 192 (D.R.I. 2003)   3 n.8, 27 n.43, 132 n.230, 29 n.52

Stop & Shop, 239 F. Supp. 2d at 189-91   133 n.231

Stop & Shop, 239 F. Supp. 2d at 193   133 n.233, 134 n.236

Sugarbaker v. SSM Health Care, 190 F.3d 905, 912 (8th Cir. 1999)   59 n.203

Summit Health Ltd. v. Pinhas, 500 U.S. 322 (1991)   2 n.5, 15

United States v. HealthCare Ptrs., Inc., 1996-1 Trade Cas. (CCH) ¶ 71,337 (D. Conn. 1996)   84 n.60

United States v. Heffernan, 43 F.3d 1144 (7th Cir. 1994)   45 n.127

United States v. Hutcheson, 312 U.S. 219, 236 (1941)   56 n.190

United States v. Lake Country Optometric Soc'y, No. W95CR114 (W.D. Tex., Jul. 9, 1996)   11 n.33, 80 n.46

United States v. Lake Country Optometric Soc'y, No. W95CR114 (W.D. Tex., Jul. 9, 1996), *summarized at* [1988-1996 Transfer Binder] Trade Reg. Rep. (CCH) ¶ 45,095, at 44,781   130 n.216

United States v. Long Island Jewish Med. Ctr., 983 F. Supp. 121, 136, 149 (E.D.N.Y. 1997)   108 n.129, 114 n.160, 115 n.166

United States v. Marine Bancorp., 418 U.S. 602, 618 (1974)   17 n.8, 142 n.266

United States v. Mass. Allergy Soc'y, 1992-1 Trade Cas. (CCH) ¶ 69,846 (D. Mass. 1992)   80 n.46

United States v. Med. Mut., 1999-1 Trade Cas. (CCH) ¶ 72,465 (N.D. Ohio 1999)   101 n.110

United States v. Mercy Health Servs., 107 F.3d 632 (8th Cir. 1997), *vacating as moot and remanding with instructions to dismiss,* 902 F. Supp. 968 (N.D. Iowa 1995)   108 n.129

United States v. Mercy Health Servs., 902 F. Supp. 968, 976-87, 980-81 (N.D. Iowa 1995), *vacated as moot and remanded with instructions to dismiss,* 107 F.3d 632 (8th Cir. 1997)   112 n.152, 114 n.162

United States v. Microsoft Corp., 253 F.3d 34, 51, 58, 68, 69 (D.C. Cir. 2001) (en banc) (per curiam)   35 n.77, 132 n.229, 36 n.81, 48 n.146

United States v. Mont. Nursing Home Ass'n, 1982-2 Trade Cas. (CCH) ¶ 64,852 (D. Mont. 1982)   80 n.47

United States v. Mountain Health Care, P.A., 2003-2 Trade Cas. (CCH) ¶ 74,162 (W.D.N.C. 2003)   81 n.52, 84 n.60, 91 n.76

United States v. Ore. State Med. Soc'y, 343 U.S. 326, 336 (1951)   129 n.212

United States v. Penn-Olin Chem. Co., 378 U.S. 158 (1964)   120 n.183, 142 n.266

United States v. Portac, 869 F.2d 1288 (9th Cir. 1989)   45 n.127

United States v. Realty Multi-List, Inc., 629 F.2d 1351, 1363 (5th Cir. 1980)   30 n.57

Williamson Oil Co. v. Philip Morris USA, 346 F.3d 1287, 1301-03 (11th Cir. 2003)   27 n.44

Williamson v. Sacred Heart Hosp., 41 F.3d 667 (11th Cir. 1995) (per curiam unpublished opinion reprinted at 1995-1 Trade Cas. (CCH) ¶ 70,905)   140 n.259

Willman v. Heartland Hosp., 34 F.3d 605, 610-11 (8th Cir. 1994)   69 n.2, 74 n.20

Willman v. Heartland Hosp., 34 F.3d 605, 611, 612 (8th Cir. 1994)   27 n.43, 72 n.13

Wisconsin v. Kenosha Hosp. & Med. Ctr., 1997-1 Trade Cas. (CCH) ¶ 71,669 (E.D. Wis. 1997)   115 n.168

Wisconsin v. Marshfield Clinic, 1997-1 Trade Cas. (CCH) ¶ 71,855 (W.D. Wis. 1997)   109 n.138

Woman's Clinic, Inc. v. St. John's Health Sys., Inc., 252 F. Supp. 2d 857, 865 (W.D. Mo. 2002)   48 n.144

Xechem, Inc. v. Bristol-Myers Squibb Co., 274 F. Supp. 2d 937, 943 (N.D. Ill. 2003)   62 n.218

Zinzer v. Rose, 868 F.2d 938 (7th Cir. 1989)   105 n.119

INDEX

horizontal market-allocation agreements 44
horizontal mergers 46
horizontal price-fixing agreements 42
tying agreements 47
vertical mergers 46
vertical price-fixing agreements 47

B

business records, management of 150–151

C

Clayton Act 8, 10, 12, 17, 21, 41, 56, 67, 118

E

exclusionary conduct 132–46
 "all-products" provisions 135–36
 full-line forcing 142–44
 hospital impedance of medical-staff competition 140–41
 opposition to certificate-of-need applications 138–39
 pharmaceutical industry collusion 144–46
 selective and exclusive managed-care contracting 132–35
exclusive contracts between hospitals and physicians
 challenges to 76
 effectiveness of 76
 relevant geographic markets 78

F

Federal Trade Commission 9–12, 83
 Antitrust Division 9–11, 83

G

geographic market 19
 defined 16, 19
 health-care contexts 19
government enforcement in health care 13–14

H

Hart-Scott-Rodino Antitrust Improvements Act of 1976 9
 premerger notification provision 118
health care
 competition in 4–8
 government enforcement in 13
 market characteristics 5–8
Health Care Quality Improvement Act of 1986 59, 103
health maintenance organizations 1

I

independent practice associations (IPAs) 12
interstate commerce 15–16

L

Local Government Antitrust Act of 1984 58

M

market power 21–24
 health-care issues 23
 market-share thresholds 22
 monopsony power 23
 proof of existence 22

ABA SECTION OF ANTITRUST LAW
COMMITMENT TO QUALITY

The Section of Antitrust Law is committed to the highest standards of scholarship and continuing legal education. To that end, each of our books and treatises is subjected to rigorous quality control mechanisms throughout the design, drafting, editing, and peer review processes. Each Section publication is drafted and edited by leading experts on the topics covered and then rigorously peer reviewed by the Section's Books and Treatises Committee, at least two Council members, and then other officers and experts. Because the Section's quality commitment does not stop at publication, we encourage you to provide any comments or suggestions you may have for future editions of this book or other publications.

Defending Liberty
Pursuing Justice